HyperTalk Disk

Utilities
Large Book Programs
XCMD's
Surprises
(Everything that will fit on an 800K disk!)

Only $15

Supercharge your HyperTalk programming with this disk. Lots of good things to make your programming easier and more powerful. It will help debug your typos too!

✂ ---

Name _____

Address _____

City _____State ـــــZip _____

Make checks payable to **Sandlight Publications**.
✂ --

Send orders to:
    Sandlight Publications
    17857 Aguacate Way
    San Diego, CA 92127

HyperCard
Made Easy,
Second Edition

William B. Sanders

Scott, Foresman and Company
Glenview, Illinois   London

Apple®, ImageWriter®, LaserWriter® and MacPaint® are registered trademarks of Apple Computer, Inc.
Macintosh™, Finder™, HyperCard™, HyperTalk™, MultiFinder™ and StackWare™ are trademarks of Apple Computer, Inc.
Word and Excel are trademarks of Microsoft Corporation.

Library of Congress Cataloging-in-Publication Data

Sanders, William B.,
    HyperCard made easy / by William B. Sanders. -- 2nd ed.
    p.   cm.
    Includes index
    ISBN 0-673-38577-9 :
    1. Macintosh (Computer)--(Programming. 2. HyperCard (Computer program) 3. HyperTalk (Computer program language) I Title.
QA76.8.M3S27 1988b
005.265--dc 19   88-18525
                                   CIP

1 2 3 4 5 6-MVN-93 92 91 90 89 88

ISBN 0-673-38577-9

Notice of Liability

Scott, Foresman Professional Publishing Group books are available for bulk sales at quantity discounts. For information, please contact Marketing Manager, Professional Books, Professional Publishing Group, Scott, Foresman and Company, 1900 East Lake Avenue, Glenview, IL 60025.

Table of Contents

Preface

HyperCard has enjoyed an unprecedented acceptance from its introduction. With Version 1.2 (or Version 1.21, as was used for this book), a whole new subset of commands, functions and properties have been made available. This edition covers the new features of HyperCard and HyperTalk along with the standard features. To make this book more useful for readers who are familiar with HyperCard and want to quickly find the new features, look for the graphic disk as pictured below:

That disk will mark a discussion of some new Version 1.2 feature of HyperCard. If you have an older version of HyperCard, the new features will not work. You can get an updated version from the store where you bought your computer. However, you can use all of the other features of HyperCard not marked by the graphic disk with the old version. Also, all of your old stacks will work with the new version.

HyperCard Made Easy: Second Edition also has a new chapter on using the extra commands (XCMD's) for HyperCard. Chapter 12, *Using XCMD's*, explains where to get XCMD's, how to install them and how to use them.

Introduction

What's It All About?

This book is primarily about a new kind of computer application base called **HyperCard, Version 1.2.** HyperCard is used to organize information into discrete units called stacks that can be linked to other stacks of information. We will examine how to create stacks with a special emphasis on practical uses. The last chapter of the book examines **MultiFinder**. MultiFinder is an environment in which several different applications, including HyperCard, can be used at the same time. That is, you can use one application, and then switch to another, without closing down the first one, and then switch back to the original application. Also, it allows certain types of "multi-tasking" to occur. For example, while your Mac sends something to the printer, simultaneously, you can work on another project on your computer.

Special Note: Any model of Macintosh, including the Macintosh II, will work with HyperCard and MultiFinder. However, to use HyperCard your Mac should have at least one megabyte of RAM memory, and for using MultiFinder, at least two megabytes is recommended. A Mac Plus, SE or II right out of the box will work fine for HyperCard applications and programming, but to use MultiFinder, you should have your memory upgraded to at least two megabytes. Apple Computer and other companies make RAM memory upgrades for all models of the Macintosh, from the Mac 128 to the Macintosh II. Before proceeding further, check to see if your memory is sufficient.

Welcome to HyperCard

HyperCard is a whole new way of approaching how computers are used. In some ways it is exactly like any other computer application such as word processors, database programs, spreadsheets and educational programs. All you do is to learn how to enter information in the form of written text, names and addresses, numbers, graphics, sound or any other kind of information. Depending on what you enter, the computer will respond with information on the screen that can be saved to a disk, printed on paper or sent over telephone lines to another computer. All you need to know is how to use your computer and the special commands for the application.

User Levels

Since there are several different levels of experience on the Macintosh computer, you can get the most benefit from this book by understanding it in terms of levels of expertise. Before going on, be sure determine the level or levels that best describe you. This will save you a good deal of time.

> **Special Note:** The term "stackware" denotes an application written with HyperCard. "HyperTalk" is the programming language used to write HyperCard "scripts" or "programs."

New to Macintosh

If this is the first time you've used a Macintosh computer, even if you're familiar with other types of computers, including the Apple II family of computers, it is very important to understand the underlying philosophy of the Mac.

Basically, the philosophy is that of a desktop analogy. Your computer's applications should be as intuitive and simple to use as possible, just like getting what you need from the top of a desk. The mouse should be an "arm" used to get things that you need, moving around the desktop of your screen and drawing graphics. Your keyboard is for entering text and numbers as you would on a typewriter or calculator. This makes it very easy for the person using the application. To become familiar with the general tools on your Mac, you should go over the manual that comes with your computer and experiment with the mouse, the menus and the keyboard. The rest of this book assumes you've done that.

You should go over all sections of this book very carefully, and give yourself plenty of time. Go through all examples and stop where you feel comfortable before continuing. Experiment a lot, and see what you can do at all levels. You will be able to start doing productive work with the example programs in this book and on the sample Stackware that comes with your HyperCard from Apple Computer, Inc. very quickly. However don't expect to start writing HyperTalk scripts (the highest level of HyperCard) right off the bat. All of the examples in this book work fine, and you can copy them and use them with no problems. However, when you get to the tougher aspects, which give you far more control, first be sure to have a clear grasp of one level before going on to the next. For example, go through all of the material on "authoring" before jumping ahead to "scripting."

Experienced Macintosh Application User

If you've used different Macintosh programs, such as MacWrite, Microsoft Word, MacDraw, SuperPaint, Excel or any other Macintosh program, you will find HyperCard both familiar and different. It should be familiar in that it is easy to use. HyperCard has the same overall feel because you choose various options from menus and the graphics work very much like other Macintosh applications. However, it is different with respect to power and flexibility.

First, you should find applications which most closely fit something you would like to use on a regular basis. Much of the stackware that comes with HyperCard can be used "as is" with no modification at all. However, to fine tune a HyperCard application to do exactly what you need, you can begin "authoring" applications. That means you can change existing HyperCard stacks to make them do what you want. You can even take something from one stack and integrate it into another. The section on "authoring" will be of primary interest to you. First, though, be sure to completely cover the sections on how to use HyperCard. For further fine tuning of a HyperCard application, you can begin writing your own scripts. By combining "authored" stacks with "scripted" stacks, you can ease your way into programming if you so desire.

Programmers

If you already have a grasp on computer programming, there is the temptation to immediately jump to the section on writing your own "script", the term Apple Computer, Inc. introduced to describe programming with HyperCard. My advice is to understand first how HyperCard applications work and spend some time with "authoring" before attempting to write your own script.

Programming is encapsulated into buttons, fields, backgrounds, cards and stacks. You don't write a big long program as with other programming languages to produce an application. Rather, scripting entails placing scripts in different parts of a stack, either in individual cards and buttons or in a stack's background. HyperTalk looks something like a combination of Forth, BASIC and C. It is a fairly high level language and very modular. Since a good portion of this book is dedicated to writing scripts, further details will not be covered here. However, you should become familiar with how HyperCard applications are organized and the fundamentals of "authoring" before jumping into scripts.

Outline of System

We will begin with an overview of HyperCard. Figure 1-1
shows the basic components of HyperCard

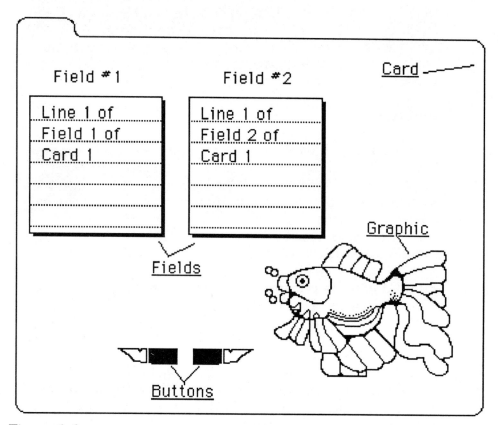

Field #1   Field #2   Card

Line 1 of   Line 1 of
Field 1 of   Field 2 of
Card 1   Card 1

Graphic

Fields

Buttons

Figure 1-1

Cards
The basic organizing component of HyperCard is the card
itself. Cards contain information in the form of text and

graphics. The user adds text and graphics with the keyboard or the mouse.

Buttons

The buttons on each card can indicate some action relevant to the stack or to a specific card. Buttons are represented by a labelled or unlabelled graphic of some sort that indicates what "pressing the button" will do. Buttons are "pressed" by pointing to them with the "browse tool" and clicking the mouse button.

Browse Tool

In the Figure 1-1 example card, the fountain pens are pointers to the next or previous card in the stack. If the pen on the right is "clicked" then the next card in the stack appears, and if the left pen is chosen then the previous card appears. Buttons can do other things as well, and they are key elements in authoring your own stacks.

Fields

Fields are categories on cards. If you think of each card as a record in a file cabinet, the fields are categories that each record might have. For example, schools might have records with information about students. Each student record (card) may have a separate *field* for name, address, who to contact in an emergency, class level, and medical information. When you use a stack of cards, the fields help organize information, and make it easy to find what you need. The browse tool changes to an "I-beam" cursor when it enters the field area, and you can write text in the field when the browse tool changes to the I-beam.

Special Note: There are two different tools with which to write. The browse tool is used for writing in fields, and the text tool is used as a graphic element to write on non-field areas of a card and in the background. In the above sample card the information outside of the field boxes was written with the text tool and the information inside the boxes was written with the browse tool. The text written with the browse tool is much easier to change and manipulate than that written with the text tool. It is possible to write on fields with the text tool, but as we will see further on in the book, text written in fields with the text tool cannot be used in calculations.

Text Tool

Browse Tool

Linking Cards: Stacks

The goal of HyperCard is to allow the user easily to arrange information on cards and retrieve that information. Each card in a stack may have the same background or common features, but the individual cards have unique information or even special fields or buttons. For example, a stack of cards for business may have general information for each employee, as well as specialized information for different categories of the employees. Executive, staff and line workers all have names, addresses and telephones in common, but certain executives and sales representatives may have a travel expense category that would not pertain to other employees. Thus, a special field for travel may be introduced only on certain cards. Likewise, specialized buttons may be required on certain cards to provided added information about the card or to take a special branch to another card. For example, if a sub-category is required to explain more optional details about a card a *card button* will provide the needed option just for a single card, without it unnecessarily cluttering up the other cards.

Stack

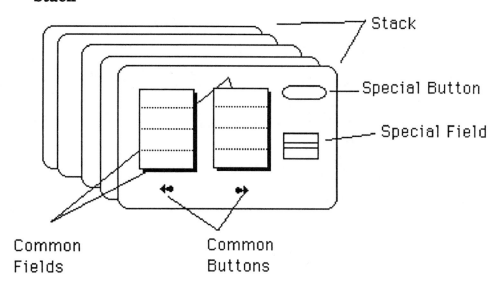

Figure 1-2

The card immediately after the last card is the first card of a stack. So instead of a "stack", a stack is more like a "ring" of cards. However, since there is a sequential order to stacks, it is better to think of them as a stack with a top and a bottom; a beginning and an end in most cases.

Linking Stacks

In certain applications, it will be useful to link one stack with another. In these circumstances, each separate stack might be thought of as a separate subroutine, in dealing with specialized options for single cards, one stack is a subroutine of another stack. For example, the following shows two independent stacks linked by buttons.

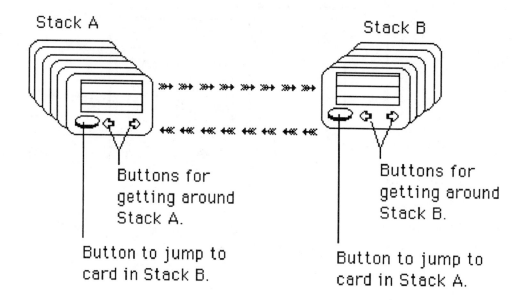

Figure 1-3

The above example shows two wholly independent stacks linked by buttons telling HyperCard that the next card is specified in another stack. For example, one stack might be a calculation stack and the other a class list stack. Teachers using the class list stack have all of a student's grades on a single card. To determine the average grade, another stack is used to do various types of mathematical calculations. Supposing there is another stack that does calculations written for another application; instead of re-authoring a field or special card to do calculations, the teacher just installs a button to jump to that other stack. In the calculation stack, a button is installed to jump back to the class list stack. Of course, if the teacher had wanted, a stack could have been developed that took care of both recording grades and calculating final averages. However, by using the existing stack along with the new one, the teacher saved authoring time.

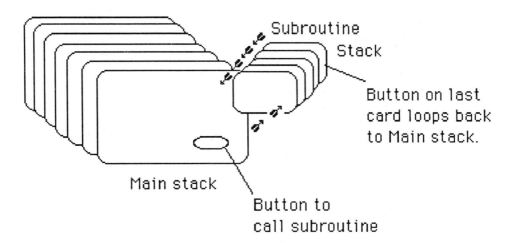

Figure 1-4

The second example shows a situation where the "subroutine" stack is used. All a subroutine stack is is a stack that is dependent on a main stack for it to be of any sensible use. For example, an extended footnote describing a point that is important only to a few of the stack's users might be placed in such a separate stack. When the button to the subroutine is pressed, it calls up the subroutine stack. The button on the last card of the subroutine stack cycles back to the main stack. As in the first example, the user could just as well have placed the "subroutine" stack into the main stack. Figure 1-5 shows how this would conceptually look.

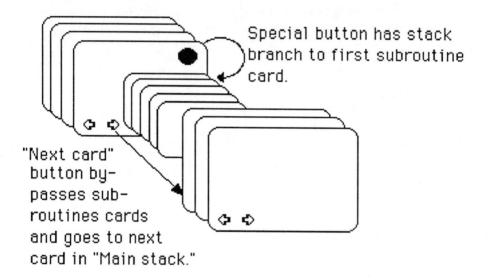

Special button has stack branch to first subroutine card.

"Next card" button by-passes sub-routines cards and goes to next card in "Main stack."

Figure 1-5

As you can see, HyperCard provides a lot of flexibility. There is no reason that several stacks cannot be linked together by including buttons that indicate the next place to get a card is another stack. Figure 1-6 shows connections between five stacks, each linked to every other stack directly and indirectly.

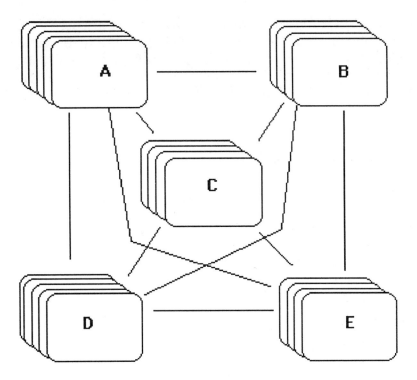

Figure 1-6

The card and stack concepts suggest modularity and linkage. Think of using, authoring and scripting in Hyper-Card in terms of small, discreet parts that can be linked to form larger wholes.

Working With Menus

Those familiar with the Macintosh should be familiar with using menus. Basically, a menu is selected by clicking and holding the mouse button down and then dragging the pointer to the desired option. The option is selected when the option is highlighted (inverse)and the button is released. If the menu option is a light gray ("ghosted") it cannot be selected. Depending on which mode you are in and/or which tool you are using, certain options will be ghosted. Likewise, the menu bar across the top of the screen will show different menus and menu options depending on your mode and tool use.

The opening menu bar on HyperCard stacks appears as follows:

 File   Edit   Go   Tools   Objects

As long as the browse tool is selected this menu bar will be visible and available for use. If the File menu is selected, it will look like the following and present eleven options.

```
File
   New Stack...
   Open Stack...    ⌘O
   Save a Copy...
   ............................
   Compact Stack
   Protect Stack...
   Delete Stack...
   ............................
   Page Setup...
   Print Card       ⌘P
   Print Stack...
   Print Report...
   ............................
   Quit HyperCard ⌘Q
```

Figure 1-7

As soon as one of the other tools is selected, both the menu bar and the options change. For example, if the paint brush tool is selected the menu bar changes to this,

 File   Edit   Go   Tools   Paint   Options   Patterns

making a different set of menus and menu options available. Note that the **Paint**, **Options** and **Patterns** menus now appear but the **Objects** menu is no longer there. When the menus are open, there are also changes. For example, instead of looking like the File menu that was available when the browse key was selected (Figure 1-7), it changes to the one seen in Figure 1-8.

File

New Stack...
Open Stack...   ⌘O
Save a Copy...

Import Paint...
Export Paint...

Compact Stack
Protect Stack...
Delete Stack...

Page Setup...
Print Card   ⌘P
Print Stack...
Print Report...

Quit HyperCard ⌘Q

Figure 1-8

Ten of the options have been "ghosted" and cannot be selected. When using HyperCard decks, it is important to keep in mind what options are available with different tools. As we continue the examination of various aspects of HyperCard, we will discuss how and when to use the several options on the menus and how to get to required menu options.

The Tools

> **Special Note:** In order to see the toolbox (**Tools** on the menu bar) the User Preferences must be set at least to the level of "Painting". To get to the User Preferences, go to the Home card and press the left pointing arrow. (The left arrow takes you to the last card in the stack if you click it from the first card of the stack. Alternatively, you could choose "Last" from the **Go** menu.) Then choose Painting, Authoring or Scripting. To be on the safe side, choose Painting, otherwise you may accidentally change a button or script in one of the sample stacks.

Here there will be a brief introduction to the tools. In the next several chapters, the tools' uses and effects will be explained in detail. To get to the tools, you can do one of three things:

1. Select the Tools Menu and click a tool.
2. Pull the Tool Menu off the menu bar by dragging it to the desktop by the lower right hand corner.
3. Pressing the Option and Tab keys simultaneously from the keyboard.
4. Using a script to make it appear and disappear.

The toolbox has 18 tools, each one represented by an icon in the box and an icon that appears when that tool is selected. Sometimes the icon is identical to the tool that appears in the tool box and sometimes different. For example, the browse tool appears the same in the toolbox as it does on the desktop, but the selection tool (the box made up of broken lines) has a cross with a dot in the center. However, if you're ever unsure of what tool is currently selected, the toolbox icon menu has the selected tool in inverse graphics. You can see this with the browse and selection tools in the illustrations in Figure 1-9.

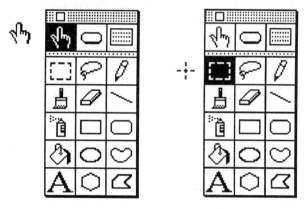

Figure 1-9

Notice the broken line between the top three tools and the bottom 15. The bottom part of the toolbox has all of the graphic tools. They are all employed in drawing or creating graphic text. The top three tools are used in either moving around (browse tool) or working with buttons or fields. We'll briefly introduce all tools here, and expand on them later. Do not be concerned at this point if you do not understand what they do. At this stage, all we're doing is introducing them.

Operational Tools

> **Special Note:** On the left side of the tool icon there will be the desktop icon of the tool, if the desktop icon is different from the tool icon.

Browse Tool   This tool is the major "selection tool" for pressing buttons and moving around the different cards and stack and writing text in fields.

Button Tool The button tool brings the arrow pointer to the desktop. It is an important authoring and scripting tool that we cover in Chapter 3.

Field Tool   The field tool, like the button tool, brings the arrow pointer to the desktop. This tool is an important one for setting up fields on cards and in the stack background.

Paint Tools

Select tool As mentioned previously in this chapter, the select tool is used for selecting a graphic area.

Lasso   The lasso is like the select tool except it can select an irregular area whereas the select tool only carves out a rectangular area. It automatically shrinks to fit around the selected area.

Pencil The pencil draws flexible lines, very much like a free hand drawing. If it draws across a previously drawn line, it erases the line.

Paint brush The paint brush has several different shapes that appear on the cards, depending on what brush shape and/or pattern is chosen.

Eraser The eraser tool removes graphics from the cards.

Line Tool various types of straight lines are drawn with the line tool in different line widths.

Spray can The spray can works like the paint brush in placing solid or patterned graphics on the screen, except it does so in a spray-like fashion.

Rectangle tool For drawing squares and rectangles, either filled with the selected pattern or not, use the rectangle tool.

Rounded rectangle tool Same as the rectangle tool except the corners are rounded on rectangles or squares.

Bucket   Enclosed areas, including outlined alphabet and number characters, are filled with the current pattern with this tool.

Oval tool   This tool draws ovals and circles.

Curve tool   This tool acts something like the pencil in drawing free form shapes, but in the pattern fill mode, it automatically draws a line from the last point to the first point when the mouse button is released.

I A

Paint text tool   This tool writes text on cards and buttons, but not in the field spaces. The browse tool does that.

Regular polygon tool   There are six different regular polygons from which to choose from the Options menu when using this tool.

Irregular polygon tool Like the polygon tool but is used in drawing polygons with irregular sides.

A couple of new features for getting tool is the use of the key combinations -- Command-Tab (browse), Command-Tab-Tab (button) and Command-Tab-Tab-Tab (field). These short-cuts will become more evident when you start authoring stacks.

The purpose of this first chapter was to introduce the general elements of HyperCard. We can boil it down to six key elements:

1. Cards
2. Buttons
3. Fields
4. Backgrounds
5. Stacks
6. Tools

Buttons and fields make up global and local elements of stacks and cards, and backgrounds define general proper-ties of cards. The tools are used to create the buttons and fields and type and draw on the cards.

By beginning with these fundamental elements, it will be easier to use HyperCard and create your own HyperCard stacks. This chapter did not attempt to explain all of the nuances of the tools, buttons, fields and everything else that goes to make up HyperCard. As we go further into HyperCard and its applications, we will explain differing functions and characteristics of the primary elements. For now, you should have a general idea of what a card, stack, button, field and tool is. In the next chapter we will get into using HyperCard ap-plications that are made up of the features this chapter intro-duced.

Getting Started With HyperCard

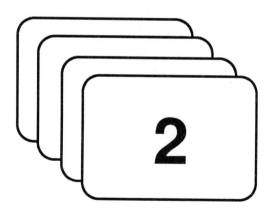

Setting Up For HyperCard

The very first thing to do is copy protect all four disks of the HyperCard set and make back ups. To copy protect a disk, flip open the window in the upper right hand corner of the 3 $1/2$ inch disk. Use the standard copy procedures to make copies. Install all four on a hard disk, and then use the Startup file to get it all going. If you do not have a hard disk, turn on your Mac and place the copy of the Startup HyperCard disk in the internal drive, and it will automatically initiate the Home Card. Do not copy protect the copies you will be using.

One 800k Disk Drive. If all you have is a single 800k disk drive, it would be best to use the single HyperCard System file and remove all files from the startup disk except the System, HyperCard and Home files. That will give you enough room to create some new stacks of your own, but it would be very cramped and you could not use the Help cards. At a minimum two floppy drives are strongly recommended.

Two 800k Disk Drives. With two 800k drives, place a recent Finder and **non**-HyperCard System file on the Startup disk. This will let you quit HyperCard and use another application without going through shut down/restart on your Mac. The second drive can be used for the HyperCard Help disk, a file storage disk or another HyperCard disk, especially the Hyper-Card Help disk while you're getting started. The Startup disk will have to have minimum files; so only the Finder, System, HyperCard and Home files should be there.

RAM disk Setup. If you have two megabytes or more of RAM on your Mac, you might want to use a RAM disk. A RAM disk is a program that organizes your RAM memory so that part of it acts just like a disk drive. This will significantly increase the speed of going between stack and different applications.   Set the

Startup disk with a copy of the RAM disk, a recent Finder and System file along with HyperCard and the Home file. Then when the system is turned on, all of the key programs and files will go into the RAM drive, and you will have the other drives free for more disks in a much faster environment. If you use MultiFinder, a RAM disk is not recommended.

MultiFinder Setup. If you are planning to use HyperCard with MultiFinder, you will need at least two megabytes of RAM memory, and a hard disk is strongly recommended but not absolutely essential. For details on installing HyperCard and MultiFinder, please turn to Chapter 11 and go over the section on installing and using MultiFinder.

Going Home and Leaving Home

HyperCard automatically goes to the Home card when you start from the HyperCard icon. From the desktop, your HyperCard program file looks like the following:

HyperCard

HyperCard Icon

By double clicking the icon, you can start HyperCard and automatically go directly to the Home card. Alternatively, you could click any other HyperCard file icon and open it's stack instead of the Home stack.

Home   PracticeStack

HyperCard Stack Icons

The above two icons show different stacks. Double clicking (opening) the Home stack will start with the Home screen. If you open the other stack, PracticeStack, it will bypass the Home stack and go directly to the PracticeStack. (The file PracticeStack is not on the original four disks that come with HyperCard.) However, there *must be a stack named Home* either on the desktop or an available disk file. It does not have to be the original one that came with HyperCard Startup disk. In fact, if you renamed the PracticeStack to "Home", and the original Home stack to "XYZ", it would work fine. HyperCard would use the contents of the original PracticeStack as the Home stack. Later when you're more experienced using HyperCard, you'll probably want a customized Home stack of your own.

What is the Home Card?

The Home card is part of a Home stack. The card itself is a collection of buttons that transfer control to a number of different stacks. Figure 2-1 gives an idea of what the Home Card looks like.

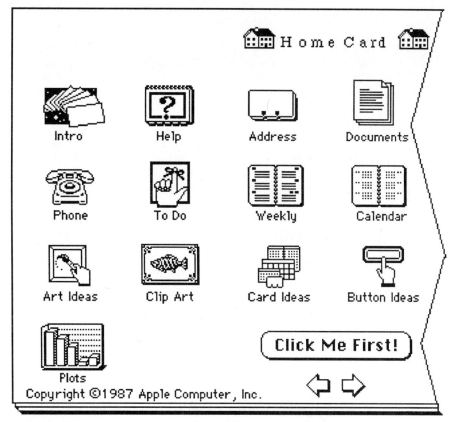

Figure 2-1

The separate icons are buttons. When a button is pressed by pointing to it and clicking the mouse button, the program transfers to the stack named in the button. The left and right arrows at the bottom of the screen also are buttons, but instead of going to another stack, they go to the next (right) or previous (left) card in the Home stack. If you click the left arrow you will be transferred to the last card in the stack. When you arrive there, you will see the following card:

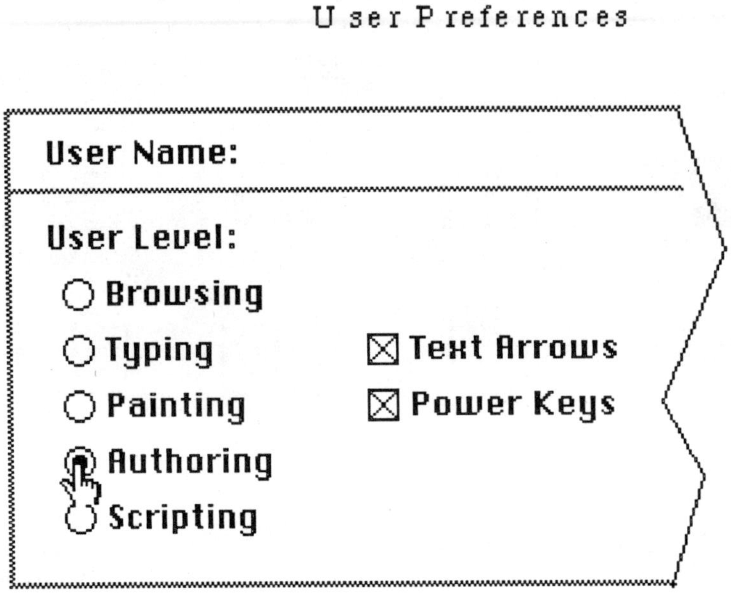

User Preferences

```
User Name:

User Level:
   ○ Browsing
   ○ Typing          ⊠ Text Arrows
   ○ Painting        ⊠ Power Keys
   ◉ Authoring
   ○ Scripting
```

Figure 2-2

The User Preference card is an important one since it controls what level you can work in. For this chapter, you will need to be at the "Painting" level. So click Painting with the Browse tool as shown on the card. After that is done, you will see these menus on the menu bar.

```
  🍎   File   Edit   Go   Tools
```

Depending on what the previous level was, you will be able to see more or fewer menu choices. The Authoring and Scripting are higher levels, and the Browsing and Typing are lower levels. This level will allow you to do everything planned in this chapter, but for the next chapter, you will have to go to the next higher level.

Once you leave the Home card, there are a number of different ways to get back. Most cards in most stacks will have a home icon on them somewhere so that whenever need be, you can return Home. These are a few of the common Home icons you will see:

It is easier to use the Command-H sequence to get Home since you don't have to look for a different Home icon on all the different cards.

Moving Around With Buttons

The graphic icon associated with a button can be anything. The Button Ideas stack is a good place to begin looking at some things that buttons can be. Make sure your HyperCard Ideas disk is in a drive and click button ideas. You'll see several, including these:

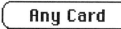

Figure 2-3

If you don't happen to like those, or you want to make your own button icons, Figure 2-4 shows some other ideas created with the paint tools:

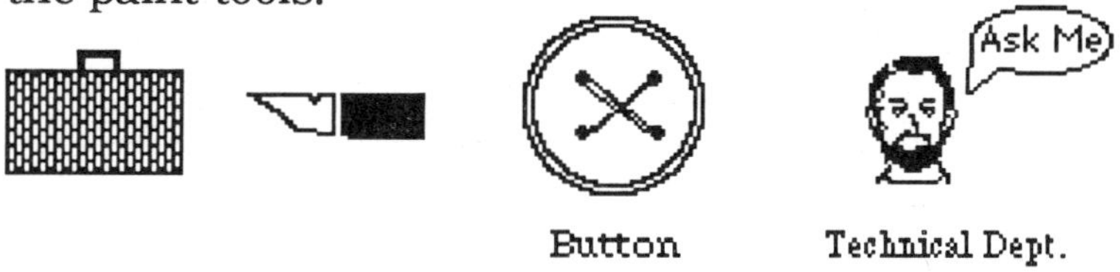

Button   Technical Dept.

Figure 2-4

Further on in this chapter we'll use the paint tools, and in the next chapter, see how they can be made into working buttons.

Exploring and Using Help

The HyperCard Help stack is accessed in a number of different ways. Some cards may have a help buttons and by clicking them the program will jump to the Help stacks. You can always get to the Help stacks by choosing Help from the Go menu or pressing the Command Key and question mark (?) keys.

Place the HyperCard Help disk in one of your drives or make sure it is on your hard disk and click the Help button from the Home Card. Figure 2-5 shows the first Help card.

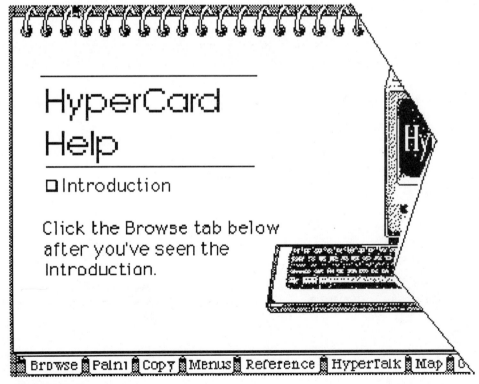

Figure 2-5

Each file tab at the bottom of the card is a button. By clicking one of the tabs, you will be taken to the named information. Start with the "Browse" tab and work you way to the "Menus" tab. Use the Index and Map tabs for finding different elements of HyperCard as you begin learning more features of the program.

Where Buttons Can Go

There are four different places a button can take the program. First, a button can cause a jump to another card.

Card to card

Figure 2-6

Second, a button can go to another stack.

Card to stack

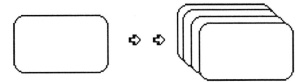

Figure 2-7

Third a button can make visible text and/or graphics on a card.

Card to message on card made visible

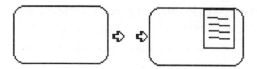

Figure 2-8

Fourth, a button can go to an exit. The exit can cause HyperCard to quit or even shutdown.

Figure 2-9

Other Button Activities

Buttons also can do other things besides going to different stacks. Pressing a button can operate options from the different menus, including many of the Paint menu options. An interesting view of this use of buttons can be seen by bringing the Tools menu to the desktop and then pressing a button. As the button functions use the different paint tools, they will be selected (darkened) as the button uses them. Behind each button is a script or program. The underlying script is what makes all the buttons work. We will get to that in Chapter 4, the first chapter on scripting.

To see this work, go to the Plots stack, and when it comes up with the bar graph pictured, bring down the Tools and Pattern menus. Press the Pie button with these two menus on the side of the card. Now you will be able to see graphically how the pie graph is drawn with the different tools initiated by the script generated by the Pie button.

> **Special Note:** A shortcut for bringing down the Tools is to press the Option-Tab key combination. For the Pattern menu, press the Tab key while a paint tool is selected.

Using the Go Menu

Another way to get around in HyperCard is with the Go menu. Usually the cards will have various buttons to move from one place to another on a stack, but with new stacks and in other situations the Go menu can be a big help. Since this menu is used a lot for global and local movement, it would be a big help to remember the Command key sequences.

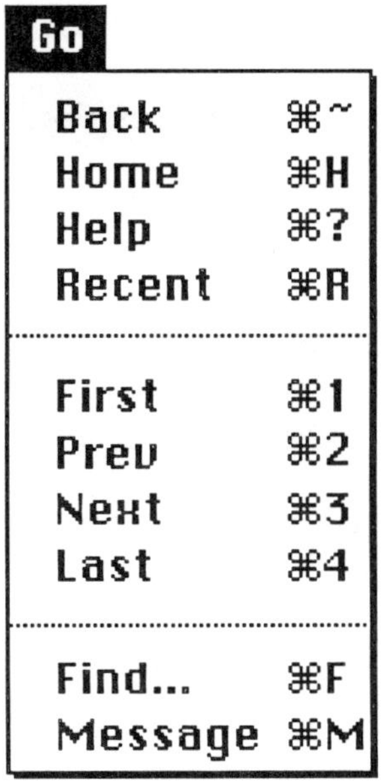

Go	
Back	⌘~
Home	⌘H
Help	⌘?
Recent	⌘R
First	⌘1
Prev	⌘2
Next	⌘3
Last	⌘4
Find...	⌘F
Message	⌘M

Figure 2-10

The first four options in the Go menu are for global expeditions through one or more stacks.

Back. This command goes to the previous card used; not the previous card in the stack. It can go from stack to stack and keep 100 cards in memory.

Home. Jumps to the Home Card.

Help. Jumps to the Help Stack

Recent. This provides a pictorial of the recent cards you've used. The cards are very small and you have to recall key features of the card's graphics to find the card to want. It takes a while to get used to, but it can be very useful for making big jumps.

The next four commands on the Go menu are for local explorations of a current stack.

> *First.* This goes to the first card in the stack.

> *Prev.* The program goes to the previous card in the stack.

> *Next.* The program goes to the next card in the stack.

> *Last.* Jumps to the last card in the stack.

The final two commands in the Go menu are for more particular movements. Both require the user to type in specific words for these two operations to do something.

> *Find...* This locates matching words in the current stack. A message box appears at the bottom of the screen for the search word or phrase. HyperCard 1.2 has more options with "find" that will be discussed further on in the book.

Message. The message box appears and scripted messages send commands to HyperCard. In Chapter 4 we will delve into using HyperCard script, but for now here are some examples.

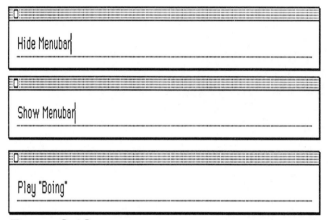

Figure 2-12

The first command in the message box will hide the menu bar across the top of your screen. Not surprisingly, the second message brings it back. (Be sure to write in the second message if you write in the first.) Finally, the third message will play a single "boing" that sounds something like a cartoon version of a spring popping out of a sofa. Once you put the third message in, it will produce a "boing" sound each time you press the Return key when using the Browse tool. You can erase it just by backspacing over it in the Message Box.

Text: Writing in Fields

In addition to buttons, there are a number of different types and styles of fields that can be used in HyperCard. In Chapter 3, we will examine how to create different types of fields, and here we will see what different types of fields look like. To write in all types of fields, use the Browse tool ; not the paint text tool . Both the Browse and Text tools will show an I-beam symbol when placed on a card in an appropriate place to enter text. The paint text tool can write anywhere on the card, but the Browse tool will show the I-beam symbol only when it is in a text area.

The first basic difference in fields is whether or not they scroll. A scrolling field can handle more text since both on and off screen text can be viewed by scrolling. However, while non-scrolling fields can hold off screen text, it cannot be viewed. Scrolling is accomplished by dragging the box in the right margin or pointing to the top or bottom arrows and holding down the mouse key as illustrated in Figure 2-12.

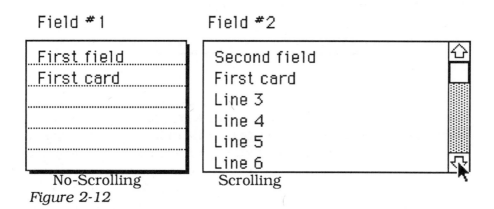

Figure 2-12

Field #1 in Figure 2-12 has lines as part of its style and Field #2 does not. Other standard formats include opaque, transparent and non-shadowed rectangles. In transparent fields, any kinds of graphic may make up the field.

To move from one field to another, press the Tab key. For example, a common set of fields would be Name, Address, City, State and Zip Code. To move from one field to another, press the

Tab key. Tabbing on the last field will cause the cursor to jump back to the first field. If a number of fields are compressed together for purposes of style and function, you may see something like the following on the screen:

```
Joe Bloue
9191 Frisbrane Road
Santa Hono          CA    92123
```

That looks like a single field, but in fact there is a separate field for Name, Address, City, State and Zip Code. The spacing was made up by putting five fields in the following arrangement:

```
Joe Bloue
9191 Frisbrane Road
Santa Hono          CA    92123
```

To the user, this will be invisible, but such a style would certainly come in handy for mailing labels and similar applications. Therefore if you are writing in a field and pressing the Return key does not get the expected results, try pressing Tab.

"Auto Tab" now allows the user to substitute the Return Key for the Tab Key in non-scrolling fields that go beyond the bottom line of a field. Instead of disappearing off the bottom of the field, the Auto Tab makes the cursor jump to the next field down when Return is pressed.

For example, if the Auto Tab were on in the above example, after typing in "Joe Bloue," the user pressed the Return Key, the cursor would jump to the next field down where the address is listed. This gives the option of using the Return Key instead of the Tab key to go from one field to another. Chapter 3 explains how to turn the Auto Tab on and off.

In HyperCard, the individual lines can be of major importance in a field. Calculations in scripts are often based on information in a *certain field on a specific line.* For example, the sample stack, "HyperCalc", uses numbers on specified lines in various fields. By changing the numbers on the specified lines, different results are obtained. However, if the same information is entered on different lines, then the calculations will not work. Line numbers are consistent in fields from top to bottom beginning with number one.

> Line 1
> Line 2
> Line 3
> etc....

Each time the Return key is pressed a new line is created. The text continues and is preserved even if the text exceeds the limits of the field box. That text can only be seen again, though, if the field is one that can be scrolled.

Painting and Drawing

In Chapter 1, we had a quick introduction to the Paint tools, and in this chapter we will look at their use more closely. We will do this in conjunction with the special effects that are available in the Paint and Options menus and on the separate tools. There are several effects available on the Paint and Options menus, and we will introduce these as we go along interspersed with the various tool. We will begin by looking at the Paint and Options menu shown in Figure 2-13.

```
┌─────────────────────────┐     ┌─────────────────────────┐
│ Paint                   │     │ Options                 │
├─────────────────────────┤     ├─────────────────────────┤
│ Select           ⌘S     │     │ Grid                    │
│ Select All       ⌘A     │     │ FatBits                 │
│ ·························│     │ Power Keys              │
│ Fill                    │     │ ·························│
│ Invert                  │     │ Line Size...            │
│ Pickup                  │     │ Brush Shape...          │
│ Darken                  │     │ Edit Pattern...         │
│ Lighten                 │     │ Polygon Sides...        │
│ Trace Edges             │     │ ·························│
│ Rotate Left             │     │ Draw Filled             │
│ Rotate Right            │     │ Draw Centered           │
│ Flip Vertical           │     │ Draw Multiple           │
│ Flip Horizontal         │     └─────────────────────────┘
│ ·························│
│ Opaque                  │
│ Transparent             │
│ ·························│
│ Keep             ⌘K     │
│ Revert                  │
└─────────────────────────┘
```

Figure 2-13

We'll begin with the tools used for free hand creations and the Patterns menu.

Special Note: There are many "power keys" associated with different functions of the Paint and Options menus. While using a paint tool, pressing a power key will choose the menu option for you without having to use the pulldown menus. Throughout the discussing of painting and drawing there will be references to these power keys and the letters or numbers associated with the characters and paint functions.

Eraser   To get started, knowing how to use the eraser is important. By choosing it and dragging it over painted areas, everything will be erased. A double click of the eraser while it is on the menu will erase the whole page. It is a simple tool but very important.

> **Special Note:** While drawing on a card, the paint tools will paint right over fields and buttons, but while drawing in the background, the graphics effects go underneath buttons and fields.

Pencil   The pencil is used for two important drawing functions. First it is used for general free hand drawing. It draws at one pixel and second, it is used for fine narrow lines. By dragging it across the screen, different pictures can be created. For example, Figure 2-14 needs some touch up work on the woman's left shoulder.

Figure 2-14

We can use the pencil for touch-up. The best way to touch up a drawing with the pencil is to use **Fat Bits** from the Options menu or press the Option-F while in the paint mode. The portion of the drawing on which you are working is magnified and a miniature of its picture is shown so that you can see what the larger picture section looks like. Zooming in on area needing touch up work is seen in Figure 2-15.

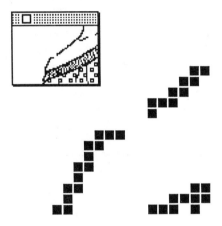

Figure 2-15

The pencil is then used to fix up the little missing section. Also, the pencil erases one pixel (little block) at a time. So if you have some very small area you want to edit, use the pencil instead of the eraser.

Special Note: To zoom in on the area you want of a picture, first touch the spot with the pencil. Then the Fat Bits will take you right to that point.

Paint brush The paint brush differs from the pencil in two important ways. First, it has many different brush shapes.

Depending on which brush shape you choose, your brush line will have a different pattern when dragged across the screen. Either double-click the brush icon on the Tools menu or choose **Brush Shape...** from the **Options** menu. The shapes include the following on the Brush Shapes dialog box:

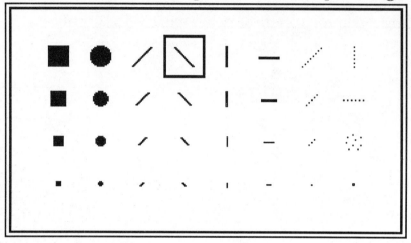

Figure 2-16

Choose the desired brush shape by pointing and clicking. A box surrounds the chosen shape. Above you can see the left leaning slash has a box around it. Once that is chosen, the "\" will be the brush cursor until another shape is picked. Figure 2-17 shows lines created with different brushes:

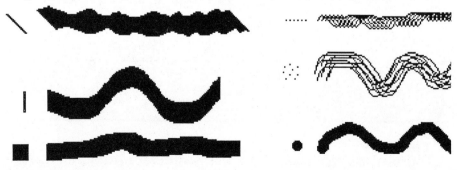

Figure 2-17

Depending on what you want to draw, different brush shapes are best suited.

A second feature of using the paint brush is the ability to use different patterns as a brush. Choose a large square brush pattern, and then once the Brush Pattern dialog box is put away, press the Tab key to bring down the Pattern menu. Choose the brick shape pattern and paint something. The paint brush now draws bricks on the screen canvas.

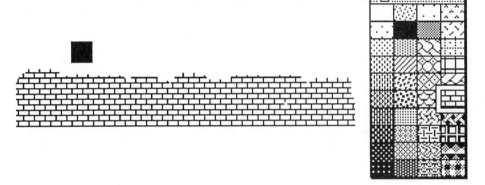

Figure 2-18

Even though the brush shape looks like a solid black square, you can see on the Pattern menu that the brick pattern has been chosen. The effect is that of a crumbling brick wall.

The patterns used in drawing can be customized to any shape you can get into the little box. From the Options menus choose "Edit Pattern..." You will see the current pattern blown up in the Pattern editor. By clicking the dots in the left box, you can change the pattern to whatever you want.

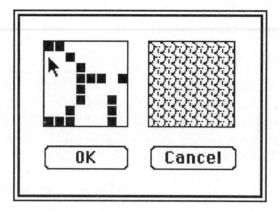

Figure 2-19

The above pattern in Figure 2-19 was created to make a wave-like pattern. The trick is to watch the box on the right while drawing in the box on the left. The pattern is saved with the stack when you quit drawing.

Line Tool   The line tool is a good one to use with either the brush or pencil to make starlight lines. With the pencil and paintbrush, it can be difficult to get a perfectly straight line, but with the line too, it's simple. Just hold down the mouse button at the point to begin the line and drag it to ending point and release the button. There are six different line widths you can use. Choose **Line Size...** from the **Options menu** or use power keys 1, 2, 3, 4, 6, or 8 to increase the line widths.

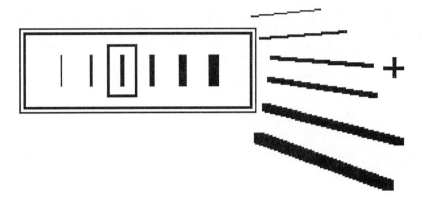

Figure 2-20

The cursor changes to a cross the width of the chosen line. In that way it is easy to tell what size straight line you will draw. The line width is also used with tools that surround areas such as circles and the several polygon tools.

Spray can The spray can works similarly to the paint brush except it only has one shape, and it "sprays" instead of "brushes" on the current pattern. By pressing the Shift key while spraying, you can get straight vertical or horizontal lines, and it acts like a "spray eraser" if you press the Command key and drag it across a painted surface. Figures 2-21 -2-23 show some applications for the spray can. The first is an "old rustic brick walk" and the second shows two smoke stacks sprayed with different patterns. The "rustic" effect was done with the brick pattern sprayed on rather than placed with another tool that gives a solid effect. The different "smoke" effects were accomplished using the solid black pattern, and then one of the dotted patterns.

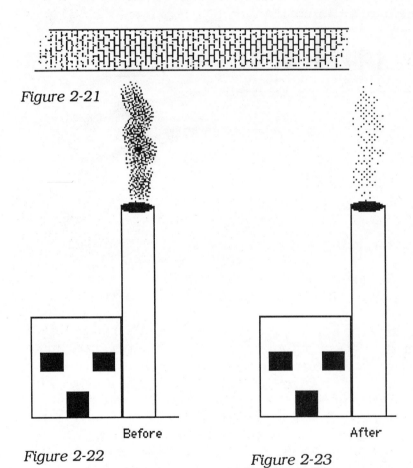

Figure 2-21

Before

After

Figure 2-22

Figure 2-23

Choosing a Regular Polygon Side. When the regular polygon tool is double clicked, the dialog box for the shapes appears on the screen. (The Polygon Shape box can also be brought to the top by choosing it from the Options menu.)   Figure 2-24 shows the available choices.

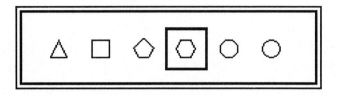

Figure 2-24

All of these shapes are drawn from the center instead of from a corner as with the Circle and Rectangle tools. They also rotate on an axis. If you need a box shape on its side, like a diamond, then use the polygon tool instead of the rectangle tool. The sides can be made fatter by increasing the line width.   Figure 2-25 shows some different regular polygon figures.

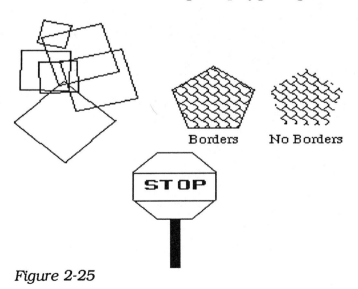

Figure 2-25

Another trick that can be done with filled shapes is to make them without borders. By holding down the Option key while dragging the shape, they will appear with no borders as can be seen in the pentagon above.

Irregular Polygons and Curves. For drawings that are not limited to regular shapes, the irregular polygon and curve tools are used. Both tools can be used for non-surrounding shapes. However, when used in the fill mode, the last point of the line automatically will be connected to the first point. That forces one or more enclosed areas that can be filled.

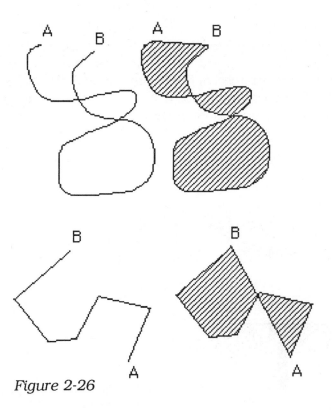

Figure 2-26

In the above examples, the figures on the left were drawn in the non-fill mode, beginning at point A and ending at point B. In the fill mode, a line connects A and B, and all of the surrounded areas are filled with the current pattern.

Some Special Effects

All drawings can be manipulated in ways that cannot be done easily with pen and paper. These effects involve either the use of the Select or Lasso tools or the Paint or Options menus.

Special Note: When you want to surround something with the Lasso, it is easier in many applications to surround it with the Select tool and then press power key S. The select box will Lasso the object, and the icon will turn into the Lasso.

Multiple Images. The first effect is done with the Lasso or the Select tool. By holding down the Option key while dragging a selected area, the original stays put and a copy of the original appears. If both the Option and Command key are held down, repeating copies are created. In the second case, the space between the images is controlled by pressing the Option key and numbers 1-8.

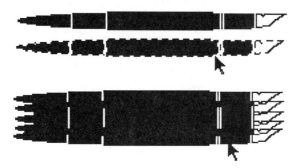

Figure 2-27

Note in Figure 2-27 the arrow cursor is on the screen. In using the Lasso or Select tool, the arrow appears when there the pointer is at a spot it can drag the object.

Another way to get multiple images is to select Draw Multiple from the Option menu or use the power key M. Figure 2-28 shows a "tornado" drawn with the oval tool with the Draw Multiple selected.

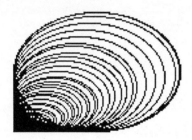

Figure 2-28

Pattern Borders

Lines can be drawn in the selected pattern by holding the option key as you drag the line or border tool. Figure 2-29 shows several examples using a wide border and different patterns with the line tools and tools that draw borders.

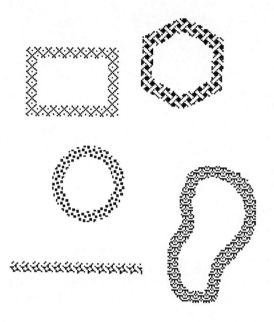

Figure 2-29

Stretching, Shrinking and Enlarging

By pressing the Command key while dragging a picture after it is selected with the Lasso or Select tool, you can enlarge or shrink it. If dragged from a corner, the picture is proportionately enlarged or shrunk. If dragged from a side or the top or bottom, it will be stretched.

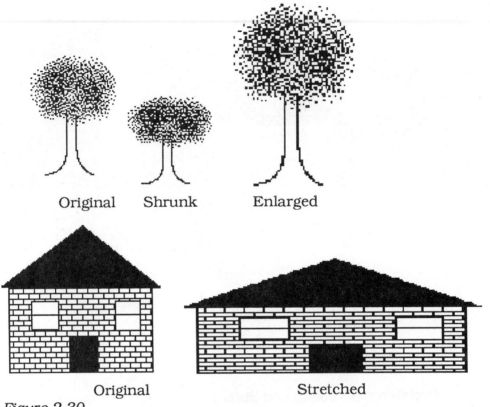

Original   Shrunk   Enlarged

Original   Stretched

Figure 2-30

Notice the distortion which occurs when changing size and stretching in Figure 2-30. Some drawings will look better than others using these techniques. For best results in changing the size of an irregular figure, center it using the Select tool, and then point the arrow at one of the four corners of the Select box around the figure.

Pattern Pickup. Substituting one pattern for another is simple. Draw the object, drag the object onto the pattern, either choose Pickup from the Paint menu or press power key P. Then drag the shape off the pattern. Figure 2-31 shows the three steps to create a cat made up of diagonal lines.

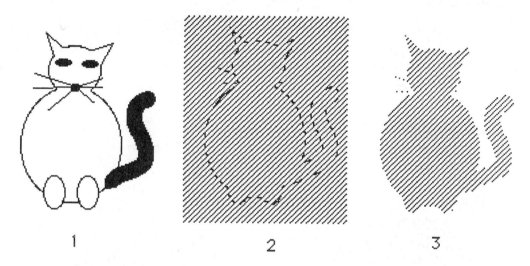

Figure 2-31

A somewhat related function involves using an automatic select of the last figure drawn to get your graphics away from a pattern. For example, you decide you want to label a pattern, and, using the paint-text tool write on a pattern. It does not look like you want, and you want to get it off the pattern without destroying the pattern or the label. By pressing command-S or the power key S, your last drawing will be selected and you can drag it away.

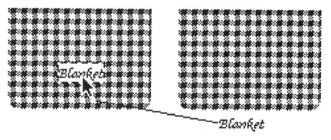

Figure 2-32

Changing Positions and Shading

In the Paint menu there are a number of different effects for changing the position and shading of figures. Figure 2-33 shows how they appear and the associated power key with each.

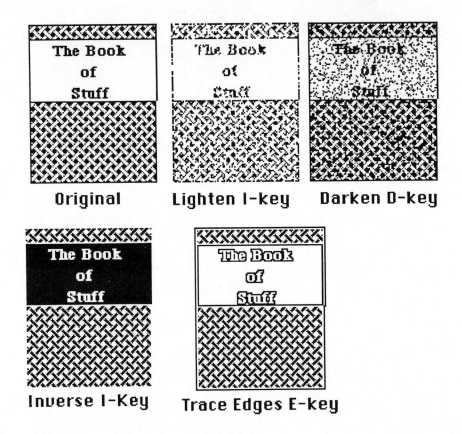

Original Lighten I-key Darken D-key

Inverse I-Key Trace Edges E-key

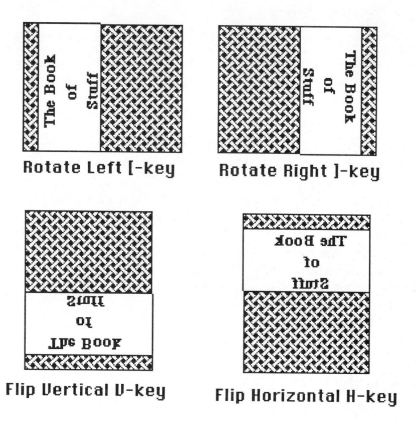

Rotate Left [-key

Rotate Right]-key

Flip Vertical V-key

Flip Horizontal H-key

Figure 2-33

Centered Drawing: If you want to draw relative to the center with tools that normally draw from an edge or corner, use the power key C or choose Draw Centered from the Options menu. In Figure 2-34, the big asterisk (S) character is the point where both rectangles began. The centered rectangle's sides are equidistant from the asterisk, while the rectangle not centered shows the sides drawn away from the upper left hand corner of the rectangle.

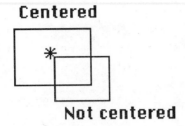

Figure 2-34

Remember that the regular polygon tool does not require the Draw Centered option since it does that anyway.

Opaque and Transparent Transfers: When non-filled drawings are transferred onto a filled image, they can be either opaque or transparent. If opaque, they cover over the portion of the pattern they are placed upon, while if transparent, only the outline of the drawing is visible.

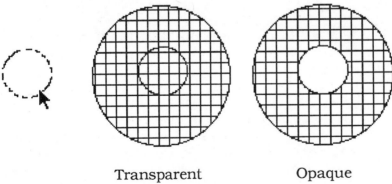

Transparent   Opaque

Figure 2-35

After selecting the shape to be dragged onto a pattern, choose opaque or transparent from the Paint menu. The default is transparent.

Keep and Revert. Keep and revert are two options for maintaining a drawing so that if you work on it and mess it up, you can get the original one back. To preserve the drawing, choose Keep from the Paint menu or use Command-K. After you've worked on the graphic and decide you want to get the latest "kept" version back, choose Revert from the Paint menu or use power key R.

Importing and Exporting Files

There are a number of different applications where you will want to place graphic files in HyperCard prepared with non-HyperCard tools. This section discusses different ways to use non-HyperCard files saved in MacPaint format imported to Hyper-Card.

Scanner Pictures. Most scanners that work with the Macintosh can save their output as MacPaint files. If your application requires drawings that are difficult for you to do yourself, scanning the art from another source can get the job done. For example, the following card shows art scanned from an art book of public domain art nouveau drawings. (Such books are known as "clip art" books.) The required section of the art was then saved as a MacPaint file. A paint tool was selected from HyperCard and Import Paint was chosen from the File menu and the scanned art file was selected. Once the artwork was on the HyperCard card, it was clipped and positioned on the card. The unwanted portion of the art was removed.

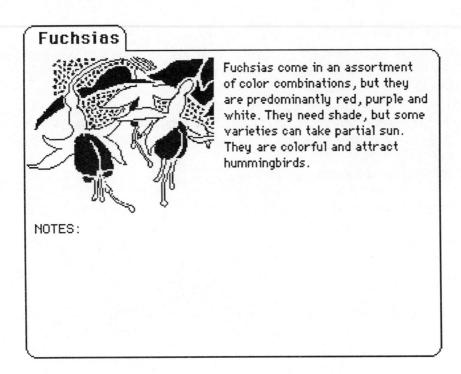

Fuchsias come in an assortment of color combinations, but they are predominantly red, purple and white. They need shade, but some varieties can take partial sun. They are colorful and attract hummingbirds.

Figure 2-36

Digitized Pictures: Another powerful tool that can be used in conjunction with HyperCard is a video digitized file in MacPaint format. By photographing objects and people with a video camera and digitizing the results into a format the Macintosh can read, you can organize your output with a HyperCard file.

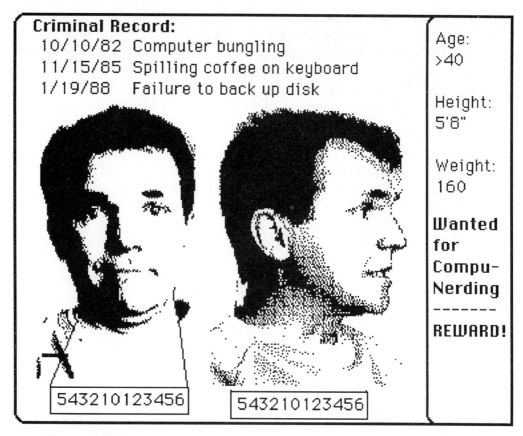

Figure 2-37

For example, a Realtor could keep an index of real estate for sale with digitized pictures of houses on separate HyperCard cards, or the police could keep criminal records using digitized photos of felons as shown in Figure 2-37

Computerized "Clip Art." Several companies make "clip art" or "click art" as it is sometimes called. This is copyright free art that can be used for different applications. For example, in putting an ad or flyer together, many businesses will use clip art. This is less expensive than hiring an artist every time advertisements are prepared A HyperCard file could be built to organize and keep track of it, and then it easily could be found for a specific ad or flyer. Similarly, the art could be used to illustrate another HyperCard file. So if you like art, but you're not an artist, there are a lot of ways to get it on disk and into HyperCard.

Exporting Art. Any art work done on HyperCard can be exported by choosing the Export option under the File menu when a paint tool is being used. The Export option takes a snapshot of the screen and places it on the current disk. In this way, you can use the tools in HyperCard to work on a picture and then have them available to paste into another application, such as a word processor or page makeup program. Since it takes a snapshot of the screen, it exports the text as well. Many of the illustrations in this book were done using Export.

Special Note: It also is possible to export shots of the current screen to the disk by pressing the following:

Command key + Shift + 3

It is not necessary to be using a paint tool or any other tool using this method.

Another way to export art is simply to use the cut and paste method. Before leaving HyperCard, any art that is copied or cut stays in a buffer which can then be pasted in another Hyper-Card or non-HyperCard application. Similarly, you can import art that way as well from card to card or from a non-HyperCard application.

Printing With HyperCard

HyperCard has a very powerful print manager providing the user with numerous printing options. If you are familiar with other general Macintosh printing applications, some of the options will be familiar, but there are so many printing possibilities with HyperCard, it is important to go over this section very carefully.

To get started, be sure your printer icons are on the startup disk or with the startup system files. If using a LaserWriter, be sure that *both* the LaserWriter and the LaserPrep files are in place. If using the Finder and/or MultiFinder, instead of the standard System on the HyperCard StartUp disk, be sure to pull down the Apple menu and select "Chooser". Then indicate what type of printer you wish to use. Using the HyperCard Startup disk, the printer icon on the disk will automatically choose the printer for you.

The Page Setup routine is standard, but if using the Laser-Writer, things will be slowed considerably if the smoothing or flipping options are used. Furthermore, the reduce or enlarge options do not work with HyperCard, but as we will see, such options are available, to some extent, in printing stacks.

Printing Single Cards, Stacks and Reports

Printing Cards. From the File menu, there are options for printing a single card, a stack or a report. Printing single cards is very useful for getting precise information without having to print the whole stack, such as a single address or phone number required for out-of-office use or a daily schedule.

However, if a card has more information than fits on the screen, which is common with cards that have scroll bars, the results may end up looking like the card in Figure 2-38, one from a fictitious personnel file.

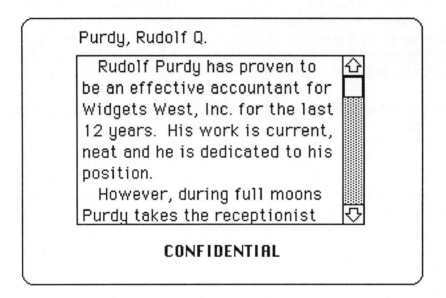

Purdy, Rudolf Q.

Rudolf Purdy has proven to be an effective accountant for Widgets West, Inc. for the last 12 years. His work is current, neat and he is dedicated to his position.
However, during full moons Purdy takes the receptionist

CONFIDENTIAL

Figure 2-38

In these circumstances, where only part of the information is visible, it is necessary to choose Print Report from the File menu. When printing a report, all of the information in the selected fields is printed. For example, if the card in Figure 2-38 were printed out as a report, with the chosen field named "Personnel", it would look like the following:

Personnel
 Rudolf Purdy has proven to be an effective accountant for Widgets West, Inc. for the last 12 years. His work is current, neat and he is dedicated to his position.
 However, during full moons Purdy takes the receptionist

to a cabin in the woods and performs spreadsheet calculations in front of her. She seems to enjoy it, and it has not had a negative effect on either Purdy's or the receptionist's work.

The dilemma in printing reports when all that is required is the information on a single card is that all the information in the selected fields of the entire stack is printed. Thus, if the Personnel field were chosen, not only would Purdy's file be printed; so too would all of the others. In the next chapter you will see how to cut a single card and place it into a new stack all by itself to be printed as a report. At this point, all you need to know is that it is possible to get all of the information in a single card even if that information is not visible on the screen. We will return to printing later on in this chapter and discuss printing reports in detail.

Stack Printing. The next level of printing after single cards is printing the entire stack. The stack printing option in the File menu will do that for you. When you select the Print Stack... option there are several ways to print the cards. Whatever method is used, each entire card is printed as it appears on the screen. In choosing the stack printing option, the choice is one of how many cards you want on a single page and the size of the card. The smallest size you can print and still read the text is the half size. This will put eight cards on a single page, and is a very efficient and effective way of making hardcopy of the cards. Full sized cards placed two to a page are easier to read and are still more economical than than a single card to a page, but it is more difficult to get an overview of the stack. A "snapshot" of the page is shown with a rough representation of what a page of cards will look like. In some cases it may be useful to print quarter sized cards, especially for an overview of the stack. If the cards have large graphics or type, it would be possible to read individual cards as well. Try printing them in different sizes to see what best suits a particular application.

The icon options from left to right at the bottom of the screen next to **Header**, provide the option of placing the date, time, page number and stack name, respectively. Likewise, you can type in information yourself for the header title.

The standard format option stacks cards on top of one another on a single page. The split-page format does the same thing except it adds a dotted line and space for punch holes at the top and bottom of the page for placement in min-binders. Figure 2-39 shows the appearance of two cards on a page with the split-page format. (The "holes" are not printed, but they illustrate where mini-binder holes might go.)

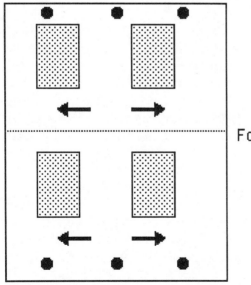

Fold line

Figure 2-39

Report Printing. Returning again to printing a report of a stack, the options range from lists to mailing labels. After choosing Print Report... from the File menu, the dialog box provides three basic styles; labels, columns and rows. The left side of the box shows a reduced outline of the page in the selected style as shown in Figure 2-40. On the right side of the box are the fields in the stack and you select the one you want printed. In the example in Figure 2-40, the Name and Address fields have been selected, but the date was not. The column format was chosen for the style.

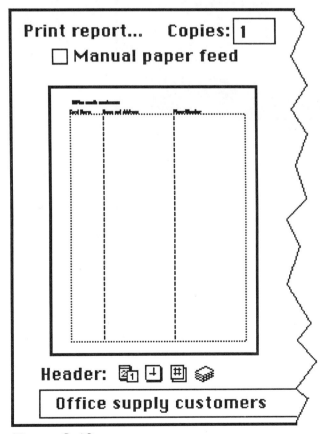

Figure 2-40a

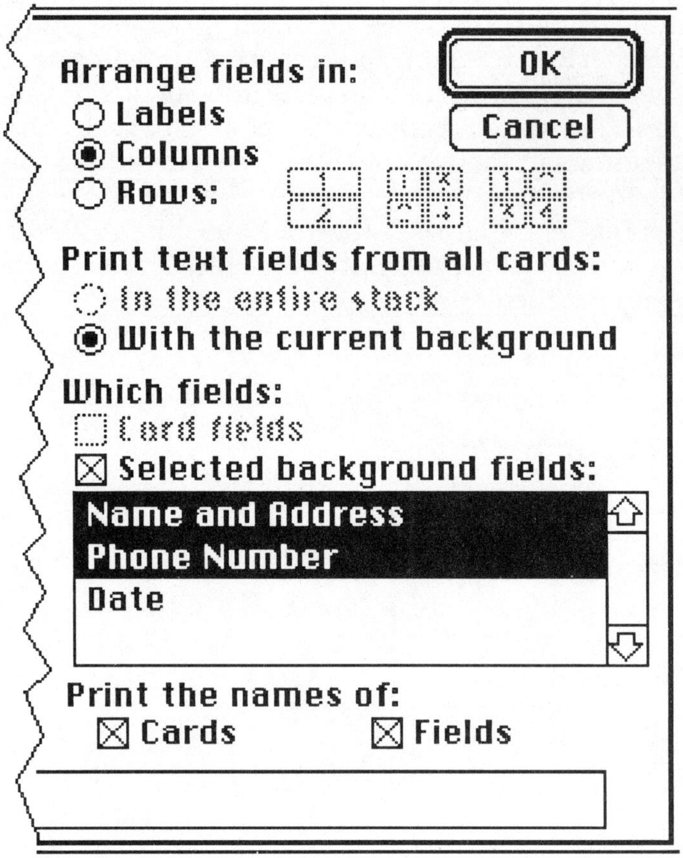

Arrange fields in:
○ Labels
◉ Columns
○ Rows:

[OK]
[Cancel]

Print text fields from all cards:
○ In the entire stack
◉ With the current background

Which fields:
☐ Card fields
☒ Selected background fields:

Name and Address
Phone Number
Date

Print the names of:
☒ Cards   ☒ Fields

Figure 2-40b

If, instead of columns, rows are chosen, there are three row styles. The first style places the fields on top of one another. The second two styles arrange the rows in two columns. The first two-column style is essentially like having two columns, with the second one beginning after the last entry has been entered in the first column. This is like a telephone book arrangement. The second style of two columns of rows orders the data from column one to column two alternating columns as it goes through the sequence of data. The broken vertical line shows the division between field/card information, which can be optionally omitted and in most cases will be, and the data in the fields. Figure 2-41 shows an example of one arrangement using standard row and card information.

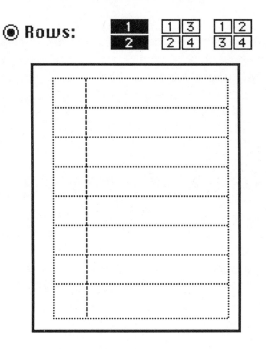

Figure 2-41

One of the nice things about the printing options in HyperCard is the ability to print reports of the same data in so many different ways. In a stack, information for one aspect of a general use may be needed only in part of a printout, while another part may be required in a separate printout. For example, a stack may have project information for a given task coupled with the name and department of the individual responsible for accomplishing the task. The project information can be printed in one printout, and then the labels for sending the information to the correct person and department could be printed out in a second printout. All of the information is taken from the same stack, and HyperCard allows the flexible printing required for different purposes of the printed material.

In preparing labels, the two fundamental differences are between printing with an ImageWriter or a LaserWriter. Dot matrix printers and daisy wheel printers (letter quality) use tractor fed labels that usually are in single label columns, while with a laser printer, there are several columns of labels on a single label sheet. So, depending on which one you use, check the format and adjust the label size before printing.

Special Note: Before wasting labels, make some test runs with ordinary paper in your printer to make sure that the output conforms to the type of labels you are using. Place the trail sheets next to the labels and check to see if they align correctly. When the printout on the labels matches the trial ones, place the information on a HyperCard card so that whenever you need to use the same label format again, you will have it. HyperCard retains the last printing information for a stack automatically, but if you use another printing option in the meantime, you may have to re-figure the labels all over again if you do not make a note of them somewhere.

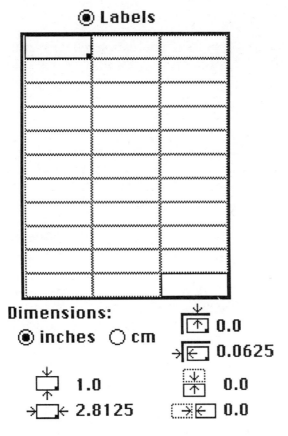

Figure 2-42

Getting the knack of preparing labels for a report format printing is simple but requires some practice. The format in Figure 2-42 shows the label printing tools that appear on the screen when the label option is selected.

Place the pointer in the little black box in the label in the upper left hand corner. Holding the mouse button down, drag the label to the size you want. You will be able to see the size in inches or centimeters in the boxes below the label box.

Summary

There is a lot you can do with HyperCard as we have seen from this brief examination of what tools and options are available with the program. At this point you should be able to use Hyper-Card stacks to get information, and add text and graphics to a card. Likewise you should be able to use all of the tools dealing with text and painting. In other words, you can use HyperCard applications, and you've seen some of the many different things possible. Experiment with different parts of the HyperCard applications that come with HyperCard. Use them and try different things to see what you can and cannot do.

Once you've done all sorts of different things with the different HyperCard applications, go on to the next chapter. There, you will see how to begin making your own HyperCard applications. This is called "Authoring," and it is as easy to learn as using HyperCard itself. However, unless you understand the basics of how to work with HyperCard, it will be confusing if you begin making your own application. Therefore, take some time to go through the various stacks on your disks before starting the next chapter.

Authoring

What is Authoring?

Authoring in HyperCard will be a unique experience since it is a new form of creating programs for microcomputers. It is something like programming, but it is far simpler. It is something like configuring an applications program, but it is far more flexible and powerful. Basically, authoring is making your own HyperCard stacks, cards and buttons. As a matter of fact, it is so simple that you can develop and market professional quality software in a very short period of time.

An overview of authoring involves four key elements:

      1. Creating a new stack
      2. Adding buttons
      3. Adding fields
      4. Adding cards

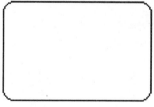

New Field

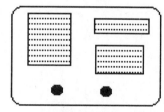

Add Fields

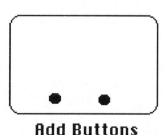

Add Buttons

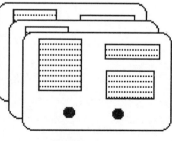

Add Cards

Figure 3-1

Setting Preferences for Authoring

The first thing to do is to re-set the preferences to "Authoring." Go to the Home stack and go to the last card in the stack as described in Chapter 2 and change from "Painting to Authoring."

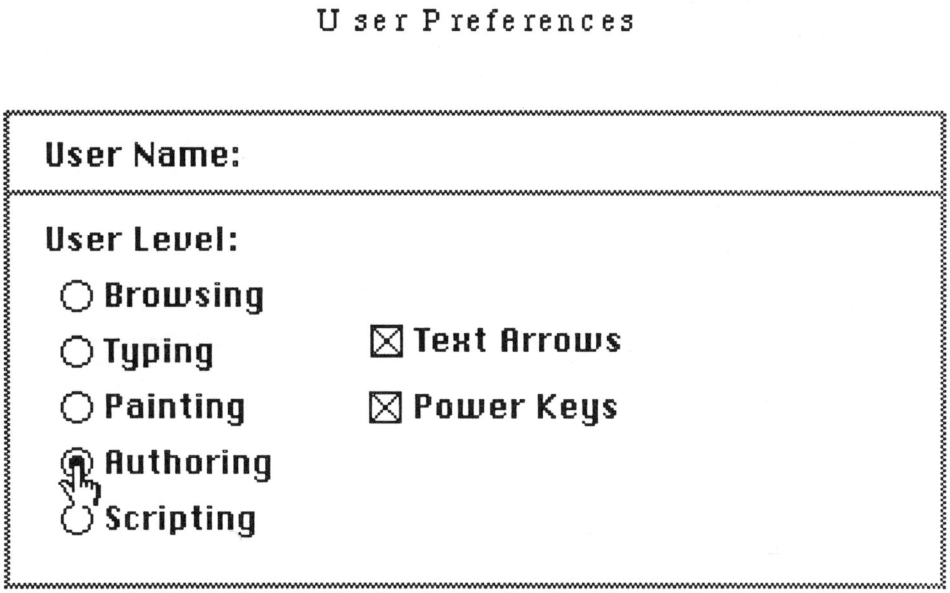

U ser P refe rences

```
User Name:

User Leuel:
  ○ Browsing
  ○ Typing          ⊠ Text Arrows
  ○ Painting        ⊠ Power Keys
  ◉ Authoring
  ○ Scripting
```

Figure 3-2

Once that is done, you're all set to create a brand new stack and begin authoring.

New Stack

To create a new stack, simply click New Stack. When you do that the following dialog box appears on the screen:

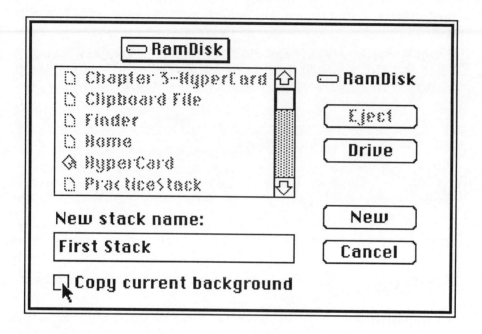

Figure 3-3

Same or different background?

The first decision to make is whether or not to use the same background, including all graphics, fields and buttons in the background. For this first stack, click the "Copy current background" box so that the "x" in the box is removed as shown in Figure 3-3. (The default is to copy the current background; so whenever you want a new stack, be sure to click this box if you do not want to duplicate the background.) Next, name the stack "First Stack" as was done in the example or any other name you want. Then click "New" and you will see a blank screen with the menu bar across the top. This is the first card of your new stack.

Stack Info... Pull down Objects menu and choose Stack Info.... You will be shown a dialog box that looks like Figure 3-4.

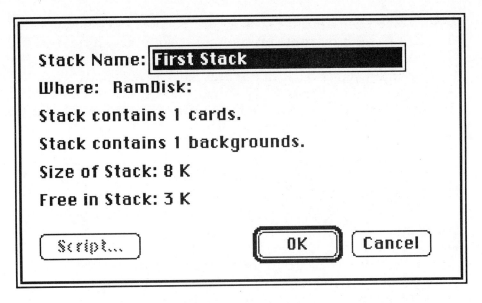

Figure 3-4

This box provides information about the stack. The ghosted Script... button can be used when developing your own script which we will cover in the next chapter.

New Cards

With an existing stack you want to use or a new stack being developed, adding new cards is a simple matter. To add a new card, either press Command-N or choose New Card from the Edit menu. Before adding any new cards, first use the paint text tool and write,

> This is Card #1

on the only card in your new stack. Now, add a new card.

Your screen will appear blank again. You've added a new card, but since you only wrote on the first card, you will not be able to see anything. Using the Go menu choose First or press Command-1 to get back to the first card. Now, you will see the message, "This is Card #1." To get back to the second card, choose Last from the Go menu or press Command-4. On it, using the paint text tool, write,

This is Card #2

For now, this is all you need.

Card Info

Go back to the first card in the stack, choose the Browse tool and select Card Info.. from the Objects menu. The Card Info dialog box appears and you will see the dialog box shown in Figure 3-5:

```
┌──────────────────────────────────────────────────┐
│                                                    │
│   Card Name: │Uno                            │    │
│   Card Number: 1 out of 2                          │
│   Card ID: 2844                                    │
│   Contains 0 card fields.                          │
│   Contains 0 card buttons.                         │
│                                                    │
│   ☐ Can't delete card.                             │
│                                                    │
│   [ Script... ]      [[  OK  ]]   [ Cancel ]       │
└──────────────────────────────────────────────────┘
```

Figure 3-5

There will be no name next to "Card Name." You can name it whatever you want, but it is optional to do so. The information tells you that this card is the first in a stack of two cards. Since there are no fields or buttons on the card, it indicates that there are zero. If for some reason you do not want a specific card deleted, and there will be many applications where this will be important, just click the "Can't delete card" option. If at some later time you want the card deleted, just click the same option again, and it can be deleted. The Card ID number is 2844, which at this time should be noted but is not vital until you get to scripting. (Your Card ID may be different, but don't worry if it is.) Click OK and go to the second card in the stack and do the same thing. Note there is a different ID number for the second card that is not in sequence with the ID of the first card. That is as it is supposed to be.

If you ever want to get rid of a card, from the Edit menu you can choose either Cut Card or Delete Card. If you use Cut Card, the card is placed on the clipboard so that it can be pasted elsewhere if you want. Delete Card gets rid of the card and does not place it on the clipboard.

Background and Foreground

Thus far, we've been working only in the foreground. That is, we've been writing on top of individual cards, and we have not been adding anything to the underlying layer that is common to all cards in a stack. Whatever you put in the foreground applies only to a single card, but what you put in the background is common for all cards.

To see how the background and foreground differ, from your "First Stack" choose any one of the paint tools and select Background from the Edit menu or press Command-B. You know you are in the background since your menu bar will change and anything you wrote or drew in the foreground will disappear.

 File   Edit   Go   Tools   Paint   Options   Patterns

Background Menu Bar

Figure 3-6

Now, using the paint brush tool, draw a big "X" at the bottom of the screen. Press Command-B to go back to the foreground (Command-B toggles the background and foreground) and you will see something like the Figure 3-7:

This is Card #1

Figure 3-7

Go to the second card, and you will see the same "X", but it will show that you are on the second card. Take the eraser tool from the Tools menu and try to erase the "X." It cannot be done since it is in the background and will appear on every card that is added to the stack. In authoring, most of the buttons and fields will be in the background. Likewise, many HyperCard stacks you author will be enhanced by background graphics and paint. To easily identify a stack, for instance, you might want to label it with the paint text tool and add a little graphic frame.

Return to the background of the stack and erase the "X" with the eraser tool. Using the filled paint rectangle tool and the paint text tool draw the "First Stack" graphic shown in Figure 3-8 in the background:

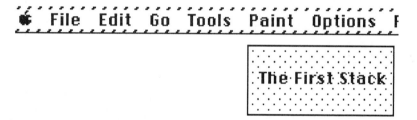

Figure 3-8

After using the text tool to write "The First Stack" on the screen, choose Transparent from the Paint menu so that the rectangle and text merge. Now, whenever you are in the stack called "The First Stack," you'll know it by glancing at the label. There are other, more subtle, ways to do the same thing. For example, you could have a "file card" background or some similar graphic that would show what the stack was about. For example, a stack for sales calls might have a briefcase background with no labels as shown in Figure 3-9.

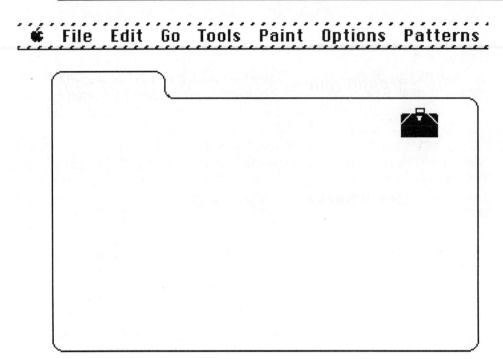

Figure 3-9

Look at the various HyperCard example disks to see what they have used for the background, and look at non-computer documents that use cards, pages, folders or anything else as well to get some more ideas.

Background Info

Like the cards, there is also a set of information about the background in the Objects menu. You can optionally give the background a name to protect it against deletion by clicking the "Can't delete background" option in the dialog box. Otherwise, it just gives the same information about the background as the other "Info" boxes have.

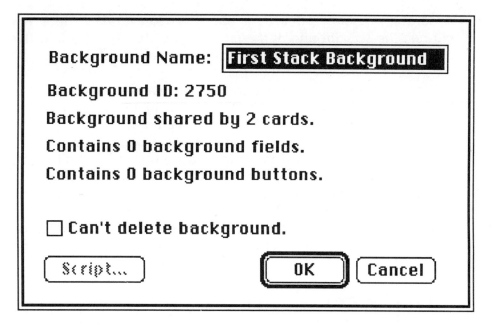

Figure 3-10

Special Note: It is probably a good idea to click the "Can't delete background" option in the Background Info dialog box. If you want to change the background, you can always un-protect it, but to avoid accidentally getting a new background where you don't want one or accidentally zapping an old one, it's best to protect it.

New Background

In a single stack, there will be applications where you will want to change backgrounds. This might be done for a "subroutine" that goes off and does something different and then returns to the original background further on in the stack, or it could be for a general change at some point in the stack. From the Objects menu if you choose "New Background," HyperCard generates a new card with a blank background. *It does not change the background of the previous cards.* You can add the new background and then add cards as you go along.

To revert to the original background, the easiest way to do it is to select a card with the original background, choose Copy Card from the edit menu and then paste it in after the last card. Now all of the new cards will have the original background again. This will require erasing any information on it you don't want, but it is easier than going through the process of re-designing the background all over again. Alternatively you can go to the last card with the original background, select New Card, and then cut the card just created and paste it after the card with the background you wish to change from. Using this second method does not require erasing any information on the card.

Creating Buttons

Placing buttons on a stack is the first real step in making an operating, original stack. At the level of authoring, it is very simple but somewhat limited. However, we will see what can be done and how to use buttons to their maximum potential.

Using the Button Tool

Click the button tool on the tools menu. You will see the arrow pointer. At this point most of the activities that pertain to text, graphics and other operations now apply to buttons. For example, cutting and pasting is used for cutting and pasting buttons, not text and graphics. This can be tricky to remember at first, but in time you will get used to it.

Using your "First Stack" stack, we will now put a button on it and make the button do what we want. Usually buttons are simply used for moving from one card to another, and that is exactly what we will do. We will create a set of buttons that will move us back and forth through the stack.

New Button. To get started, go to the first card in the stack and click the Objects menu and choose "New Button." When you do that, you will see the screen shown in Figure 3-11.

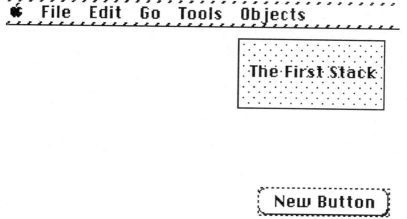

Figure 3-11

Button Info: Pull down the Objects menu and select Button Info. You will see a dialog box like the one shown in Figure 3-12:

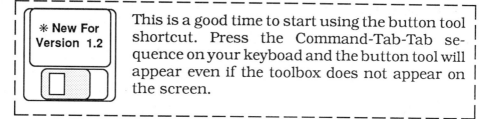

* **New For Version 1.2**

This is a good time to start using the button tool shortcut. Press the Command-Tab-Tab sequence on your keyboad and the button tool will appear even if the toolbox does not appear on the screen.

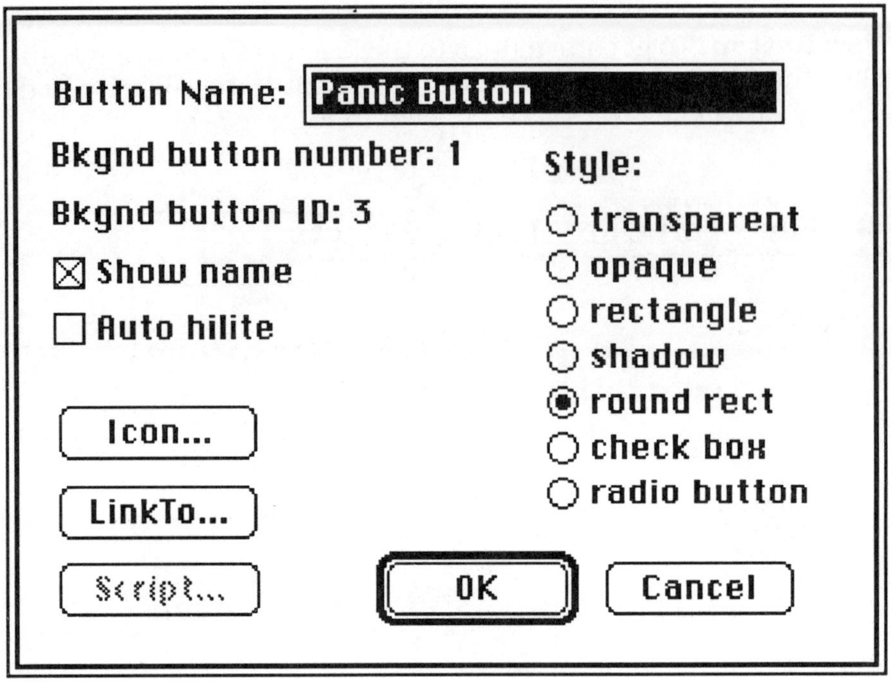

Button Name: **Panic Button**

Bkgnd button number: 1

Bkgnd button ID: 3

☒ Show name

☐ Auto hilite

[Icon...]

[LinkTo...]

[Script...]

Style:
○ transparent
○ opaque
○ rectangle
○ shadow
◉ round rect
○ check box
○ radio button

[OK]   [Cancel]

Figure 3-12

This button is going to take you to the Help Stack, and so we'll call it a "Panic Button". Type that in next to Button Name. Notice that the circle with "round rect" is darkened. That is the shape of the button, and for this first one we will stick with it. Also note that there is an "X" in the box next to Show Name. That means that the name next to Button Name will be shown on the button.

Next, make sure your HyperCard Help disk is in one of your drives or on your hard disk. Click the "Link To" button and the following box will appear:

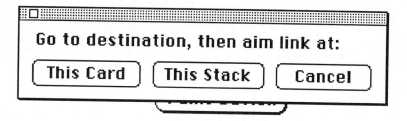

Figure 3-13

At this point, you can go to any other card or stack you want. Since the button we're working on will cause HyperCard to go to the Help Stack, press Command-? or choose Help from the Go menu. Then your screen will appear as shown in Figure 3-14.

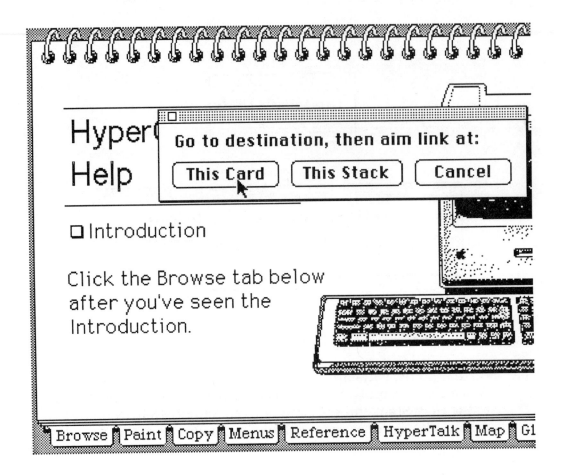

Figure 3-14

Place the arrow pointer on the "This Card" option and click it. That sets the destination of your "Panic Button." The program returns to the card with the button with which you were just working. Move the button so that it is directly under the "First Stack" label. Be careful in moving buttons. They can also be stretched and shrunk without the Command or Option keys pressed. Drag the button from its center to move it as shown in Figure 3-15.

Figure 3-15

That is all you have to do. Select the Browse tool, and try out your new button. It will find the Help Stack and take you to the card you selected. At its most basic level, that is all there is to creating buttons and linking cards and stacks through buttons. At the authoring level, you can link any card with any other card in any stack.

In summary, there are five essential steps for creating buttons and linking them to another card or stack:

> **Step 1:** Select the Button Tool from the Tool menu.
> **Step 2:** Select New Button from the Objects Menu
> **Step 3:** Select Button Info from the Objects Menu
> **Step 4:** Select Link to... in the Button Dialog Box
> **Step 5:** Go to the desired card and select the card or stack as the destination.

Now that the basics are completed, let's return to the Button Info dialog box and examine the options available.

Button Styles

There are seven button styles available from the Button Info style selection. Any style can be used for your buttons.

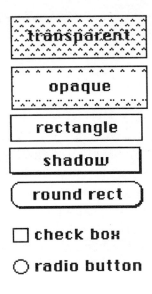

Figure 3-16

The transparent and opaque buttons work very much like the transparent and opaque options available in the Paint menu. The transparent buttons blend in with their surroundings and the opaque covers them up.

Likewise, you can exercise your options to not have a name at all. If you do not wish for a text name, click the "Show name" box in the Button Info dialog box to remove the "X". If you use too long of a button name, it may not fit in your name box.

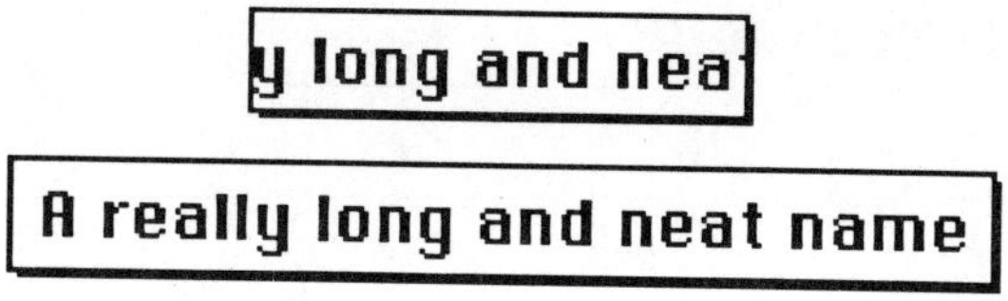

| y long and nea |

| A really long and neat name |

Figure 3-17

As soon as the name has been entered, you can see it will not
fit. Using the Button tool, select the button and drag it from the
corner until you can see the entire button name as shown in
Figure 3-17.

Button Icons

In the Button Info dialog box, one of the options is "Icon..." The
Icon... option will show you several different types of button
styles you can use. When you select Icon..., you will see the
screen shown in Figure 3-18.

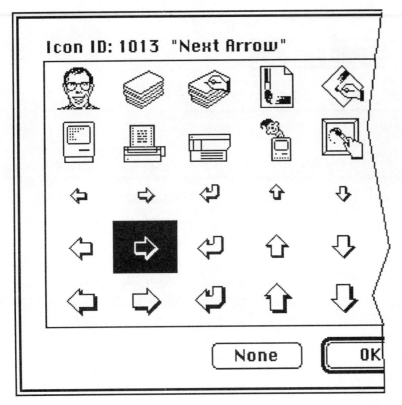

Figure 3-18

Use the scroll arrows on the side to see all the different icons available. If you decide to choose this option, use the "transparent" option from the Button Info dialog box, and then your icon will appear without any boundary. (Of course if you want it mixed in with one of the seven styles in the dialog box, by all means feel free to mix the styles.) For developing the "First Stack" stack, choose the right pointing arrow. It will be highlighted as shown in the above figure. When it is placed on the first card, return to the Icon... set and choose the left pointing arrow. Place both arrow buttons at the bottom of the card as shown in Figure 3-19:

Figure 3-19

These buttons go in the *foreground*; not the background. You want these buttons to go to the next card. If they are placed in the background; then all the arrows would make the "next card" to be a single card that was selected in the Link to... operation in the Button Info option. Do nothing with these buttons now, but when you add cards, use the Link to... operation to have the buttons connect to the next and previous cards. Later on we will learn how to make buttons that will go to any *next* or *previous* card; not just a specified card generated in the Link to... operation. Then we can put the buttons in the background in a single effort rather than having to go through a new definition process every time a new card is added to the stack.

Customized Button Icons

Using the button icons available on HyperCard will suffice for many applications, but customizing icon buttons allows you to best communicate the button's function. For example, working on Project A, Project B and Project C in HyperCard concurrently, it would be very useful to have unique button icons for each project. In that way, it is simple to keep them separate and show others who may use the stacks developed exactly what the buttons do through an icon representation. We'll start by examining how to make unique icons from existing button styles.

Creating New Styles from Existing Styles. The easiest way to make a new button style is to take an existing one and add some changes to it. For example, we could take the radio button and generate several different styles.

○ original radio button

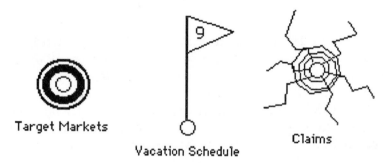

Target Markets

Vacation Schedule

Claims

Figure 3-20

In the examples in Figure 3-20, the hole in the "glass", the target's "bull's eye" and the "golf hole" are the original radio button. By using the paint tools around the radio button, or any of the other button styles, you can incorporate the button's shape into entirely new and different shapes.

Special Note: Remember that buttons and graphics are moved using different tools. Try to position the button where you want it on the card, in the background or foreground, *before* adding the paint graphics around it.

Making Button Graphics From Scratch. Take a look at the buttons on the Home Card in the Home Stack. Those buttons are original designs. There are two ways to make originally designed buttons. By choosing the **transparent** style from Button Info, simply draw the figure you want around the transparent area for the button. When the button tool is selected, even with transparent buttons, you can see the area encompassed by the button. This area can be increased or reduced by dragging the sides and corners of the button. Then place the graphics on top of the button area.

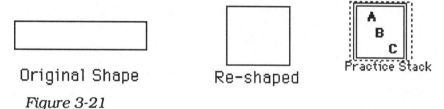

Original Shape   Re-shaped   Practice Stack

Figure 3-21

The original shape of the transparent button is a long rectangle. Using the button tool, the button is first selected and then re-shaped into a box. Finally, the graphic is drawn on top of the button. (In Figure 3-21, the button is the dotted square beneath the graphic "ABC Block." The label was added using the Paint Text tool.)

Using the above method, the graphic and button are actually separated. Basically, the graphic serves to pinpoint where the transparent button is located on the screen. This works fine, but if you want to make a copy of the button and use it on another stack, it is necessary to copy both the button and the graphic. Since the button is transparent and can only be viewed when the Button tool is selected, this procedure is tricky.

Making Customized Button Icons. Go to the Home Card of the Home Stack and click the button tool. Select and move some buttons back and forth. If the graphic stays in one place and the button moves; then the above method has been used to create the button. On the other hand, if the button and graphic move together, then the button is an icon. We saw that by choosing the Icon... option from Button Info, it was possible to select an existing button icon and make graphic buttons. How is it possible to make customized button icons that are actually part of the button?

In order to make your own icon buttons, it is necessary to have a "resource editor" for the Macintosh. The most widely distributed such editor is "ResEdit," a resource editor available through Macintosh computer clubs or Macintosh dealers. There are other resource editors, but for the examples here, we will use ResEdit.

Special Note: Before proceeding with this project, make a special backup of HyperCard and use the special backup for this example. This procedure will change permanently one of the HyperCard icons. Also, there are many different versions of ResEdit. The version you get may work slightly different from the one in the examples here, but in general, the procedures are similar.

Place HyperCard and a disk with ResEdit in your Macintosh. Launch ResEdit, and a series of windows will appear on your screen. Find the HyperCard window and select "Icon" as shown in Figure 3-22.

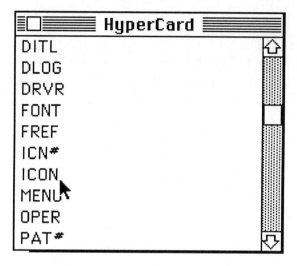

Figure 3-22

Next, a window with the various icons will appear on the screen. Select a simple icon, such as the one with the page with a folded corner.

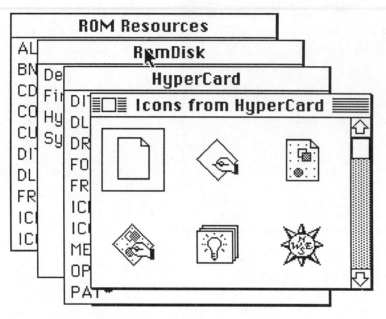

Figure 3-23

Open the selected icon by double clicking it, and trace over it with the arrow pointer to erase it as shown in Figure 3-24.

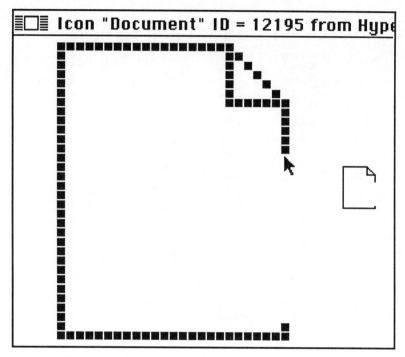

Figure 3-24

Using the same arrow pointer in the same way as the HyperCard Pencil Tool, draw the icon you want in a button. For example, for some financial application, a big dollar sign might be appropriate.

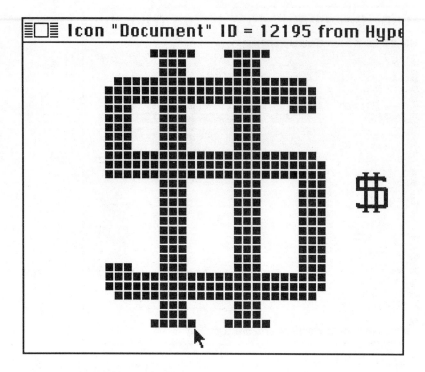

Figure 3-25

To help give you a better idea of what your icon will look like when completed, there is a small view of it on the right side of the screen. Drawing in the ResEdit editor is very much like HyperCard drawing with the pencil when in the Fat Bits mode. When completed, click the box in the upper left hand corner of your screen to close it. When it is closed, the Icon screen shows the dollar sign character instead of the document character.

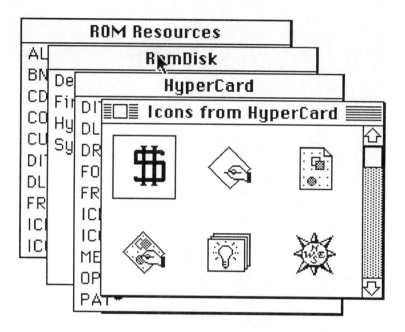

Figure 3-26

Finally, when the dialog box queries whether to save or not, respond with Yes.

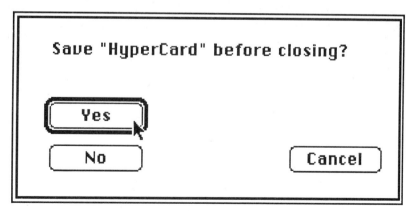

Figure 3-27

To check and make sure that everything worked out as expected, launch the special HyperCard you used with ResEdit. Using the Button tool, create a new button and choose transparent for the style, and then click "Icon... " Scroll the icon window until you come to the bottom. You should see the dollar sign icon as shown in Figure 3-28.

Figure 3-28

If you place that icon on a card as a button, it will be treated as a button item and not a paint item. Therefore, if you want to use it again or move the whole thing to another card, it can be done in a single step.

Copying Existing Buttons

Perhaps the most powerful operation at the authoring level is using the copy function while the Button tool is selected. Not only can you get the button that way, you can also get the *script*. The script is the underlying program that tells the button what to do. Even though we have not yet discussed the process of writing scripts, there is no need to do so as long as you know what a button does. For example, one of the most useful things a button does is simply go to the next or previous card. As we saw in the Link to... operation, we could designate a specific card as the button's target, but we could not make the button go only to *any* next or previous card. By copying and pasting buttons that are already scripted to go to any next or previous card, we can create buttons that will do the same operation.

To prepare for this change, delete the arrow buttons from the "First Stack" demonstration stack we've been using. After choosing the Button tool, just click each arrow button, and when it is selected choose Cut from the Edit menu or press Command-X. Then follow these steps:

1. Go to the Home Card.
2. Choose the Button tool.
3. Select the left arrow button by placing the pointer on it and clicking it.
4. Choose Copy from the Edit menu or press Command-C.
5. Go to the "First Stack" stack and go to the back ground (Command-B).
6. Choose the Button tool and paste in the button by choosing Paste from the Edit menu or press Command-V.
7. Follow steps 1-6 except select the right arrow from the Home Card.

When completed, the background on the First Stack should look like Figure 3-29 when the Button tool is selected. (The squares around the arrows will disappear when another tool is selected.)

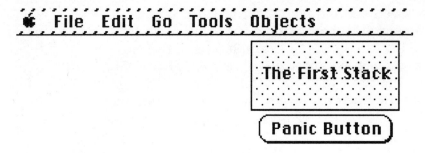

Figure 3-29

Every time a new card is added, the left arrow button will point to the previous card and the right arrow button will point to the next card. Since the new card is added to the end of the stack, the next card is the first card of the stack. Go through the sample disks that come with HyperCard and select a number of different buttons to cut and paste.

The Field Tool

The field tool is very much like the Button tool except instead of making buttons for communications between cards, it makes areas where you can put and recall messages, calculations and other information to be used. Fields are set up so you can easily get into and out of them with a minimal fuss. That means they must be set up in a way that is "intuitively natural" to anyone who uses them. By "intuitively natural" we mean that they should be set up in a way that people generally expect them to be. For example, it might be a very good idea to place a Zip code before a name and address for arranging fields to be sorted for mailing. However, people (including the post office) expect the Zip code to "naturally" appear after the name and address. Thus, while there might be a lot of practical reasons for placing fields in non-standard orders, keep in mind that the more "natural" it feels to someone, the easier and more efficient it will be to use.

For the most part, fields will be placed in the background and are not limited to a single card. Naturally there will be exceptions to this, but for the most part, fields will be a background item.

Adding fields

Adding fields is very much like adding buttons. After selecting the Field tool from the Tool menu, pull down the objects menu and click New Field. Using the "First Stack" again as an example, we'll add some fields. In the background, the screen will look like Figure 3-30 when the field is first added:

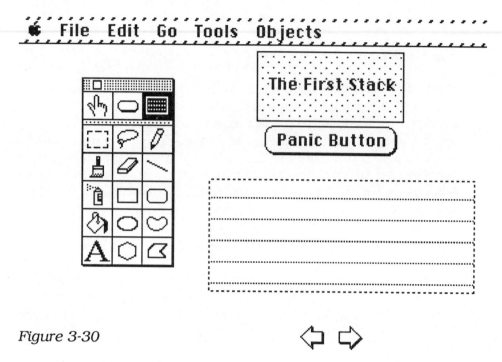

Figure 3-30

Before looking at Field Info from the Objects menu, we'd better stop a minute and plan what we want to do with the fields for the First Stack. Keeping it simple, we will make First Stack a name and telephone number stack with an added memo field where we can jot down information we may use in talking with someone or make notes on what they last said. We will order them as follows:

1. Name field
2. Phone field
3. Memo field

Since we already have the first field on the background, it will be the name field. However, it is far too big for a single name; so the first thing to do is to change its size to a single line for the name.

With the field tool selected, place the pointer at the lower right corner of the field and drag the field so that it is only one line tall as shown in Figure 3-31.

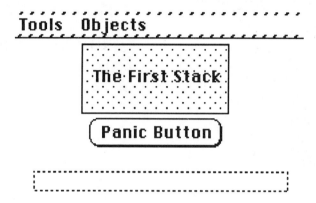

Figure 3-31

Next, go to the foreground, and see what it looks like. There is no visible Name field. That is because the default condition for field style is transparent. Now it is time to get Field Info from the Objects menu and fix that. Remember to select the field with the Field tool before choosing the Field Info option from the Objects menu. The field menu looks like the one in Figure 3-32.

Field Name: **Name**

Bkgnd field number: 1

Bkgnd field ID: 4

Style:

☐ Lock Text
☐ Show Lines
☐ Wide Margins
☒ Auto Tab

○ transparent
○ opaque
◉ rectangle
○ shadow
○ scrolling

[Font...]

[Script...]

[OK]   [Cancel]

Figure 3-32

Since this will be the name field, use "Name" for the name of the Field Name. In order to see where the name goes, choose the rectangle style. That should be enough for this first field.

For the second field, first type the word "Phone:" directly under the rectangle showing the first field's location. Then, using the Field tool again, make a new field and shrink it and place it right next to the word "Phone:" as shown in Figure 3-33.

* New For
Version 1.2

Remember to use the Command Tab-Tab-Tab shortcut to select the Field tool. Also take note of the Auto Tab option on the field dialog box shown in figure 3-32. If you click the box next to Auto Tab, in non-scrolling fields, the cursor will jump to the next field when the last line of the field is reached and the Return key is pressed.

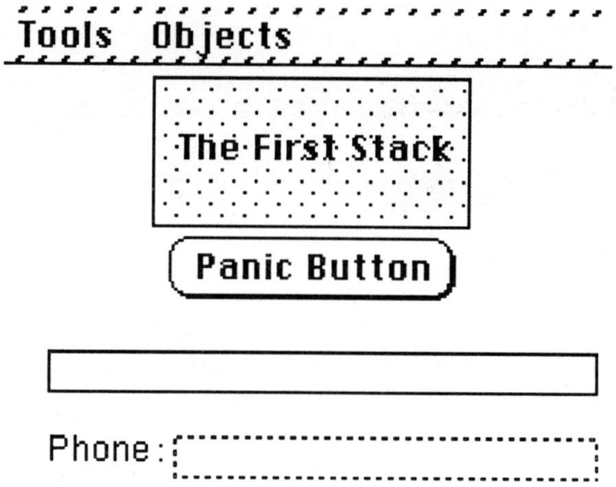

```
Tools  Objects
```

```
: The·First·Stack :
```

```
( Panic Button )
```

```
Phone :
```

Figure 3-33

This time, we will leave it as a transparent field. Now place parentheses using the Paint Text tool next to the word "Phone" for a place to put area codes. When you use the Paint Text tool, you will not be able to see the area for the Phone field, as shown in Figure 3-34.

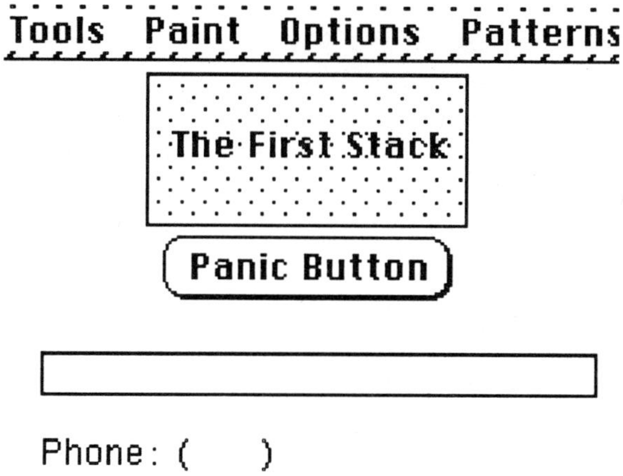

```
Tools  Paint  Options  Patterns
```

```
: The·First·Stack :
```

```
( Panic Button )
```

```
Phone : (    )
```

Figure 3-34

Now, let's take a look at Figure 3-35 to see the Field Info for this second field.

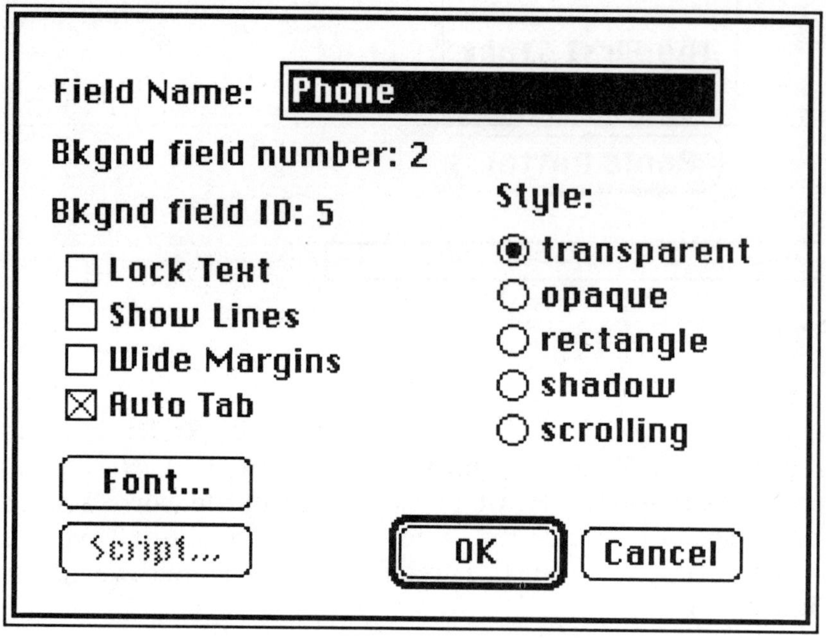

```
┌──────────────────────────────────────────────────┐
│                                                    │
│   Field Name: │Phone                        │      │
│                                                    │
│   Bkgnd field number: 2                            │
│                              Style:                │
│   Bkgnd field ID: 5                                │
│                              ◉ transparent         │
│       ☐ Lock Text            ○ opaque              │
│       ☐ Show Lines           ○ rectangle           │
│       ☐ Wide Margins         ○ shadow              │
│       ☒ Auto Tab             ○ scrolling           │
│                                                    │
│      ┌──────────┐                                  │
│      │ Font...   │                                 │
│      ├──────────┤        ┌────────┐  ┌──────────┐  │
│      │ Script... │       │   OK   │  │  Cancel  │  │
│      └──────────┘        └────────┘  └──────────┘  │
│                                                    │
└──────────────────────────────────────────────────┘
```

Figure 3-35

The Field Info is about the same except the style is transparent. The important element is the Background Field Number. It is 2 instead of 1. With fields, this number is more important than with buttons since it represents the "tabbing order" of the fields. Each time the Tab key is pressed while entering data into a field, the cursor jumps to the next field in order of field number. Since we want to first enter the name and then the phone number, everything is in the correct order.

For the memo field, we are going to want some field elements different. We will want scrolling so that we can write longer memos if we need them, and wide margins for a better appearance. This field will be placed to the left of the current fields and buttons.

Select the Field tool and create a new field. Move it to the left side of the screen and then drag it so that it looks like a tall narrow rectangle. Now, select the new field and double-click it. That is a short cut to bring up the Field Info dialog box. Now choose "scrolling" and "Wide Margins" from the options in the box, and name it Memo as shown in Figure 3-36.

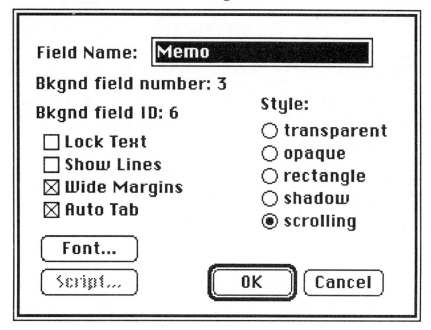

Figure 3-36

 Next return to the background of the stack and using the Paint Text tool, write in "Phone Memo" above the memo field. Now, your background should appear as shown in Figure 3-37.

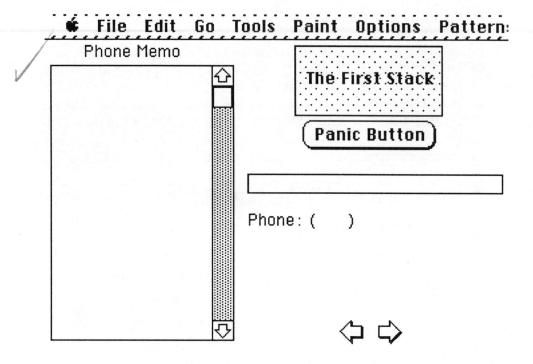

Figure 3-37

With the addition of the "memo" field, you have completed authoring your first stack. This is a working, practical stack that you can use to keep phone numbers and jot down notes. Later on, you can add other features to the background and easily change the buttons and fields so that it does more.

The remaining field styles, opaque and shadow, provide two more options. Opaque will cover up any text or graphics, so it would not be a very good choice where you want to have the field mixed in as we did with the parentheses for the area code in Phone field in the "First Stack" example. However, if a background pattern is desired and you do not want the text to be lost in the pattern, an opaque field would be a good style as shown in Figure 3-38. In the same figure, the "Show Lines" option was used, and the Chicago font for writing in the field with the Browse tool was chosen also. Choosing a different font from the default Geneva font allows you to have more precise options. Whenever you write in a field with the Browse tool, that font will appear automatically. If the field is going to be routinely printed by a printer, be sure to choose a font that will look good on the printer. For example, LaserWriter printers have certain Post-Script fonts, such as Times, Helvetica, Palatino, Bookman and others that may not look as good on the screen as the Chicago font does. However, Chicago is not a PostScirpt font and does not look very good when printed by a laser printer. Although a font may look good on the screen, it may not be the best choice for a certain type of printer.

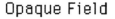

Opaque Field

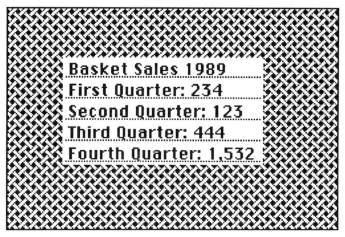

Figure 3-38

The shadow style is very useful for setting up things like organizational charts where each field is clearly separated from the other. It looks a little nicer than the rectangle field and is "intuitively right." For example, Figure 3-39 uses the shadow field for showing how HyperCard fields might be used for an organizational planning guide.

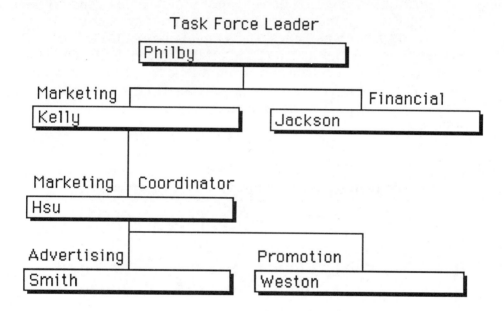

Figure 3-39

In the last analysis, the author of the stack makes aesthetic decisions regarding how a card will look. Also, remember the paint tools considerably extend the available styles using opaque and transparent fields.

The Order of Fields

In designing a stack, it is easy to get fields out of order after moving them around, changing stacks and using the flexibility that is built into HyperCard. Imagine working from the inside of HyperCard outwards when thinking about the order of fields. For example, the following five fields on a card show where they are in terms of being "near" or "far" from the top. This order affects the position the cursor will jump when the tab key is pressed.

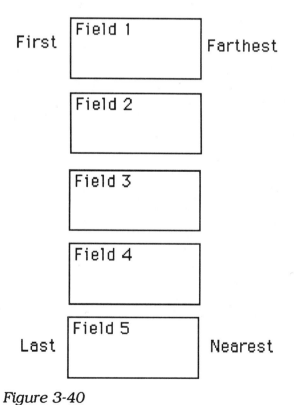

Figure 3-40

When typing on the cards with the Browsing tool, the first one will be Field 1. When you press the Tab key, the cursor will jump to Field 2 and so on until it reaches Field 5. Notice that it goes from the farthest field to the nearest.

To re-order the fields, select the Field tool and pull down the Objects menu shown in Figure 3-41.

```
┌─────────────────────────────┐
│ Objects                     │
├─────────────────────────────┤
│ Button Info...              │
│ Field Info...               │
│ Card Info...                │
│ Bkgnd Info...               │
│ Stack Info...               │
│·····························│
│ Bring Closer        ⌘+      │
│ Send Farther        ⌘-      │
│·····························│
│ New Button                  │
│ New Field                   │
│ New Background              │
└─────────────────────────────┘
```

Figure 3-41

Suppose you want to take Field 5 and make it the fourth field. In other words, you want to switch Fields 4 and 5. You can take either Field 4 and select Bring Closer or Command + or select Field 5 and use Send Farther or Command -(minus). Go ahead and do it. Start in Field 1 and press the Tab key until you have tabbed through all of the fields. After Field 3, the cursor should have jumped first to Field 5 and then to Field 4.

Special Note: If it is a little confusing having "Send Farther" mean that the field is "brought closer" to the front of the line, think of fields as a stack of fields. The first one you put in is the "farthest" away from the top and the "first." To bring it closer to the last fields you put on the stack, you would use "Bring Closer" to *place it nearer to the last field*. Figure 3-42 gives another conceptual view to help better visualize the arrangement.

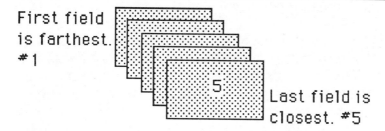

First field is farthest. #1

Last field is closest. #5

Figure 3-42

Field Numbers, ID's, Locking Text and Line Numbers

At this stage of the game, the field numbers are the only thing you need to be concerned about since they can be manipulated at the authoring level of HyperCard. Going back to Figure 3-36, note that the third field (the Memo field) we put in the First Stack example referred to the **Bkgnd field number: 3**. That should make sense because we have just discussed the order of fields.

However, there is another notation referred to as **Bkgnd field ID:6** (background field identification) as well. That little note tells you something about HyperCard we have not yet discussed. Each time a field or button is added it is "laminated" onto the background or foreground. Each button *and* field is counted in order of its position from the bottom to the top. As we saw with the layering of fields, each one has a relative position number from the farthest to nearest. The background field ID is the field or button position relative to other fields and buttons in the same background. Since we used three buttons (the Panic Button and the next and previous card buttons) and three fields, the last field would be 3 + 3 or 6. Unlike the position of the background field number, the background field ID cannot be changed by moving it closer or farther with the Object menu options. Thus, while both button and fields can have their background field numbers changed from the Object menu, their background ID remains constant.

A final note before closing this chapter regards the line numbers in each field. In authoring, the line numbers are not important unless one of the fields has been cut from another application that used scripting in its creation. Each field, as was explained in the last chapter, has unique lines numbers. As we will see in the next chapter, each line number is a possible reference point. Thus, if you cut and paste a field and you get a message indicating an error when you enter text, it may be because the line was expecting a number for a calculation. In the next chapter, we will begin examining how to write script in Hyper-Talk, the programming language of HyperCard.

✳ New For Version 1.2

To change the line spacing in fields independent of the menus, a quick shortcut is to select the field and press,

> Shift-option > (more space)

or

> Shift-option < (less space)

The only difference between the 1.2 method and the older method is that now it is necessary to press the Shift key along with the other keys.

Summary

Basically this chapter has been an introduction to authoring HyperCard stacks. Beginning with a new stack, it is a simple task to design a variety of different applications with Hyper-Card. The idea is to organize the backgrounds, buttons and fields to accomplish some kind of task. After working with an application, the author can make adjustments by adding or removing various fields and buttons. More complex buttons and fields can be added by cutting them from scripted stacks and pasting them into new ones. This limits authoring to the use of existing buttons and fields, but as more HyperCard stacks become available in the public domain and commercial channels, this problem will lessen.

Besides adding and deleting fields and buttons, their order can be changed to deal with changing requirements of an application. This flexibility allows global changes in an application without having to re-enter data or lose information. Since the background and foreground are linked in the forms and not necessarily the content, the forms can be altered without harming the foreground data.

In the next chapter, we will enter into the arena of writing scripts; the highest level of HyperCard activity. The first lesson to learn in the next chapter is to retain all of the authoring skills picked up in this chapter. While scripting provides added power and flexibility, there is no point in re-inventing the wheel every time one sits down to work with HyperCard. Therefore much of the cutting and pasting that goes on in authoring, will be just as applicable when it comes to writing a script for certain buttons and fields. Once it is written, there is no need to re-do it again if the button or field is required in another application. A simple cut and paste will suffice.

Authoring
Scripts With
HyperTalk

4

What are Scripts?

Scripts are the instructions behind the buttons, fields, backgrounds, cards and stacks that make HyperCard perform. They are short programs in an English-like language called HyperTalk. When you author a script, you're simply telling an object to do something like "Go to the next card" or "Add the numbers in column one to the numbers in column two." Since HyperTalk was designed to be as close to English as possible, it is easier than other programming languages to learn. And because HyperTalk scripts are short and modular, it is far easier to design large, practical applications without having to debug huge amounts of code.

> **Special Note**: Before you can start writing scripts, you must first go to the User Preferences card in the Home stack and select the "Scripting" User Level.

Without further ado, let's take a look at a simple script you can write that will be used a great deal when you build a HyperCard stack. Follow these steps:

1. Make a new card and go to the Objects menu and select "New Button," or press Command-Tab-Tab.
2. Place the pointer on the selected new button, press the shift key and double click the mouse button.
3. You will see
   "on mouseUp..."
   a vertical cursor and
   "end mouseUp"
4. Write "go to next card" where you see the cursor. It should now look like Figure 4-1.
5. Click "OK"

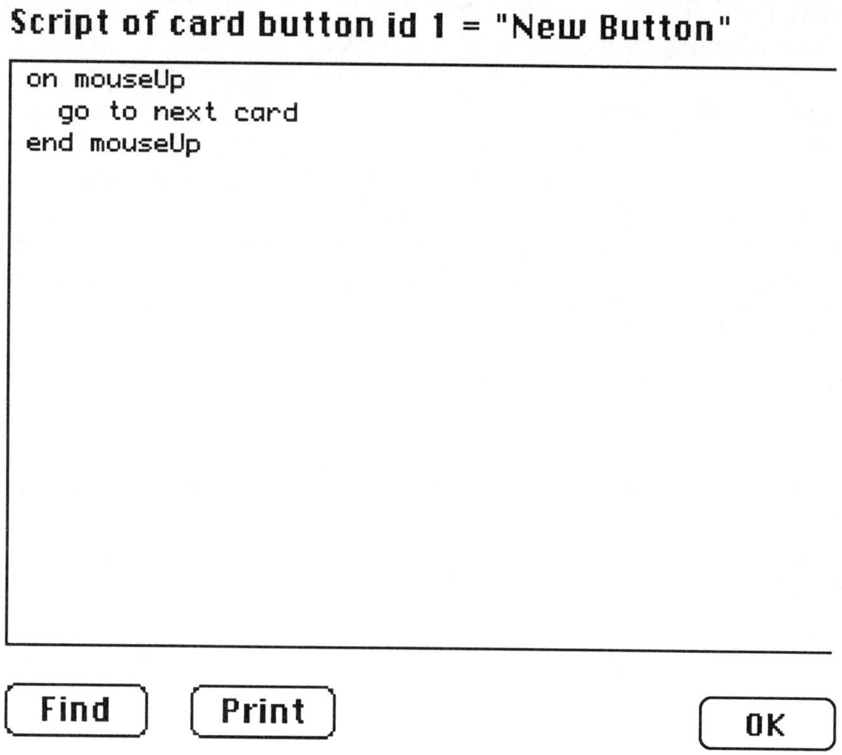

Script of card button id 1 = "New Button"

```
on mouseUp
   go to next card
end mouseUp
```

Find   Print   OK

Figure 4-1

That's it. Now whenever you press the button on that card, it will go to the next card.

Admittedly that was a very simple example, but writing Hyper-Card scripts is simple. The scripts are "modular" because they are written for discreet objects instead of entire applications. Once a script is written for an object, the object can be cut and pasted and used elsewhere in the same stack or in a different stack using the techniques discussed in Chapter 3. It is possible to write very long and complex scripts if so desired, but usually that is unnecessary. Most scripts are short, easy to write and easy to read. This can be seen by examining other scripts in the various stacks that come with HyperCard.

HyperCard Hierarchy

Scripts are written in "objects." The five objects are arranged in a hierarchy with buttons and fields at the bottom and stacks at the top. Figure 4-2 shows the objects where HyperCard scripts are written and the hierarchy in which a message moves in HyperCard.

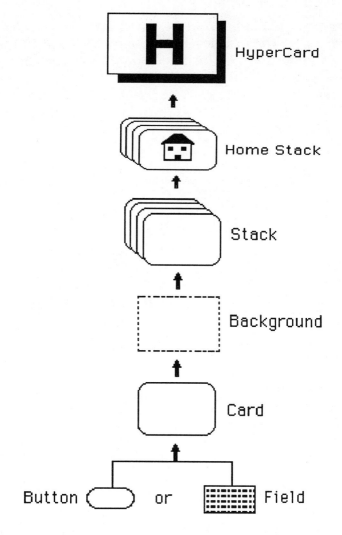

Figure 4-2

Whenever there is an action that is not found on one level HyperCard goes up to the next level. When you click the mouse or press various keys, if HyperCard does not find something to handle the message within that action, it will go up to the next level. To see how this works, we'll make a button that does nothing and a card that traps messages. The command "play boing" will make a "boing" sound. If you wrote a button script like,

```
on mouseUp
    play boing
end mouseup
```

you would hear a "boing" sound each time the button is pressed. However, if there were no "message handler" to trap the action, such as "on mouseUp" the next level of hierarchy would be examined to see if something to handle the message existed on that level.

To see how this works create a new stack. From the Objects menu, hold down the shift key and choose "Card Info...." The write the following script:

```
on mouseUp
    play boing
end mouseup
```

Click OK when you have finished, and select the browse tool. Click the mouse a few times on the card to see what happens. Now make a new button as you learned in Chapter 3. At this time, do not write a script for it or do anything else, but just create it. Again, with the browse tool, click the mouse with the pointer placed on the new button. It should still "boing." That's because, HyperCard first looks to see if there is a message handler for a mouse click on the button. There is not. Therefore, it goes up to the next level, and there is the "on mouseUp" handler, and so it sees what to do next. It's supposed to "boing", and it does.

Next, return to the new button you just made. Get the button tool, and pressing the shift key down, double click on the new button. Write the following script and press OK when it is completed ("on mouseUp" and "end mouseUp" are already written there.)

```
on mouseUp
        put "You pressed the Button" into message box
        show message box
   end mouseUp
```

Returning to the card, click on the button with the browse tool. This time, instead of a "boing" you get the message box and the message, "You pressed the Button." There is no "boing" since the mouse click was trapped in the button and did not have to go up to the card level to find a message handler that makes a "boing" sound. If you click the mouse on an area of the card not on the new button, though, the card still "boings" for you.

Using the Script Editor

The script editor short cut was used in the above examples, and now we will back pedal a bit to look at the script editor and the entry points to that editor.

On the Objects menu, there are Info... options for all five of the objects in HyperCard. The Button Info... and Field Info.. are "ghosted" until the button or field tool is chosen and a button or field is selected. Also, on the Objects menu are options for new buttons, fields or backgrounds. New cards are created from the Edit menu and new stacks from the File menu. If a new button or field selection is made, their tools are selected automatically.

When an Info... selection is made from the Objects menu for a
new or existing object, a dialog box appears with a script button.
Figure 4-3 shows the dialog box for a card.

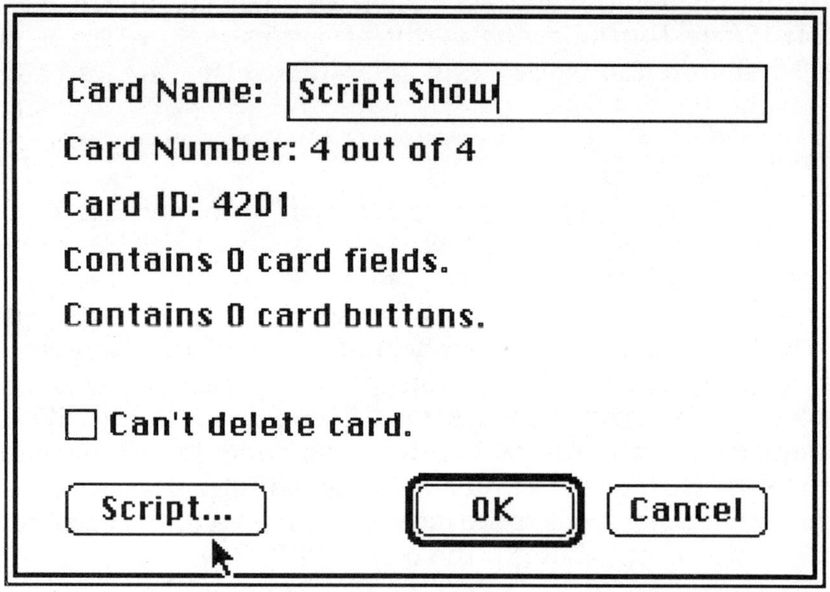

Card Name: | Script Show|

Card Number: 4 out of 4

Card ID: 4201

Contains 0 card fields.

Contains 0 card buttons.

☐ Can't delete card.

[Script...]   [OK]   [Cancel]

Figure 4-3

When the Script... button is clicked, HyperCard goes to the
script for that card only. It is not the script for the buttons or
fields on the card or the stack in which the card resides. As we
will see further on in this book, a script in a card can make a
reference to some other object, but when the script is written in
a card it is not the whole stack's script. This concept is different
from standard programming in which a single program generally references the entire file in which the program resides. Each
object's script is modular.

Special Note. The short cut for going directly to the script editor is to hold down the Shift key while clicking the Info... choice on the Objects menu. Double clicking a selected button or field while holding down the Shift key also will go directly to the script editor.

In addition to those above shortcuts, Version 1.2 has several more that will make your script work a lot easier.

Using Browse tool

Command-Option - shows all visible buttons, and clicking button will show script.

Shift-Command-Option - shows all visible buttons and fields and clicking button or field will show its script.

Using Field Tool

Command-Option - shows all visible and invisible fields. Click fields to see script.

Using Button Tool

Command-Option - shows all visible and invisible buttons. Click button to see script.

Any tool

Command-Option-C - Shows current card's script.

Command-Option-B- Shows current background's script .

Command-Option-S- Shows current stack's script.

To put the script away, press *Command-Option* and click the mouse once or press any key.

The more you work with scripts, the more you will want to use these shortcuts. Mark this page because, you will be using it as a reference for the shortcuts for a while.

Scripts written in the background affect all cards with that background in the same stack. If a button or field is created in the background, each card with that background in a stack will have those buttons and fields along with their scripts.

When writing a script, it is necessary to learn to use the various Command key control sequences for the editor since the edit menu is frozen while the script editor is in use. The following is a quick review of the editing features:

⌘ **C** Copy
⌘ **V** Paste
⌘ **X** Cut

After writing in each command line in the script editor, press the return key. If a command line is too long to fit in the screen window, the line can be extended (read as a single line) by pressing the option key when pressing return. An extended line has a break (¬) character at the end of it. For example, the line,

> put Nepal into field "Asia"

could be put in two lines as,

> put "Nepal" ¬
> into field "Asia"

and interpreted by HyperCard as a single line. However, most command lines are fairly short and easily fit into the horizontal window of the script editor.

Finally, HyperCard scripts may have comments that are not executed. Comments are ways to help you quickly evaluate a script line. A comment is made by placing two dashes (- -) before text. For example, the line,

```
        go to Help  - -This takes you to the Help stack
```

contains the comment, "This takes you to the Help stack." It is not executed even though the first part of the line, "go to Help" is. It is especially helpful on longer scripts to have comments, and while they are not essential, they are recommended.

Message Handlers: Triggering and Terminating Script Actions

Scripts are triggered by some use of **on**, one of two handler structures. Roughly translated, HyperCard's use of "on" means "When *this* happens..." The "this" can be any number of events occurring in the computer. HyperCard constantly sends system messages to objects about what's going on in the Macintosh. If someone clicks the mouse button, the mouse button goes "up" when it is released. Thus, the script segment,

```
    on mouseUp
```

triggers actions following a mouse click. We can refer to this first triggering segment as the "message trap". Thus, "on mouseUp" can be translated as "When the mouse is clicked...." There are more things to do with the mouse, as we will see, but the most common use of the mouse is to initiate some action in a HyperCard object with a simple click.

Following the initial message trap, a message handler sends out other messages to various *targets* in HyperCard. The targets are simply the objects to which the message is sent, and when the tasks are performed, control goes back to the original or *source*, object.
The most useful way to think of scripts at this stage is in terms of their beginning with a handler structure, usually "on", that traps an action. After the trap, the script has a list of statements telling the computer what to do. The message handler is

terminated when the word "end" and the name of the message handler is encountered. So, if there is the line,

> on mouseUp

there must be a termination line,

> end mouseUp.

The other of the two handler structures is called "function." We will not be using it at this stage, but further on it will be discussed. Likewise, it is possible to define your own commands with "on", but that too will come later.

Other events can be trapped as well as clicking the mouse, and there's more to do with the mouse than just clicking it. A few other events that are trapped include,

> openCard
> returnKey
> closeStack
> tabKey

For example, "openCard" triggers an action whenever a card first appears. An accounts receivable stack, for instance, may have especially bad credit risks flagged with a "boing" each time the card of a bad risk is opened. No special key or mouse action is required, and so the user is automatically reminded. As we go on, more types of message handler triggers will be introduced as needed.

Telling HyperCard What To Do

Between the beginning and ending portions of a message handler is the heart of HyperTalk script authoring. By writing a series of English-like statements, you give the computer commands it follows. These have a structure that generally begins with a command followed by various parameters and/or functions.

There are 42 commands. We will examine them separately, but it would be useful to see them here so that when reading other scripts, you can recognize them. Ones that are new or changed in Version 1.2 are indicated with (1.2) in bold face type.

Commands

add	find **(1.2)**	put
answer	get	read
beep	global	reset Paint
choose	go	select **(1.2)**
click	hide	set
close	hide picture **(1.2)**	show
convert	lock **(1.2)**	show picture **(1.2)**
deltet	multiply	sort
dial	open	subtract
divide	open printing	type
do	play	unlock**(1.2)**
doMenu	pop	visual effect
drag	print	wait
edit script	push	write

For example, we have seen the command "play" used with the parameter "Boing." That combination produced the sound of a spring popping loose. If the parameter were "Harpsichord," that would produce a sound like a note from a musical instrument. The command describes the action, and the parameter(s) specify the nature or destination of the action. The "go" command, for instance, tells HyperCard what other card or stack to go to next. As we deal with specific commands, we will deal with specific parameters.

In the parameter field, there often will be a need for functions. There are 38 built-in functions plus 17 math functions in HyperCard, and there are more you can define yourself. Functions are something like built-in sets of information that provide information relative to the parameters in a command line. Like the commands, it is a good idea to see what functions look like before we cover them individually.

Functions

charToNum	math functions-17	paramCount
clickH **(1.2)**	mouse	params
clickLoc	mouseClick	random
clickV **(1.2)**	mouseH	result
commandKey	mouseLoc	round
date	mouseV	seconds
foundChunk **(1.2)**	number of **(1.2)**	selectedChunk **(1.2)**
foundField **(1.2)**	numToChar	selectedField**(1.2)**
foundLine **(1.2)**	offset	selectedLine**(1.2)**
foundText**(1.2)**	optionKey	selectedText**(1.2)**
length	param	

For example, the script,

```
on openCard
    put the date into field 1
end openCard
```

places the current date, which is stored inside the Mac's internal clock and pulled out by the "date" function, into field 1. Thus, there is the statement combination:

```
command -function -destination
```

Not all command-function combinations are exactly like that, but most have a similar structure. As we learn more commands and functions, we will see the different forms they have.

Organizing Scripts

Most programming languages demand a "top down" structure, taking a linear approach to problem solving. Given the structure of most programming languages, this is a good idea, aiding in good clear program code that efficiently does the job. However, in the real world, people rarely think in strictly linear terms. Instead, once a goal has been identified, ideas, parts, personnel and other resources are gathered and evaluated. Different levels are set up, and then later filled in and even rearranged. That is how HyperCard is designed. It can be used in a simple linear model, but given the modular nature of HyperCard, it can be effectively used in non-linear models as well. Figure 4-4 illustrates some different configurations of HyperCard stacks.

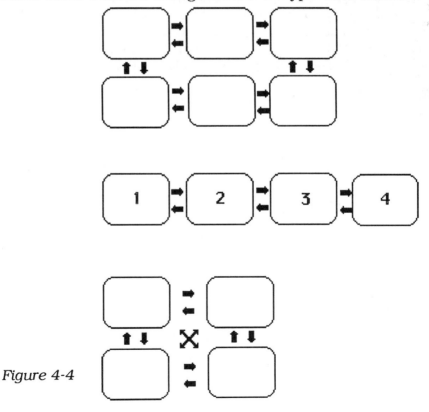

Figure 4-4

Set a Goal. In virtually every business pursuit, setting a goal is the first step in getting anything done. The same is true with HyperCard. At the outset, get a clear idea of exactly what you want done. Obviously, HyperCard cannot meet every business need. It would not make a very good word processor, for example. So in specifying a goal, be realistic in terms of what you know about HyperCard. The more you become familiar with HyperCard, the more you can extend its power. But build gradually. Do not be shy, though, for only by pushing Hyper-Card to its limits will you ever find out what those limits are.

Who Will Use It? Consider who will be using the stack being developed, and who will be seeing it. If it is used primarily by the engineering staff, the language and style would tend to be more technical, but if it is for the design staff, it would be less technical and more artistic. Get the end users point of view before completing a stack. Better yet, get their ideas and how they view the problems they must routinely solve.

How Many Stacks? Before beginning a new stack, decide whether a single stack or multiple stacks would best fit the bill. As we have seen, a stack is very flexible, and it might appear that there would be little reason to make more than a single stack. However, sometimes there will be a single core stack that can get very large, and it is better to have individual stacks access information from the core stack rather than to integrate each small stack into the larger one. For example, suppose you have a large stack with the names, addresses and other information about various clients. The stack contains several thousand names stored on a hard disk. You want to have individual stacks for sales representatives that fit on a single diskette that they can take with them. Each sales area is small enough so that the data from the big stack can fit on the small stack each sales representative needs. Evaluate the amount of disk space, the amount of data to be entered and the needs of the user in deciding how many stacks to build. And finally, if sensitive data are to be stored, discreet, independent stacks may be required so while the information is available, it is not accessible to everyone.

Write It Down. Just as an outline of a business plan or a project should be written down, write down your HyperCard plan. When you start creating your stacks, you don't have to stay with it, but a written plan or outline will give you an overall picture of what you're doing while creating the stack.

Go: Scripts for Getting Around HyperCard

The first script commands to learn are those used to move from one place to another in HyperCard. The first and most often used command for negotiating around a stack is **go**. It directs HyperCard to go to a specific card or stack. It can be in the form,

```
        go destination
or
        go to destination
```

with the "to" being optional. At the beginning of the chapter, the example,

```
        go to next card
```

was used. Similarly, a button with,

```
        on mouseUp
            go to prev card - -previous card
        end mouseUp
```

will go to the previous card. There are a number of special situations where HyperCard allows abbreviation of card destination. For example,

        go prev

will go to the previous card without the optional "to" or the word
"card." Along with "next" and "prev" (or previous), the go
command can use,

        back
        recent
        home
        help
        first-tenth
        last
        random (randomly selects a card)
        mid (goes to middle card of stack)

in reference to a card without using the word "card." The ordinal
values (first through tenth) and "last" reference the first and last
card of a *current* stack.

Cards are also referenced by card number, card ID and card
name. For example,

        go card 5
and
        go fifth

will both go to the fifth card in the current stack, and

        go card ID 2833

will find the card with the ID 2833.

In going between stacks, the destination stack name is optionally placed between quotation marks. For instance,

```
go "Organization"
```

would go to the first card of a stack named "Organization." If you want to branch to a card other than the first one in a stack, it must be specified in a different format. For example, if the card "Microflux" is in the stack, "Clients" , it would require the format,

```
go to card "Microflux" of stack "Clients"
```

to go to the desired card. Likewise, a card ID or card number can be used as well when specifying a card other than the first one of a non-current stack.

```
go third card of stack "Accounts"
go to card ID 555 of Personnel
```

Notice in the second example above, the word "stack" is omitted and so are the quotation marks around Personnel.

If a stack has more than a single background, the ordinal value of the background can be used as a destination reference. Whenever "New Background" is used in a stack, that stack is given another background. Thus, the line,

```
go to the third card of the¬
second background of stack "organization"
```

would skip the first background, and go to the third card of the *second* background in a stack named "organization." (Notice that the "line extender" (¬) was used in the last example.)

In an environment with lots of different HyperCard applications and multiple disk drives and folders, it may be necessary to specify the drive and folder path of the stack you wish to open.

For example, to get to a stack in a folder within a folder on a non-current hard disk drive, you would need something like the following:

> go "hd:Marketing:Sales:ThirdQuarterStack"

If HyperCard is not given a path to follow, it provides a dialog box for you to find the stack yourself as shown in Figure 4-5.

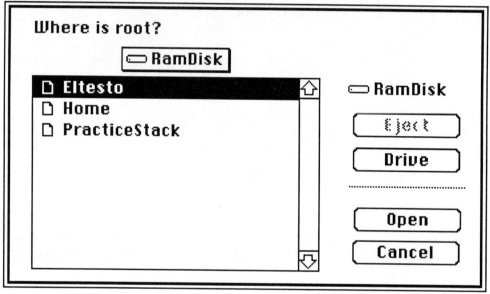

Figure 4-5

Once a stack has been found, its location is remembered by the Home stack, and HyperCard will go to the desired stack without specifying the path or bringing up the dialog box during that session of use.

With the abbreviations, the temptation is to write scripts without using the optional elements. After all, it saves time, and the optional elements do not seem to do a lot of good. For the most part, that may be true, but the options were placed in HyperCard to help make the script language more English like and to help in making lines clearer. In scripts with a lot of lines, it may be very easy to miss a mistake you made if you do not use the options. For instance, the line,

go to card "Nancy Sawyer" of stack "Personnel"

tells you more clearly what the destination is than,

go Nancy Sawyer of Personnel

It also tells HyperCard more clearly what you want, and it will go to that destination without intervention by the dialog box. Thus, while lines like

go home
go next

are fine and clear to both HyperCard and the user, more complex lines should be cleared up with the use of quotation marks and optional clarifying terms.

Special Note: To practice with the go command, you can use "blind typing" or the Message Box. To get the Message Box on the screen, press Command-M, or choose "Message" from the Go Menu. The Message Box is a little better since you can see what you type and if you make a mistake, you can see what it is. However, in using HyperCard on a daily basis, you will find blind typing much quicker. Try it by typing in a "go" command line like "go Home" on the screen. You *cannot* see what you type, but you will see the results (right or wrong) as soon as you press the return key.

Push and Pop

In getting around in a stack, there will be occasions where it is necessary to get back to a certain point after leaving it. Hyper-Card has a flag command that works like those little stickem papers used to mark files or report pages for return reference. When a script encounters he command, **push**, it places a flag on the card, and when the **pop** command is given, it automatically returns to the flagged card. Once a card is "popped," the flag is removed. Figure 4-6 illustrates how the two work together.

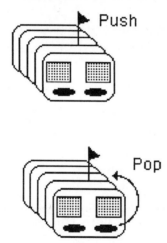

Figure 4-6

When a script pushes a card, it pushes the current card on the current stack. The pop command can be from anywhere, even another stack, and it will immediately return to the last card that was pushed. The format

        push card

is usually all that is required.

Under some circumstances, it may be a good idea to have the push command at the next card referring back to the most recent card. In this case the form,

    push recent card

may be used. Cards that serve as reminders, clarifiers, memos or footnotes that must be referenced frequently from different cards but are out of the mainstream of the stack, can be opened with a "push recent card" and then ended with "pop card" to get quickly back to the mainstream. For example, the following script could be used when opening an "off mainstream" card that returns to the last card just used.

```
on openCard
      push recent card
end openCard
```

Then on a button, put the script,

```
on mouseUp
    pop card
end mouseUp
```

to get back to the card from which you came.

Find

The **find** command may be easily confused with the go command since they both seek a destination. However, find looks for words or characters in fields while go seeks cards and stacks. **Find** is used only in the current stack; so it cannot be used by itself to find something in a field outside of the current stack.

To find a word in any field simply use the format,

find "word"

To hasten the pace of finding a word and avoiding unwanted fields, the "in field" parameter may be added to the find command. For example,

find "vessel" in field "dictionary"

would only look for the source word in the field called "dictionary." The field's number or ID also may be used in a search.

find "waffle" in field 1
find "accessories" in field ID 2833

In a word search, "word" may be optionally used in the parameter field.

find word "retired" in field "personnel"

To locate a character or characters in fields, use the **chars** parameter. This is useful for finding part of a word that may be in several whole words. For instance,

find chars "pay"

would search for all words with "pay" in it, such as "payments," "payable," "payables," "payola," "payoff," "payload," "paycheck," "payee," and "pay." The find command may also specify certain fields.

find chars "over" in field 3
find chars "dd" in field "Parts"

* New For
Version 1.2

With Version 1.2 of HyperCard come two new types of find commands. First, there is **find string**. The find string command works something like the stand find except that it will find a string of characters *anywhere* in a field. For example the entry,

   find string "hay"

will find "hay" in "**hay**stack," shas**hay**," and "oh**hay**oh." Using "find string" can also be combined with **char** to locate a given number of characters. For instance, the line,

   find string char 1 to 10 of card field 1

locates the first ten characters in card field 1.

A second new 1.2 find command is **find whole**. This command is used to find a word or word set. For example, the command,

   find whole "Jimmy Thom"

will only find the string "Jimmy Thom," but it will not find "Jimmy Thomson" as would a simple find command. A shortcut for getting **find whole** is to use the key sequence,

   Command-Shift-F

and the message box appears with

   find whole "I"

Practice with different versions of the find command to become familiar with it. Later we will see how it can be used in scripts.

Scripts for Using the Mouse and Keys

Mouse Traps. Up to this point, all of the button examples have been for clicking the mouse. Now, we will see how to use other mouse functions and certain of the keys.

There are a total of six mouse traps that can be used in handlers:
> mouseDown
> mouseStillDown
> mouseUp
> mouseEnter
> mouseWithin
> mouseLeave

The first three mouse messages relate to the mouse and its button position, and the last three relate to the mouse position within fields and buttons. Later as we progress with scripts, there will be possible applications for these mouse controlled messages, but in order to quickly see an example of how each works, making six buttons that use these mouse controlled actions will serve as reference examples. Using sounds, these buttons will show quickly what effect the mouse states have. Put each button on a HyperCard card with a field beneath each one with the script. The working script will be written in the individual button editors and duplicated on the fields. Then, the card can be used as a handy reference for seeing both the format of the scripts and the effect of using these various mouse initiated message handlers.

```
DownBeep
```

```
on mouseDown
  beep 1
end mouseDown
```

mouseDown

As soon as the mouse button is pressed down there will be a single beep. There is no sound if the button is held down or when it is released.

```
(StillDownBeep)
on mouseStillDown
  beep 1
end mouseStillDown
```

mouseStillDown

Holding the mouse down will cause a continuous beep.

```
( UpBeep )
on mouseUp
  beep 1
end mouseUp
```

mouseUp

Notice that the single beep sounds only when the button is released; not when it is first pressed.

```
( EnterBoing )
on mouseEnter
  play Boing
end mouseEnter
```

mouseEnter

As soon as the mouse cursor enters this button's outline, there will be a single "boing" sound.

```
┌─────────────────┐
│  WithinHarp     │
└─────────────────┘
┌─────────────────────────┐
│ on mouseWithin          │
│   play Harpsichord      │
│ end mouseWithin         │
│                         │
└─────────────────────────┘
```

mouseWithin

This button will emit a continuous sound while the cursor is inside the button area. It will even make sounds for a while after the cursor leaves the button area since it has to catch up with all of the commands to play the Harpsichord while the cursor was within the button's territory.

```
┌─────────────────┐
│  LeaveHarp      │
└─────────────────┘
┌─────────────────────────┐
│ on mouseLeave           │
│   play Harpsichord      │
│ end mouseLeave          │
│                         │
└─────────────────────────┘
```

mouseLeave

There is no effect when the cursor enters this area, but as soon as it leaves, there will be a single Harpsichord sound.

Key Control. As with the mouse, there are occasions where you may want special controls from the keyboard. For example, instead of clicking "OK" with the mouse, you might want the user to press the Return key. In a case of several options, pressing of several keys may be simpler than clicking one of the options. The design is up to you, and using keys instead of the mouse is simply another way of designing a stack. The keys that HyperCard traps include

```
returnKey
enterKey
tabKey
arrowKey
    left
    right
    up
    down
```

If an arrow key is used, it is important to remember that the arrow keys also are used for certain short cuts in HyperCard, and while your script can override the built-in short cuts, you may not want to. Using the arrow keys, the format is,

```
on arrowKey left  - -or right, up or down
    add 1 to total
end arrowKey left
```

Using the other keys is just like using the mouseUp trap. A useful application for the Tab or Return key would be with an application that had several cards, each with several choices. With one hand on the mouse for clicking choices and the other hand on the Tab or Return key (depending on whether the user was left or right handed) for going to the next card in the stack, it would be possible to go through the stack more rapidly. Using the scripts,

```
on tabKey      - - for righties
    go next card
end tabKey
on returnKey  - - for lefties
    go next card
end returnKey
```

it would be possible to satisfy both right and left handed users. That's a small detail, but it is one the users will appreciate when using the stacks.

Automatic Scripts

Other than buttons, every object can be opened and closed. The "automatic" scripts refer to initiating an action when the object is opened. To write a script for a card, select "Card Info..." from the Objects Menu. Click "Script..." in the Dialog Box when it appears. Then type in the example scripts shown below. For example, on opening a card with a bad credit risk, you might want the "boing" gong to sound to alert you to the client's poor performance with the following script:

```
on openCard
    play Boing
end openCard
```

Similarly, a closing can automatically trigger a script. Try the following script on a card to see the special effects it creates:

```
on closeCard
    visual effect checkerboard to black
end closeCard
```

These automatic scripts are useful when something has to be done as soon as an object is opened. The task can be a reminder, a warning or just for effect it creates. A time or date card that automatically displays the time or date when it is opened is another example.

Business Application: Organizational Mapper

This first application stack with HyperCard can be modified to fit any organization at all. The idea is to create a stack that can find people in an organization to get a job done. The bigger the organization, the more useful this stack will be since it often is difficult to find who's supposed to do what in a big organization. It also is useful for developing and analyzing a business organization since it requires the user (and creator) to stop and ask how tasks are organized. For smaller organizations, treat each position in terms of a task role. That means the same person might be in several different positions, but it will give a clear idea of what has to be done and whether there is a position for completing a task.

The stack will take a tree structure and assume a hierarchy. (This is very un-HyperCard to assume a hierarchy, but since HyperCard is so flexible, it can be used for hierarchy arrangements too.) As the stack moves toward the top there will be fewer positions, and as it moves toward the bottom it will have a greater number of positions. If your organization is different, feel free to make the necessary adjustments.

Goal: Quickly locate task fulfillment position and personnel within an organization.

Resources:
  Organizational overview card that summarizes major organizational units.
   Cards for organizational sub-units
   Cards for individual task performers
    Links between organizational levels.
    Vertical links
    Horizontal links
   Fields for task information
   Fields for personnel information
   Search capabilities

Outline

There is a single background, and all fields and other buttons are card fields. The background contains a message and two buttons as seen in Figure 4-7.

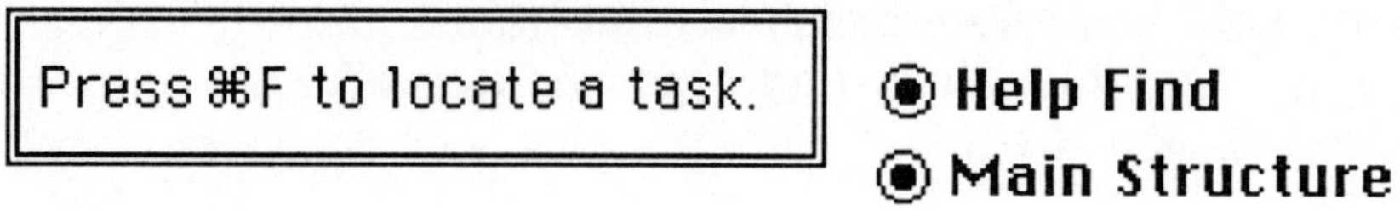

```
Press ⌘F to locate a task.    ◉ Help Find
                              ◉ Main Structure
```

Figure 4-7

Button: <u>Help Find</u>
Radio style
show name
script

>   on mouseUp
>   push card
>   go to card "Info"
>   end mouseUp
>
>   **Button**: <u>Main Structure</u>
>   Radio style
>   show name
>   *script*
>
>   on mouseUp
>   go card "StructureMain"
>   end mouseUp

The first card shows the main structure, and the card name is "StructureMain." (The button is called "Main Structure.") Pressing the Main Structure background button always brings the user back to this card shown in Figure 4-8.

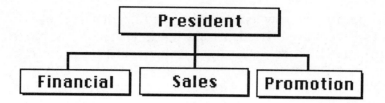

Press ⌘F to locate a task. ⊙ **Help Find** ⊙ **Main Structure**

Figure 4-8

Each box in the hierarchy is a button. When pressed, the button goes either to the person whose position is described in the box or the next organizational level down. For example, pressing the financial button leads to the financial sub-organization shown in Figure 4-9.

Finance Division

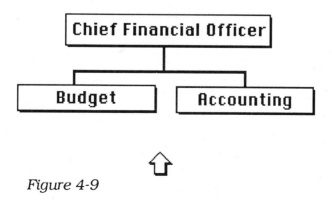

Figure 4-9

The upward pointing arrow leads to the next higher level in the hierarchy. Pressing the other buttons leads either to the next level down in the hierarchy, Budget and Accounting, or to a person. Pressing the button labeled "Chief Financial Officer," leads to a card with a field with information about what the chief financial officer does as seen in Figure 4-10.

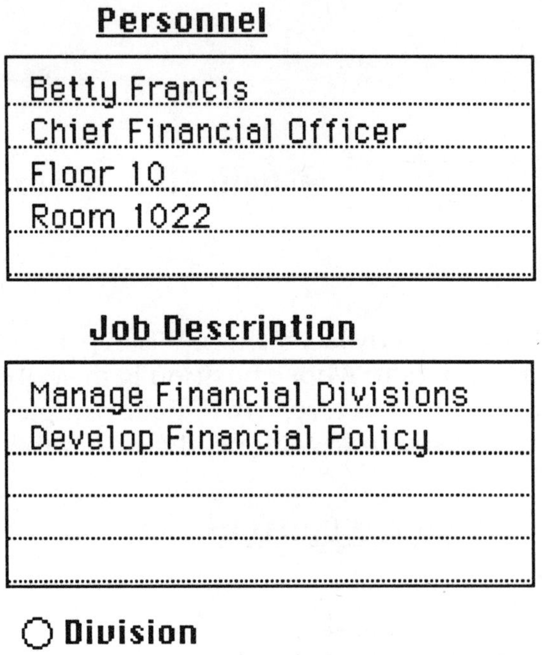

Personnel

Betty Francis
Chief Financial Officer
Floor 10
Room 1022

Job Description

Manage Financial Divisions
Develop Financial Policy

○ **Division**

Figure 4-10

The fields have no scripts. They are there for information only. The division button, takes the user to the card showing the individual's whole division. At the bottom level, there is horizontal movement between cards with individuals on the same level as shown in the example in Figure 4-11.

Personnel

Harry Worth
Budget Analyst
Floor 9
Room 911

Job Description

Analyze Promotion Division
budget

Figure 4-11

By organizing cards in this fashion it is possible to move through the hierarchy in a hierarchal fashion. However, it is also possible to move directly to a given individual using the Command-F or "find" function. To locate a given task, press the Command-F sequence and enter the task you want to find in the message box. Then HyperCard will take you directly to the task-performer.

To help the user with this, a "Help Card" is employed, shown in Figure 4-12. The script in the "OK" button automatically takes the user back to the card from whence he/she came.

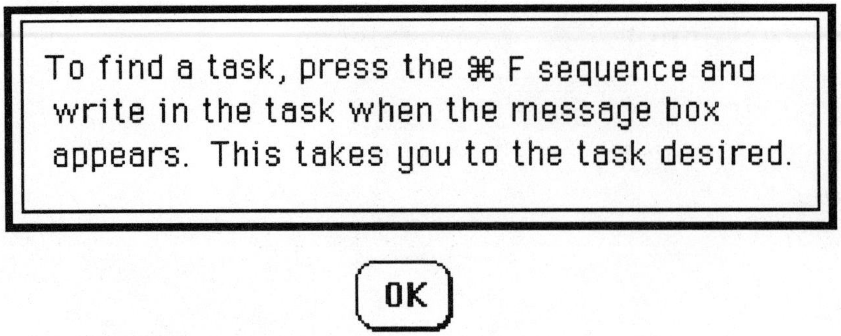

```
To find a task, press the ⌘ F sequence and
write in the task when the message box
appears. This takes you to the task desired.
```

OK

Figure 4-12

Button: <u>OK</u>
Card button oval style
script

on mouseUp
    pop card
end mouseUp

The background button "Help Find" has "push card" in its script so that whatever card the user leaves for help from, when a "pop card" is in the script, it will return to the card "pushed." That was done in this case.

All of the cards that make up this organization chart are not presented since it would take up space unnecessarily. However, from this you should be able to see how to use buttons, fields and cards creatively to move about a HyperCard stack. Change it so that you can use it in a practical way with some organization with which you work.

Organizing Elements

The Concept of "Containers"

When working with various types of data, you need a place to put it while it is being assembled, organized and displayed. In HyperCard, these places are called "containers." Both numeric and string (words, letters, etc.) data are placed into containers and manipulated until it can be used for some given purpose. For example, a container may contain a number which will be added to several other numbers and eventually be displayed as a total. Figure 5-1 shows several different numbers placed into Container A. As each number is added to Container A, its value changes. The total value of all the numbers is placed in Container B, which is a container that displays values.

Number:	Place:
55	Container A
33	Container A
44	Container A
51	Container A
82	Container A
90	Container A
355 (total)	Container B

Figure 5-1

In this example, Container A acts as a variable that accumulates added values, and Container B is both a variable and a display element. In such applications, Container B would be a field where the value 355 is displayed. As can be seen there is more than a single type of container, and depending on script requirements, one type or another is appropriate.

Container Forms

Each container form will be discussed with examples showing how to use them. There are some subtle and major differences between types of containers and how they are used. Likewise there are "chunk expressions" which involve grabbing part of a container's contents. Be sure to use the examples provided to see these differences.

Variables

Local Variables: The local variable is a non-object container which relates to a single handler. (A handler is any script that initiates action, such as "on mouseUp.") Local variables contain information in the form of values or strings. Actually, all values are stored as strings of characters, numbers included, but numbers can be treated as ordinary numeric values. If a string has quotation marks around it, then it is treated as a string and not a variable or numeric value. For example, do the following. Using a practice stack (one you can destroy), type in, blindly,

show message box

and the message box will appear. In the message box write,

```
put "word" into message box
```

as soon as you press the Return key, you will see:

```
word
```

In this instance, the message box is the container, and you can see what would happen with a local variable. (Local variables are invisible until you place their contents into a display container such as the message box or a field.) Now, write the same thing except do not put quotation marks around the word "word."

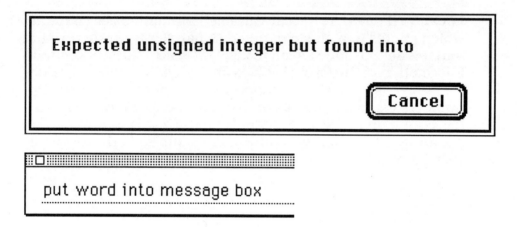

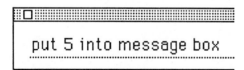

Figure 5-2

This time, HyperCard thought that "word" was a local variable with a number in it. As shown in Figure 5-2, the dialog box that appeared gave no option except cancelling the command. Finally, write,

```
put 5 into message box
```

and you will be presented with a number in the message box. With that experience, you can begin to see what is going on in variables. To create a local variable, all that is required is to use the **put** command to place something into a named container. Using the message box again, we will first put something into a local variable and then put the contents of the local variable into the message box.

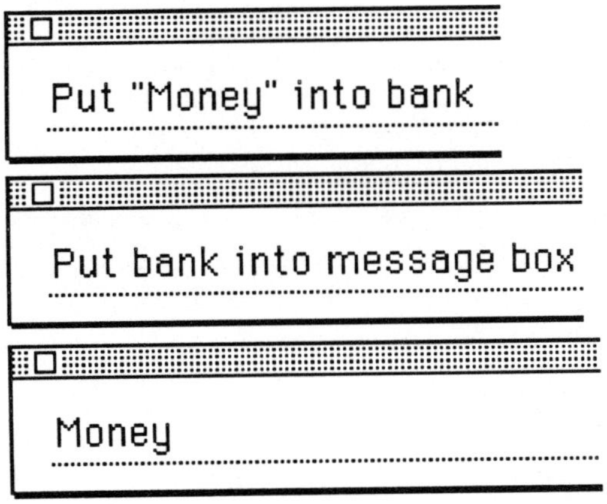

```
Put "Money" into bank
```

```
Put bank into message box
```

```
Money
```

Figure 5-3

The string "Money" is the value placed into the local variable named "bank." There is no need to declare a variable in HyperTalk. Simply by putting something into the variable creates that variable. When "bank" was placed into the message box, its contents, "Money," appeared in the box. Had the command read,

> put "bank" into message box

then the word "bank" instead of "Money" would have appeared there.

It. The "It" variable is a special kind of local variable that is automatically created when certain kinds of commands are used.

Most commonly, you will encounter it when using the **get** command, but it also is used when the commands **ask**, **answer**, **read** and **convert** are used as well. To see how it works, follow the sequence shown in Figure 5-4 pressing the return key after each entry.

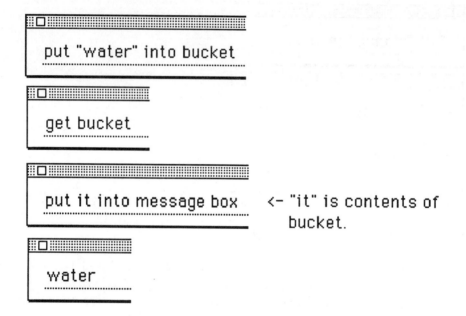

Figure 5-4

In "getting" other items that are quickly transferred, the "It" variable will be used heavily. In using it, though, remember to place whatever is in "It" somewhere that it can be kept. For example, there will be applications where you will first get the date and then the time. If you forget to put the date somewhere before you get the time, it will be lost since "It" will replace the date with the time when it is fetched with "get." Try the following example shown in Figure 5-5 to see how this works. (Notice in Figure 5-5 instead of using "message box," it was enough to use "message.")

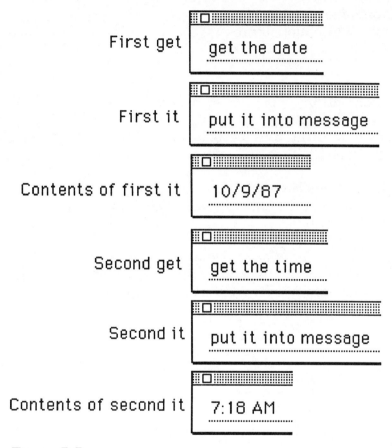

First get — get the date

First it — put it into message

Contents of first it — 10/9/87

Second get — get the time

Second it — put it into message

Contents of second it — 7:18 AM

Figure 5-5

Global Variables: Global variables can be used with different handlers. To set up a global variable, it must be "declared" with the **global** command first, and then used as a container. Each time a different handler uses the same global variable, it must first declare it with the global command. To see how this works, create two buttons named "Handler 1" and "Handler 2." Then write the following two scripts:

Handler 1 Script

```
on mouseUp            - -Handler 1
   global mousetrap
   put 22 into mousetrap
end mouseUp
```

Handler 2 Script

```
on mouseUp            - -Handler 2
   global mousetrap
   put mousetrap into message
end mouseUp
```

When finished, click Handler 1 first, and then click Handler 2. As soon as you click Handler 2, the value 22 appears in the message box.

If you changed the script so there was a local variable in Handler 1 and Handler 2, instead of getting the value of the container, "mousetrap" is treated as a string instead.

Handler 1

Handler 2

22

```
on mouseUp            - -Handler 1
   put 22 into mousetrap
end mouseUp
```

```
on mouseUp              - -Handler 2
    put mousetrap into message
end mouseUp
```

If more than a single handler is used in a single object's script, it still is necessary to declare a global variable if it is used again in a different handler. For example, if a handler is used to open and close a field any global variable used in both handlers will have to be declared within each handler routine.

```
on openField
    global drawer
    put 33 into drawer
end openField

on closeField
    global drawer
    put drawer into message box
end closeField
```

The first handler places the value 33 into the global variable called "drawer," and the second handler puts it into the message box. Without declaring the global variable a second time, however, it would not have worked. Remove the second instance of "global drawer" from the script and see what happens.

If using more than a single global variable with different handlers, a single line can initialize several variables at once. For example, if you used the global variables "retail," "wholesale" and "shippingCosts" they could be declared in the either of the following two formats:

```
global retail
global wholesale
global shippingCosts
```

or, more simply,

```
global retail,wholesale,shippingCosts
```

The second method saves time, but either method is acceptable.

Parameter variables: A final type of variable is the parameter variable. At this stage we will not be using them too much, so they simply will be introduced at this point. Later when they are employed in scripts, they will be discussed in more detail. Following a handler message, the words separated by commas are treated as parameter variables. For example, the line,

```
on fallBack, words, phrases
```

contains the parameter variables "words" and "phrases." In using the message name "fallBack", the words following that name are treated as parameter values. For example,

```
fallBack, "aunts","uncles"
```

would put the value (string) "aunts" into "words" and "uncles" into "phrases." Thus, the container (parameter variable) "words" now contains "aunts," and "phrases" contains "uncles." When parameter passing is discussed, we will examine this further.

Fields

In discussing variables, we showed an example of using field handlers. However, fields themselves are containers. Whatever is written in a field is "contained" in that field in the same way scripts put values into variable containers. Unless stated otherwise, fields are assumed to be background fields, and when writing scripts it is important to remember that. Sometimes as card will have both background and *card* fields, and unless the script specifies *card field,* there will be either an error message or the background field will be used.

Unlike variables, global or local, fields maintain information. As we will see further on in the book, there is a lot of information the user is prompted to enter. If that information is stored only in variables or places like the message box, the next time that HyperCard stack is used, the information will be gone. However, if the information is stored in a field, the data will still be there the next time that HyperCard stack is used. For a starting example, make the following field and button.

Field: Tanker
Locate field on card; not background.
shadow style
no script

Button: Loader
script

on mouseUp
    put "Oil" into storage
    put storage into card field "Tanker"
end mouseUp

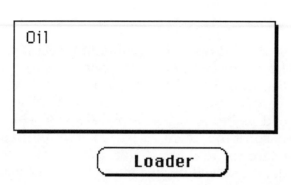

As soon as the button "Loader" is clicked, the word "Oil" appears in the field named "Tanker." If you quit HyperCard at this point, you will not lose the contents of the field called "Tanker." As soon as you re-start HyperCard, you will see the word (value) "Oil" in the card field.

Special Note: In the third line of the button script, note that the term "card field" was used instead of just "field." Even if there is only a single field on a card that is *not* in the background, it is necessary to specify "card field."

Putting something in a field is different from variables in that fields can save data after your Macintosh has been turned off. Fields are "visible varaibles" since you can see what is in them, and as such they are instructive for understanding all of the sub-parts of all containers. Each line is an independent element, and it is possible to have several values in a field. What's more, the script for a field can be placed in several different places, depending on the requirements of the application. Starting with a simple example, we can see that separate values can be placed on specified lines. Figure 5-6 shows a field with different values on different lines and the script for the button that produced the results:

Figure 5-6

Field: <u>Line Demo</u>
Locate field on card; not background.
rectangle style with lines showing
no script

Button: <u>Field lines</u>
script

```
on mouseUp
    put "One" into line 1 of card field 1
    put 2 into line 2 of card field 1
    put "four" into line 4 of card field 1
end mouseUp
```

Again a card field was used, and it was necessary to place "card field" in the button script so it would not assume the field was a background field.

Using variables, it is possible to do calculations within fields. This must be done with care, however, for each field can be treated as a single value, and it is easy to tangle up lines. Getting a little ahead of ourselves with some math commands, we will see how to write a script that uses both variables and fields as containers. It also will show how a single field can use lines as virtual fields within a field. Two scripts will be used; one in the background and the other in the field. The results will be identical, and unless you knew otherwise, it would not be possible to differentiate between the two. Make a "new background" in a practice stack with two background fields.

Field: El Taxo 1
Background field 1
Locate field in background.
rectangle style with lines showing
Script is in background
script

```
on closeField
    get value of line 1 of field 1
    put it into retail
    multiply retail by .06
    put retail into line 2 of field 1
    put value of line 1 of field 1 into whole
    add retail to whole
    put whole into line 3 of field 1
end closeField
```

Field: El Taxo 2 (Duplicate the first field and re-name.)
Background field 2
Locate field in background.
rectangle style with lines showing
Script is in field
script

```
on closeField
    get value of line 1 of field 2
    put it into retail
    multiply retail by .06
    put retail into line 2 of field 2
    put value of line 1 of field 2 into whole
```

```
        add retail to whole
        put whole into line 3 of field 2
    end closeField
```

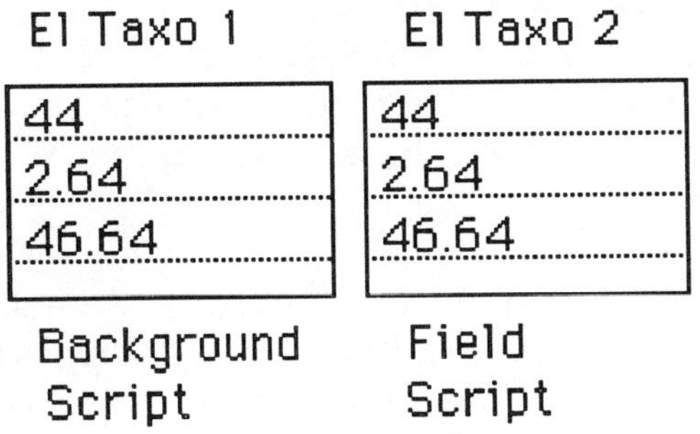

El Taxo 1   El Taxo 2

44		44
2.64		2.64
46.64		46.64

Background   Field
Script   Script

Figure 5-7

The handler used for this example was "closeField" so that as soon as the field is closed, usually caused by clicking the mouse while off the field, the calculations take place. Further on in the book, we will discuss more about calculations, but for here it is enough to know the calculations took place within *local variables* and then were placed in the appropriate places in the field. It is possible to do math with the lines themselves, but that will be covered later when discussing calculations in more detail.

The script used **add** and **multiply**. Each command does what you would expect. Using the local variables "retail" and "whole" the following sequence took place:

1. Value in line 1 was put into variable called "retail." (Figure 5-7 used 44 for value in line 1.)

2. "Retail" (44) was multiplied by .06 and so now "retail" contains 2.64 which is placed on line 2.

3. The value from line 1 (44) is now put into variable called "whole." The value from "retail" is added to "whole," so now "whole" is worth 46.64 which is put into line 3.

Label the field for "Price," "Tax" and "Total," with the Paint Text tool, and use it calculate sales tax. (If your sales tax is other than 6%, change the value in line 4 to something other than .06.) It will be a handy utility for examining how to set up scripts for using different lines in a single field.

As we begin introducing more and more commands, we will see other uses for the field object and learn how to write scripts that can use them to a fuller potential. However, even at this stage, it is important to begin thinking of where to put scripts and fields for different applications. The "deeper" the script is in a stack, the fewer times it is necessary to re-write it. At the same time, a "deep" script will affect more material in your stack; some of which you may not want influenced by a script. Selecting the right object, handler and level of depth in a stack is an art that develops with practice. With HyperCard, it is important to start that practice as soon as possible.

Selections. Another element found within fields is "selections". Selections are containers that are identified by highlighted text. For example, Figure 5-8 shows a segment of text selected. That selected (inverse) text is the container.

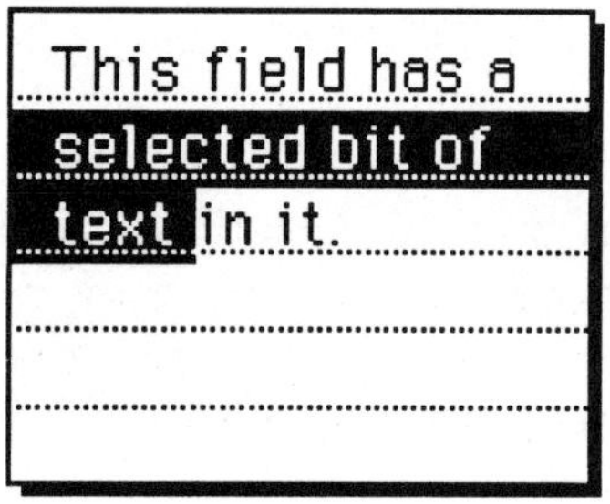

This field has a
selected bit of
text in it.

Figure 5-8

170

Using **get** and **put**, the selection can be treated like any other container in most ways. For example, if the HyperCard script,

> put "replacement" into the selection

were used in the sample in Figure 5-8, it would change to the sample seen in Figure 5-9.

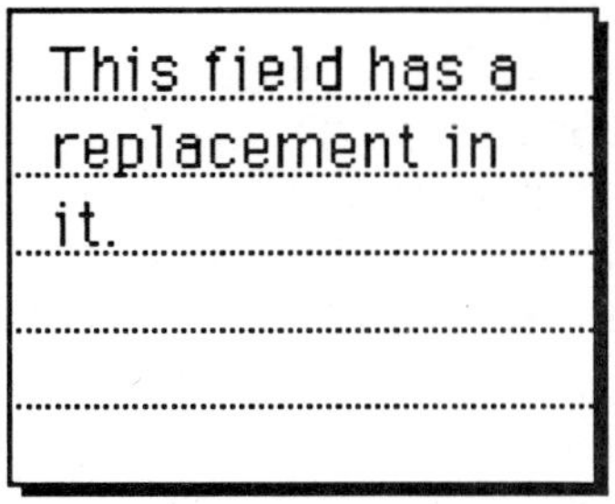

```
This field has a
replacement in
it.
```

Figure 5-9

Using selections as containers is something that requires more scripting commands than we have encountered up to this point, so we will not go further into this now. Moreover, while there are certain applications for selections as containers, variables and fields will be used far more frequently than selections.

Message Box: We have seen examples with the Message Box, and so it is familiar as a container. It is especially useful for experimenting with various script commands, and there are different applications where it will be useful as a container. It is different from a field because it does not save information after the stack has been closed, and it can be used to give commands directly to HyperCard. The abbreviations "message" and "msg" can be substituted for Message box, and "window" can be substituted for "box."

While looking at the Message box as a container, it is useful to introduce three new HyperTalk commands:

> **show**
> **hide**
> **wait**

The **show** command makes something visible. In this case, we can make the Message box visible with show. With **hide**, the opposite is true. It makes objects, such as the Message box, invisible. However, neither hide nor show affects the contents of the container they make appear or disappear. So do not attempt to use hide, for example, to change to contents of the message box. The third command, **wait**, makes the computer pause until either a certain condition is met or an amount of time passes. At this point in the book, we will introduce only the time elements associated with wait. There are two time forms, *seconds* and *ticks*. The seconds time a single second, and a tick is 1/60 of a second. Using wait, ticks are assumed to be the time element if seconds are not specified.

To see how all of this works make a button using the following script: (Note how "msg" was substituted for "message box.")

> **Button**: <u>Show/hide</u>
> *script*
>
> on mouseUp
>   put "Now watch this" into msg
>   show msg
> - -makes box appear
>   wait 5 seconds
>   hide msg
> - -makes box disappear
> end mouseUp

When you click the button, you will see the message for five seconds, and then it disappears. Using the message box this way can be useful in building stacks with reminders. For instance, when opening a field, some reminder in the Message box could tell the user not to forget to put in a person's middle initial. Figure 5-10 shows a field that uses the Message box for such a reminder as soon as the user enters the field.

```
Name:
Address:
Phone:
```

```
Don't forget the middle initial
```

Figure 5-10

Field: Reminder
script

```
on openField
    put "Don't forget the middle initial" into msg
    show msg
    wait 5 seconds
    hide msg
end openField
```

New For Version 1.2

In addition to showing and hiding buttons, the message box and fields, you can also show and hide pictures. See Chapter 10 for a complete description of how to use these new hide and show commands with graphics.

Chunk Expressions: Chunk expressions refer to a part (chunk) of a container. As we saw with fields, each individual line within a field could be accessed. In fact, lines constitute one type of chunk expressions. The complete list of chunk expressions includes,

> line
> item
> word
> character

We've discussed lines; so we will begin with "items." Items are separated by commas in a field. For example, the line,

> "pen, pencil, eraser, compass and protractor"

has four **items**:

> 1. pens
> 2. pencils
> 3. erasers
> 4. compass and protractor

The segment "compass and protractor" constitute a single item since there is no comma separating them as there are the other items.

Words are words or numbers separated by a space in a line. If you had a line in a field that read,

> "We need 15 modems"

and a script that commanded,

> get third word of line 5

the result would be "15" and it would be treated as would any of the other words in the line.

In the next example, the button called "Shift" moves various "chunks" from Field A to Field B to illustrate how chunk expressions work.

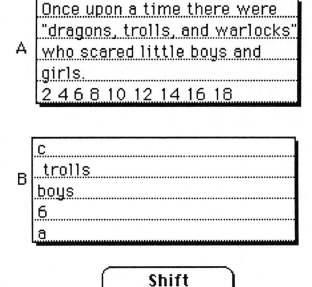

Figure 5-11

Field: A
no script
card field

Field: B
no script
card field

Button: <u>Shift</u>
script

```
on mouseUp
    get third character of line 1 of card field "A"
    put it into first line of card field "B"
    get character 11 of line 1 of card field "A"
    put it into line 5 of card field "B"
    get item 2 of line 2 of card field "A"
    put it into line 2 of card field "B"
    get word 4 of line 3 of card field "A"
    put it into line 3 of card field "B"
    get word 3 of line 5 of card field "A"
    put it into line 4 of card field "B"
end mouseUp
```

Whatever you place into the first field (Field A), determines what you will get in Field B. We will break the button script down into line pairs to see how each line in Field B was created.

Pair 1   get third character of line 1 of card field "A"
              put it into first line of card field "B"

This takes the third character from line 1 of Field A, which is the "c" in the word "Once." The "c" is placed in the first line of Field B.

Pair 2   get character 11 of line 1 of card field "A"
              put it into line 5 of card field "B"

The eleventh character of line 1 is the letter and word "a." Note that the spaces as well as the characters were counted to arrive at "a" as the eleventh character. The letter "a" is now in the "It" variable and it is placed in line 5 of Field B.

Pair 3   get item 2 of line 2 of card field "A"
               put it into line 2 of card field "B"

Instead of getting a character, Pair 3 of the script lines get an item. The second item is " trolls." Note that there is a space between the comma and the beginning of the word "trolls." Thus, when "trolls" is placed in line 2 of Field B, there is a leading space before it. When using the *item* chunk expression, you may want to omit spaces that would normally go after commas when writing lists of items that would be chosen. (Alternatively, you can get rid of unwanted spaces or other characters from items with commands and functions we will discuss further on in the book.)

Pair 4   get word 4 of line 3 of card field "A"
               put it into line 3 of card field "B"

Since "boys" is the fourth word of line three of Field A, it is placed into line 3 of Field B.

Pair 5   get word 3 of line 5 of card field "A"
               put it into line 4 of card field "B"

The fifth pair of script lines also gets a word, but this time the word is a number, 6. This makes no difference to HyperCard. It treats the "6" as a text string with no special commands required to do so.

To test that the word is indeed treated as a number, we will make a couple of simple background fields and a button which will move a "number word" and then do a simple mathematical

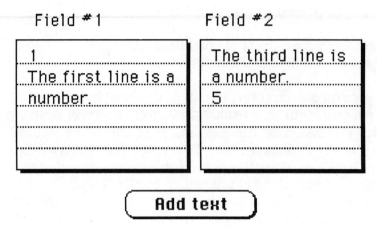

calculation. First, create the fields and buttons as shown in Figure 5-12.

Figure 5-12

Field: Field 1 (no name)
Background field 1
Locate field in background.
shadow style with lines showing
no script

Field: Field 2 (no name)
Background field 2
Locate field in background.
shadow style with lines showing
no script

Button: Add text
Oval button
   script

on mouseUp

```
            get first word of line 1 of field 1
            put it into line 3 of field 2
            add 4 to line 3 of field 2
        end mouseUp
```

Neither field has a script, but the script in the button takes the first word of Field 1 and puts it into the third line of the second field. The third line adds 4 to what had been on the first line of the first field. Try changing the number in the first field, and you will see that four is always added to it when it is placed in the second field's third position.

Accessing a Range of Chunks. When it is necessary to grab more than a single character, item or word from a field, chunk expressions use the format

```
        chunkexp A to B.....
```

where "chunkexp" is the chunk expression (word, char or item) and "A" is the beginning of the range and "B" is the end.

For example, the line

```
        get word 2 to 5 of field 1
```

would get the second through fifth words of the first background field. To see this in some immediate mode examples, use the following examples with the message box:

```
        get char 4 to 8 of "This is where I started"
        put it into msg

        get word 2 to 4 of "Frank Wilson experienced¬
         accountant"
        put it into msg

        get item 3 to 5 of "Jane Murdock, Acme Widgets,¬
```

44 Palm, Ely, NV"
put it into msg

Notice that instead of using "character" in the first of the three examples, the word "char" was substituted. This abbreviation will save time in writing scripts with chunk expressions.

To see how to use a range of chunk expressions in a script accessing a field, create the fields and button shown in Figure 5-13. (Just re-use the fields from Figure 5-12 to save time if you want.)

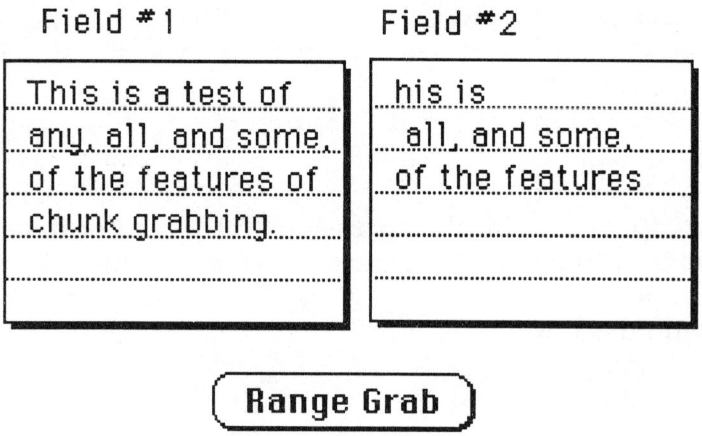

Field #1

| This is a test of |
| any, all, and some, |
| of the features of |
| chunk grabbing. |

Field #2

| his is |
| all, and some, |
| of the features |

Range Grab

Figure 5-13

Field: Field 1 (no name)
Background field 1
Locate field in background.
shadow style with lines showing
no script

Field: Field 2 (no name)
Background field 2
Locate field in background.

shadow style with lines showing
no script
Button: <u>Range Grab</u>
Oval button
   script

```
on mouseUp
    get char 2 to 7 of field 1
    put it into line 1 of field 2
    get item 2 to 3 of line 2 of field 1
    put it into line 2 of field 2
    get word 1 to 3 of line 3 of field 1
    put it into line 3 of field 2
end mouseUp
```

Using chunk expressions may not seem to useful at this point, but they will prove to have many uses as you begin using more commands in HyperCard. For example, you may have a good deal of information about a client in a line, but you only want to get their name and address from the line to use for a mailing label. By using chunk expressions, you can get the required information and use it without cluttering the mailing label with a lot of unnecessary information.

Single and Multiple Lines: When writing text in a field, a new line is recognized *only* if the return key is pressed. If there is no carriage return, even if a new line is used while writing the text, the HyperCard thinks it is the same line. Using the same fields as shown in Figure 5-13, we will demonstrate this feature. Write the material as seen in Figure 5-14, but do not use any carriage returns— don't press the return key.

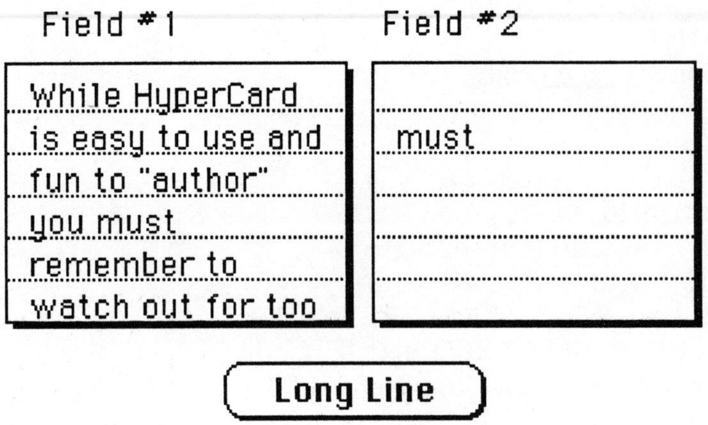

Field #1   Field #2

```
While HyperCard          must
is easy to use and
fun to "author"
you must
remember to
watch out for too
```

(**Long Line**)

Figure 5-14

Fields: Fields 1 & 2 (no names)
Background field 1 & 2
Locate fields in background.
shadow style with lines showing
no script

Button: Add text
Oval button
    script

```
on mouseUp
    get word 12 of line 1 of field 1
    put it into line 2 of field 2
end mouseUp
```

All the button script does is get the twelfth word from the first
line of Field 1 and put it into the second line of Field 2. However,
the word selected is "must," which is in the fourth line of Field
1. Try changing the script to the following and see what

happens:

get word 2 of line 4 of field 1

Since there is no "return" in the line, HyperCard treats the line as a single line (line 1), and it does not recognize any "line 4." As a result, it treats "line 4" as blank, and that is what you will get if you change the button script.

It is very important to remember that line numbers are based on the number of "returns," and not the number of visible lines in a field when writing scripts and setting up cards. This is especially important when writing scripts for fields that need to separate different numbers and words for formatting or calculations. If longer lines are required, it is a good idea to widen the field so it is easier to see that a line is a longer one. Also, knowing this information will assist in debugging scripts.

Fields: A & B

In some applications, it will be useful to have the Auto Tab function working with only some fields and not others. The new 1.2 property *autoTab* can be used for this in script control. Setting autoTab to TRUE or FALSE will turn it on or off in a script, respectively. Figure 5-15 provides a simple illustration.

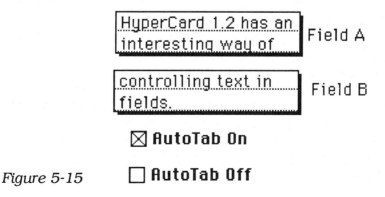

Figure 5-15

Fields: <u>A & B</u>
Card fields
shadow style with lines showing
no script

Buttons: <u>AutoTab On & AutoTab Off</u>
Check box button
  scripts

<u>AutoTab On</u>
on mouseUp
    set autoTab of card field "A" to true
    set autoTab of card field "B" to true
end mouseUp

<u>AutoTab Off</u>
on mouseUp
    set autoTab of card field "A" to false
    set autoTab of card field "B" to false
end mouseUp

At the end of the second line in Field A, press the Return key to see the different results you get with the "On" and "Off" buttons clicked.

Concatenation Using & and &&: For those unfamiliar with computer programming terms, concatenation refers to combining text strings. This allows for taking two or more text elements and combining them into a single element. In HyperCard the ampersand (**&**) operator is used for concatenation. If a single ampersand is used, the two text strings are placed adjacent to one another, and if a double ampersand (**&&**) is used, a space is placed between the two strings. For example, if you have a field that has three lines with the city, state and zip code and you want to concatenate them into a single line for printing envelope labels, concatenation will be very useful. Using two fields for illustration purposes, we can see how this can be done. Figure 5-16 shows two different shaped fields and an "Address Label" button to make the transformation.

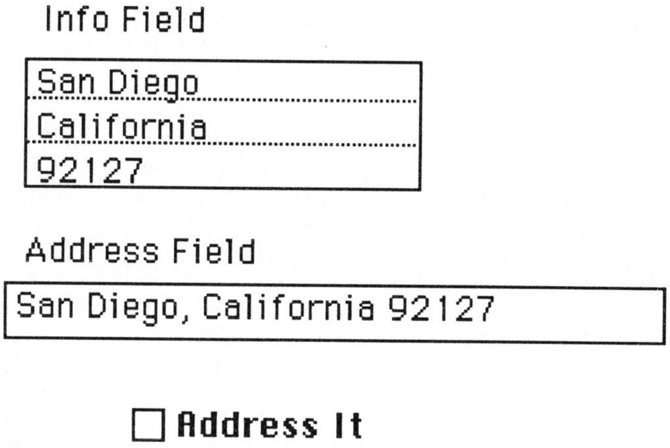

Info Field

| San Diego |
| California |
| 92127 |

Address Field

| San Diego, California 92127 |

☐ **Address It**

Figure 5-16

Field: Info
Background field
rectangle style with three lines showing
no script

Field: Address
Background field
rectangle style with no lines showing
no script

Button: Address It
Check box button
  script

```
on mouseUp
    get line 1 of field "Info"
    put it into City
```

```
        get line 2 of field "Info"
        put it into State
        get line 3 of field "Info"
        put it into Zip
        put City & "," && State && Zip into field "Address"
    end mouseUp
```

The obvious question is, "Why not put the text together the way you want it in the first place so that no concatenation is necessary?" In other words, if text has to be re-arranged by concatenation, why not put it in the desired arrangement in the first place? There are many answers to that question. The most important is the same data can be used for different purposes. Mailing labels are not the only use for which the above example information may be used, and by keeping it in separate elements, either fields or lines, it is easier to use for several different applications. For example, before putting the information into a label format, it may be necessary to first sort it by zip code. Since it is easier to sort cards when the sorting key is in a separate line in a field, having the material in the format shown in Figure 5-16 makes it easier to access items to sort.

Using Containers Between Cards and Stacks

All of the uses we have examined so far of "put" and "get" have been between fields in a single card, but it is also possible to transport data between separate cards and stacks. Basically, the sequence for getting and putting information between cards and stacks is the following:

1. **get** data
2. **go** to specified card in same or different stack
3. **put** data where you want it

Figure 5-17 shows an example moving data within a single stack.

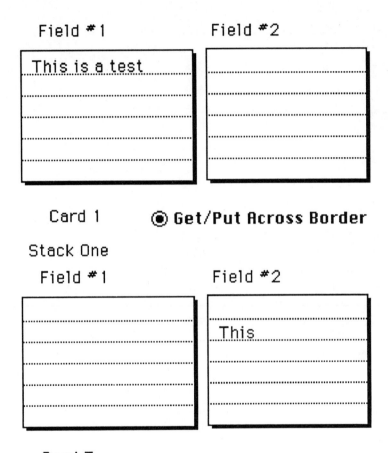

Field #1   Field #2

This is a test

Card 1   ◉ **Get/Put Across Border**

Stack One

Field #1   Field #2

This

Card 3

Stack One

Figure 5-17

Fields: <u>Fields 1 & 2</u> (no names)
Background field 1 & 2
Locate fields in background.
shadow style with lines showing
no script

Button: <u>Get/Put Across Border</u>
Radio button
script

```
on mouseUp
    get word 1 of line 1 of field 1
    go to card 3
    put it into line 2 of field 2
    go back
end mouseUp
```

When the button is pushed, the script gets the first word in the first field. The control is then shifted to the third card in the current stack. Finally, the value in the "it" variable is placed into the second line of the second field of the third card. The last line in the script, "go back," sends HyperCard to the previous card used. In this case, the card was the first card in the stack, so the script ends in the place it began.

To go from one stack to another using containers works the same way. Duplicate the stack shown in Figure 5-16, and name it "Stack 2." Change the button script to the following:

```
on mouseUp
    get word 1 of field 1
    go card 2 of stack "Stack 2"
put it into line 2 of field 2
    go back
end mouseUp
```

This time, the word "this" ends up in a different field, on a different card in a different stack. In transferring information between cards and stacks and different containers, as long as a single handler is used, it is not necessary to use global variables. Remember that global variables are only required with different handlers; not different containers, cards or stacks.

Application: Travel Expense Account

To use what we have learned in this chapter, we will make an application that keeps track of travel expenses. A new card will be used for each trip, and a special card at the end of the stack will be used to total the expenses in each category. All of the fields and buttons will be in the background so that as each new card is created for each trip, it will be unnecessary to create new fields and buttons. Even on the card that keeps totals, we will use the background for the several fields on the card in case new totals are to be maintained quarterly, monthly or whatever is useful.

The basic arrangement will be to make a single field for each card used for data entry. Each line on the card will be used for different travel expense categories. The top line will automatically enter the date, and the bottom line will be used for posting the destination of the trip. The rest of the lines will be amounts spent in each category. A button will be used to send the figures to a second card that is used for accumulating totals. The button is used instead of having the data automatically sent to the "totals" card so the user can check his/her figures before processing them. The travel expense card appears as shown in Figure 5-18.

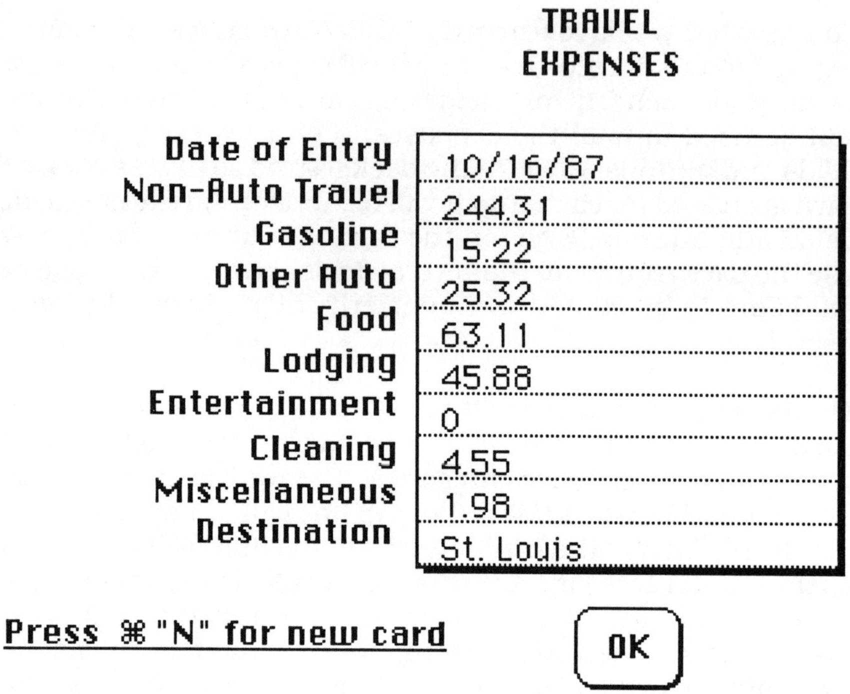

TRAVEL
EXPENSES

Date of Entry	10/16/87
Non-Auto Travel	244.31
Gasoline	15.22
Other Auto	25.32
Food	63.11
Lodging	45.88
Entertainment	0
Cleaning	4.55
Miscellaneous	1.98
Destination	St. Louis

Press ⌘ "N" for new card

OK

Figure 5-18

Field: <u>EntryField</u>
Background field
Shadow style with margin and lines showing
no script

Button: <u>OK</u>
Oval button
Button in background
script

```
on mouseUp
    get the date
    put it into line 1 of field "EntryField"
    get line 2 of field 1
- -get information
    put it into travel
- -place in local variable
    get line 3 of field 1
- -do the same for all lines
    put it into gas
    get line 4 of field 1
    put it into other
    get line 5 of field 1
    put it into food
    get line 6 of field 1
    put it into lodging
    get line 7 of field 1
     put it into fun
    get line 8 of field 1
    put it into clean
    get line 9 of field 1
    put it into misc
    go to card "Total"
- -go to the Total card
    add travel to field "Travel"
- -add variable value

    add gas to field "Gas"
- -to appropriate field
    add other to field "otherAuto" - -for all categories
    add food to field "Food"
    add lodging to field "Motel"
    add fun to field "Fun"
    add clean to field "Clean"
    add misc to field "Misc"
end mouseUp
```

Most of the work is done by the script in the button "OK." Otherwise, the only other data manipulation occurs when the "Total It" button on the "totals" card is pressed. It simply adds up the values in the eight category fields and puts the sum in the "Total Expenses" field.

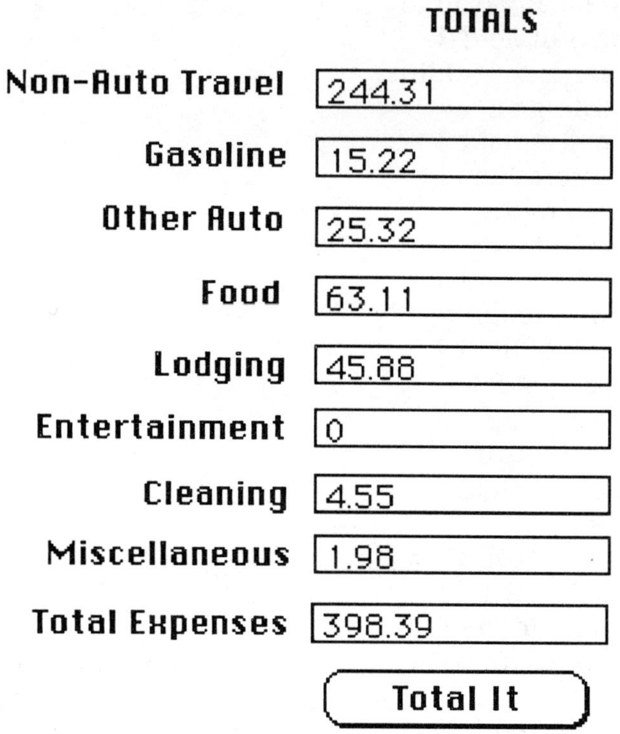

TOTALS

Non-Auto Travel	244.31
Gasoline	15.22
Other Auto	25.32
Food	63.11
Lodging	45.88
Entertainment	0
Cleaning	4.55
Miscellaneous	1.98
Total Expenses	398.39

Total It

Figure 5-19

Fields: <u>Travel, Gas, otherAuto, Food, Motel, Fun, Clean, Misc, Sum</u>
Rectangle style
No lines showing
Background Fields
no scripts

Button: <u>Total It</u>
Oval button
Button in background
script

```
on mouseUp
    put 0 into total
    get field 1
    add it to total
    get field 2
    add it to total
    get field 3
    add it to total
    get field 4
    add it to total
    get field 5
    add it to total
    get field 6
    add it to total
  get field 7
  add it to total
  put total into field "Sum"
end mouseUp
```

Both scripts are relatively long, and once we learn more commands, operations and functions, we will see how both scripts could be much shorter. In the two scripts, it is important to note how the fields were referenced in the two different scripts. In the "OK" button script, fields were referenced by their names. Using field names makes it easier to understand what the script is doing for later reference, but it is not quite as economical to program. Using field numbers, as we will see further on in the book, lets the script author order field values in a loop. Had a loop structure been employed, we could have made the "Total It" script much shorter and just as efficient. However, for from one place and use it in another on HyperCard. If you can do that, then you understand a core element of HyperTalk scripts.

As a final note for the "Travel Expense" stack, see if you can create another button that will total the sum of each single card. In that way, you will have a stack that not only keeps a running total of all expenses, but it will keep "trip totals" as well. Also, add and change categories to better suit your own actual expenses.

Summary

This chapter takes the second major step in using HyperTalk scripts; using containers. In Chapter 4, we saw how to author scripts that moved between cards and stacks. This chapter showed how to place things into containers and use the information in the containers with other containers on the same and differents cards and stacks. Since containers are the basic unit of organization in HyperCard, they will be used heavily in creating your own stacks. In fact, once you master the concepts of movement and use of containers in HyperCard, you're 90% competent in fully understanding how to use HyperTalk scripts and HyperCard.

Of the many containers, variables, including local and global and the special "It" variable, fields, the message box and selections, most of the container work in HyperCard deals with variables and fields. Within fields, individual lines are "sub-containers" along with the several chunk expressions within lines. Organizing data within these containers allows accessing and using the data for a nearly infinite variety of applications. And while most of the chunk expression examples used in this chapter involved field, remember that *all containers* have separate lines, words, items and other chunk expressions.

Calculations

HyperCard Calculations

In Chapter 5, we introduced some basic calculation commands: add and multiply. In this chapter, we will look at other calculation commands as well as various **operators** and how to use them in **expressions**. Operators in expressions derive values from other values and have several forms. These allow several different types of sophisticated mathematical and logical formulations in HyperCard. We will examine these in detail in this chapter.

In addition we will be looking at the ways in which numbers, as well as time, date and text, can be formatted. There is much more we will do with formatting in Chapter 7, but here it is important to get started learning a little about formats so you clearly can see the results of any calculations.

Calculation Commands and Functions

There are four basic arithmetic commands:

> **add**
> **subtract**
> **multiply**
> **divide**

We've seen how add and multiply can be used with containers. When using add, the conjunction *to* is used, while multiply uses *by*. Thus, with containers labelled "Time" and "Money" we would use the formats,

> add Time to Money
> multiply Time by Money

Similarly, **subtract** uses *from* and **divide** uses *by*, the same as multiply does. For example,

subtract Time from Money
divide Time by Money

would perform subtractions and divisions respectively. All of
the commands must be used with values *with containers*.
Thus, the statement,

subtract 10 from 20   ←**This will not work**

would not work in HyperCard. Use the following field and
script in Figure 6-1 for some illustrative practice:

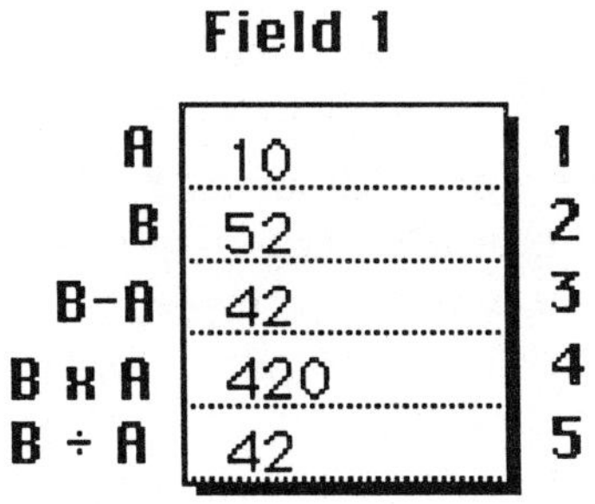

Field 1

Figure 6-1

Field: Field 1 (no name)
Shadow with lines showing
background field
script

```
on closeField
    get line 1 of field 1
    put it into A
    get line 2 of field 1
    put it into B
    subtract A from B
```

```
        put B into line 3 of field 1
        multiply B by A
        put B into line 4 of field 1
        divide B by A
        put B into line 5 of field 1
    end closeField
```

This exercise is similar to those in Chapter 5 using add and multiply except that we've added the new commands divide and subtract. When you finished entering numbers in the first two lines, place the pointer outside of the field and click the mouse. Remember when examining the results that the values of the container B changes with each calculation.

Operators

In Chapter 5 we introduced two operators, "&" and "&&" used in text concatenation. Here, we will examine the other operators and learn how to use them. As you will see, there are many mathematical operations and calculations possible without using containers as the source and destination, even though containers certainly will be used for storage of results. First, we will provide an overview of HyperCard operators in order of precedence and a classification of operator type.

Order of Precedence for Operators

Operator	Type
( )	Grouping
-	Negative value for number
not	Logical value negate
^	Exponentiation (power of...
div mod * /	Division, modulo, multiplication of numbers
& &&	Text concatenation
< > <= >= ≥ ≤	Numeric logical
is in contains	Text logical

= is <> ≠	Text & numbers logical
and	Logical
or	Logical

Table 6-1

Depending on the type of expression, one or another type of operator is required. Operators are commonly used in evaluative and conditional expressions. These are expressions where an "If....Then..." condition is set up. Later on in the book we will examine conditional expressions in detail, but in some of the examples in this chapter we will be using them.

Groupings: When several different operators are used in a single line, parentheses set up the order of precedence and separate operations. The innermost groupings are calculated first moving outward and left to right until the outermost calculations are completed. For example in the grouping,

$$((10 * 5) / (3 * 4) + 96)$$

the calculations would be made in the following order:

1. $10 * 5 = 50$
2. $3 * 4 = 12$
3. $50 / 12 = 4.166667$
4. $4.167 + 96 = 100.166667$

The expression,

put ((10 * 5) / (3 * 4) + 96) into can

would place the value 100.166667 into the container (local variable) called "can." Using the message box, practice with some of the following groupings:

```
put (14 + 3 / ((8 * 9) / (5-11)) into msg
put ((33/11) + (3 / 9)) / (2^4) into msg
put (25 div 4) && "and" && (25 mod 4) into msg
```

It is also possible to take the **value** of a grouping from a line and put it somewhere else. Using the function **value**, the calculated results of a grouping on a line can be placed in another line, in another field or in any other container. For practice, the little card shown in Figure 6-2 can be used to take the value from a field's line and put the results into a message box.

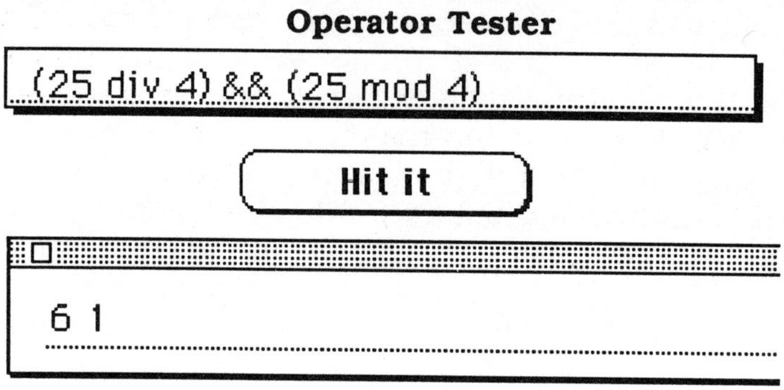

Operator Tester

(25 div 4) && (25 mod 4)

```
        Hit it
```

6 1

Figure 6-2

Field: Field 1 (no name)
Shadow with 1 line showing
background field
no script

Button: Hit It
Oval button
script

```
on mouseUp
    get value of line 1 of field 1
```

```
        put it into msg
    end mouseUp
```

Try different groupings in the field and click the button to get the value in the message box. In most applications, the formulas for the calculations are kept invisible inside scripts, but while you are learning how to use groupings, you might want to create some cards with visible calculated fields as in the Figure 6-2 "Operator Tester" example.

Logical Expressions : In addition to being used with arithmetic, operators can also be used in logical expressions. Both text and numbers have logical operations. The operators indicate some condition that can be evaluated as true or false between two numbers or strings.

<u>Numeric Logical Operators</u>
>	greater than
<	less than
<= ≤	less than or equal to
>=≥	greater than or equal to

Using the Operator Tester, try some of the following operations. Notice that the message box will either come up with "true" or "false"

22 > 21
833 ≥ 831   {**Note:** Use option + > to get ≥}
(2 * 5) < (3 * 3)
(3 + 3) => (2 * 3)

Later, you will be able to write scripts that will make a choice depending on whether the results of a calculation are true or false.

Text Logical Operators

is in	right element has the left element in it
contains	left element has the right element in it

Logical operations with text deal with locating parts or all of a text string within another text string. The two operators, **is in** and **contains** are similar operators using opposite arrangements. To visibly see how this arrangement works out to be true, look at Figures 6-3 and 6-4.

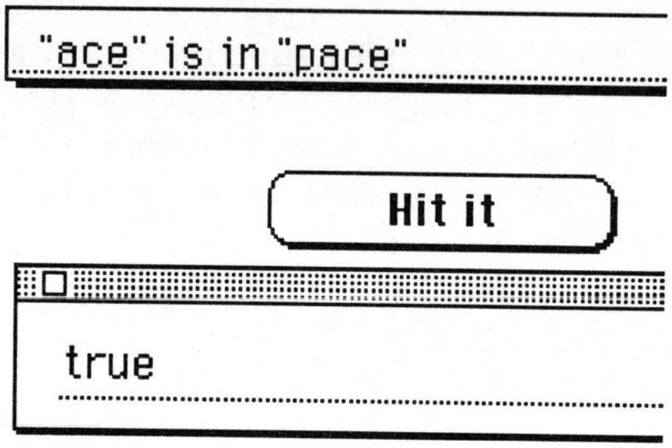

```
"ace" is in "pace"
```

```
    Hit it
```

```
true
```

Figure 6-3

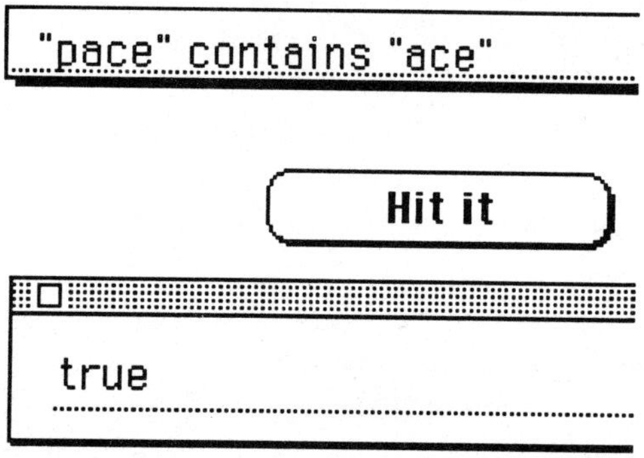

```
"pace" contains "ace"
```

```
    Hit it
```

```
true
```

Figure 6-4

In Figure 6-3 "ace" is the *right element* and Figure 6-4 it is the *left element*. It is equivalent to saying,

The word "ace" is in the word "pace."

and

The word "pace" contains the word "ace."

When in doubt with a HyperTalk script, just see how it sounds in normal English, and chances are you will be able to get the containers or words in the order you want. Try some of the following in the Operator Tester (Figure 6-2):

"apples" is in "oranges"
"rain" contains "i"
"I love a parade" contains "love"
"Buy low, sell high" contains "high"
"The check" is in "the mail"

Text and Number Logical Operators
=	Equal value
<>	Not equal
is	Same as equal
≠	Same as not equal
not	Logical negate
and	Both true
or	One is true

Most of the text and number logical operators are fairly self-explanatory, but sometimes there is confusion as to when to use the logical negate and the and/or comparisons.

Think of **not** as a "double negative" in logical operations. For example, the following expression is logically false:

"apples" = "oranges"

However, the expression,

not ("apples" = "oranges")

is true. In other words, it's like saying,

#1. "The statement 'apples equals oranges' is <u>not</u> true."
#2. "Statement #1 <u>is true</u>; thus, the results are true."

There may not be a lot of uses for the logical not, but in some applications it may be handy; so you might as well know how to use it. If using logical not is confusing, you can get a true result with a statement like,

"apples" ≠ "oranges"   (**Note:** option + = make ≠)

and be just as efficient.

Using the Operator Tester, try the following:

"Fun" is "Fun"
"Far" is "Out"
"Money" ≠ "Happiness"
not ("Hot" = "Cold")

With the logical **and** and **or**, the choices depend on one or both expressions being true. With **and**, they both have to be true, and with **or**, only one has to be true. For example, using the message box, put in the following sequence, pressing the return key after each line.

(9 > 10) and (10 > 9)

(3 > 5) or (5 > 3)

```
put 5 into pot
put 7 into can
put 10 into boot
(pot < can) and (boot > can)
```

Precedence

Precedence refers to the order in which operations will be calculated. In Table 6-1, near the beginning of this chapter, the operators are listed in order of precedence. To re-order precedence, use the parentheses, and the innermost expressions within parentheses will be executed first, then work outward, moving from left to right. For example, suppose you wanted to add 50 to 30 and then multiply that number by 10. If you wrote,

$$50 + 30 * 10$$

precedence would first multiply 30 by 10 and then add the 50. To re-order precedence, you would write,

$$(50 + 30) * 10$$

and that would generate the desired results. If you start getting unusual and unexpected values in your calculated fields, check the precedence and how the numbers, text and containers are arranged.

Setting HyperCard Properties With Scripts

Up to this point, the various object properties of HyperCard have been set with the menus. *Properties* refer to how objects appear and how they perform. For example, we can change the property of a font to make it appear **bold**, and we can change the property of the user level so that the user can only use the Browse tool. This can also be done from a script using the **set** command. As we will see as we go along, there are many levels and categories of properties. They include the following:

global	window	painting	field
stack	background	card	button

It is important to be aware of the different script forms to use with different properties. Some properties are in more than one category and must be treated somewhat differently in each one. For example, as you will see further on in this chapter, there are text properties for both window and paint categories. Depending on how the script is written, the text will either be treated as paint text or field text. Otherwise, setting properties is fairly straightforward and simple.

The primary word for installing a property is **set**. You can either set a *property* to a value or the *property of an object* to a value or condition. For example,

    set userLevel to 2

places the user in the "Typing" level. This would be useful in a script in a stack where you do not want anyone doing anything other than entering text data and browsing. Even if the user changed the level from the Home stack, the script could change it back as soon as the user opened the stack.

Property values also can be true or false. For example, if you want to have the name of a button appear or disappear, you can set the **showName** to "true" or "false." For example, the following script will show the name of a button named "Correct" when it is clicked and will make the name disappear when the button is released.

    on mouseDown
        set showName of button "Correct" to true

```
    end mouseDown

    on mouseUp
        set showName of button "Correct" to false
    end mouseUp
```

Several other characteristics of property values also exist. These will be introduced along with the property further along in the book.

Number and Text Formats

A global property of HyperCard is **numberFormat**. This controls what is displayed on the screen and how a value is calculated. Since HyperCard stores everything as text, the combination seen on the screen is the combination that is used in calculations. An important feature to be aware of when changing number formats is that *a change in the format only works for a current script* . For later scripts, it returns to the default precision of six digits right of the decimal.

To establish the format of the number, use **numberFormat** and **set** together along with the following three symbols:

zero	**0**
decimal point	.
pound sign	**#**

The pound sign shows the level of precision desired, whether or not the zeros are shown. The zeros establish whether a zero is placed in the position relative to the decimal point. For example, the button script

```
    on mouseUp
        set the numberFormat to "00.0000000"
        put 4/2 into msg
```

end mouseUp

would return 2.0000000 in the message box. On the other hand, the pound sign simply specifies the precision of the calculation and the script,

```
on mouseUp
    set the numberFormat to "0.#######"
    put 4/2 into msg
end mouseUp
```

would result in a simple, "2" in the Message Box. However, both would provide the same level of precision.

Leading zeros are usually placed for decimal numbers and aligning them with other value that include both whole and decimal values. For example, you could align a set of mono-spaced (e.g., Monaco or Courier font) numbers in a field such as,

```
0.55
1.76
2.11
```

by setting numberFormat to "0.00", the decimal point would be where it will align the numbers correctly. Likewise, when using money, it is important to calculate and show values with two decimal points and a dollar sign. (You can use the British pound (£) [option + 3], Japanese Yen (¥) [option + Y] or other monetary symbols as well.) For example, the script segment,

```
set numberFormat to "000.00"
put "$" & 9.95 into line 1 of field 1
put "$" & 205.19 into line 2 of field 1
```

would do just about everything you needed. However, we

would find soon that the decimal points are not aligned. The *leading* zeros do not fill the empty spaces with zeros or spaces.

One way to align decimal points with two decimal place numbers is to use the text alignment option to set the field to right align. While we're at it, we will also set the font to a mono-spaced one, Monaco. Using the *field* property (not *art* property) **textAlign** for the right justification of the text and **textFont** for the font style, we can change the alignment and font of a field for financial decimal alignment.

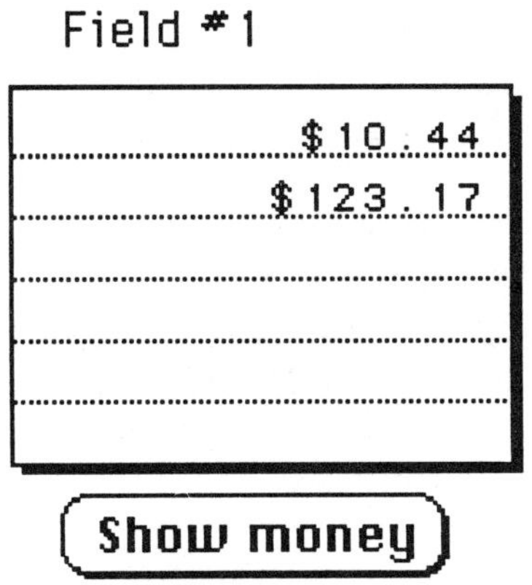

Field #1

```
              $10.44
             $123.17
```

(Show money)

Figure 6-5

Field: Field 1 (no name)
Shadow style, show lines
Background field
no script

Button: Show money
card button
oval shape
script

```
on mouseUp
    set textFont of field 1 to "Monaco"
    set textAlign of field 1 to right
    set numberFormat to "000.00"
    put "$" & 10.44 into line 1 of field 1
    put "$" & 123.17 into line 2 of field 1
end mouseUp
```

Besides controlling text alignment and font type, you can control the leading, size and style of text as well.

textHeight	leading or vertical space between characters
textSize	size of font
textStyle	available styles of font (e.g. bold, italic.)

Special Note: The term "leading" is from the old hot metal days of typesetting when varying amounts of lead were used to control vertical space between lines of text. The clarity and appearance of your text material in fields can be significantly improved by altering the **textHeight** property.

For some quick practice before we look at converting times and dates, experiment with the field shown in Figure 6-6.

Text Stuff

This should be in
bold Geneva with
the lines showing.

Figure 6-6

210

Field: <u>Text Stuff</u>
Background field
script

```
on closeField
    set showLines of field "Text Stuff" to true
    set textFont of field "Text Stuff" to Geneva
    set textStyle of field "Text Stuff" to bold
    set textSize of field "Text Stuff" to 9
    set textHeight of field "Text Stuff" to 12
end closeField
```

Change the various property values of the text to see what different results you can get.

Using Convert

To change and use different time formats, HyperCard has the **convert** command. Convert takes a *container* with the date or time and converts it to different formats. The formats include,

seconds	**long date**
short date	**abbreviated date**
long time	**short time**
dateItems	

First, we will see how to convert the time and date to different formats, and then take a look at doing calculations with time and date.

Seconds. This is the number of seconds since January 1, 1904.
Long Time. This gives the hour, minutes and seconds.
Short Time. Displays only hours and minutes.
Long Date. Shows day of week, month, date and year
Abbreviated Date. Same as long date but abbreviates day and

month. May use *abbrev date* or *abbr date* in addition to *abbreviated date*.

Short Date. Gives month, date and year in numeric values.

dateItems. Presents date *and* time as items separated by commas.

Year, month, day, hour, minute, second, day of week

Sunday, not Monday, is considered the first day of the week.

It is important to remember that the time or date must *first* be placed into a container to use **convert**. Then, using the format,

convert *container* to format

change the contents of the container to the desired format. Once the container contents have been changed to another format, you can change them again and again using the same container. For example, if you change the contents to *seconds* and then decide you want to change it to *long time,* just use convert, and it will change the seconds into the long time format.

To see how they look, make the card in Figure 6-7. Keep this card handy for a format and script reference showing how to convert time and dates.

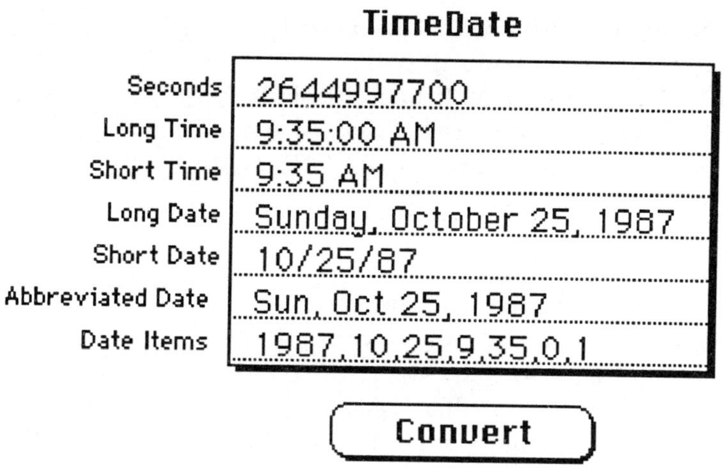

TimeDate

Seconds	2644997700
Long Time	9:35:00 AM
Short Time	9:35 AM
Long Date	Sunday, October 25, 1987
Short Date	10/25/87
Abbreviated Date	Sun, Oct 25, 1987
Date Items	1987,10,25,9,35,0,1

(**Convert**)

Figure 6-7

Special Note: The button script is pretty long, and a lot of those lines are very similar. It will save a lot of time for you if you use the cut and paste functions in your editor when writing the script.

Field: TimeDate
Shadow field with seven lines showing
Field in background
no script

Button: Convert
Oval style
Show button name
script

on mouseUp
    - -First get the Time
    get the time
    put it into clock
    convert clock to seconds

```
                    put clock into field "TimeDate"
                    convert clock to long time
                    put clock into line 2 of field "TimeDate"
                    convert clock to short time
                    put clock into line 3 of field "TimeDate"
                    - - Now the Date
                    get the date
                    put it into calendar
                    convert calendar to long date
                    put calendar into line 4 of field "TimeDate"
                    convert calendar to short date
                    put calendar into line 5 of field "TimeDate"
                    convert calendar to abbreviated date
                    put calendar into line 6 of field "TimeDate"
                    - -Note that only the clock is converted
                    convert clock to dateItems
                    put clock into line 7 of field "TimeDate"
                end mouseUp
```

Examining the script for the "Convert" button, everything is fairly straight forward until the last segment where dateItems are converted. The clock container with the time was converted, but when the contents were displayed in the TimeDate field, both the date and the time were shown. The dateItems format, takes care of both the date and time and displays them. However, if you put the date into a container and convert it to dateItems format, only the date and not the time is displayed. Therefore, remember to *use only a time container when converting dateItems*.

Calculating with Time and Date

There are two basic ways to do calculations with time and date. First, using **seconds**, it is possible to place a beginning and ending time in containers and then subtract the former from the latter. This gives the total number of seconds which can be converted into hours, minutes and seconds. Second, using **dateItems**, you can select items (remember character, word, item) from a container and do calculations with the selected items.

Seconds Calculations. Using the formula,

SecondTime - FirstTime = TimePassed

the passage of time can be measured using time converted to seconds. Then, the time can be broken into hours, minutes and seconds using the div and mod operators.

Hours = (TimePassed div 60) div 60
Minutes = (TimePassed div 60) mod 60
[Minutes *without* subtracting hours =
TimePassed div 60]
Seconds = TimePassed mod 60

We want to count the hours, then the minutes minus the hours and the second minus the hours and the minutes. To see how this might be used, make the card shown in Figure 6-8. Seconds were not calculated, but if you want them, just add them to the script.

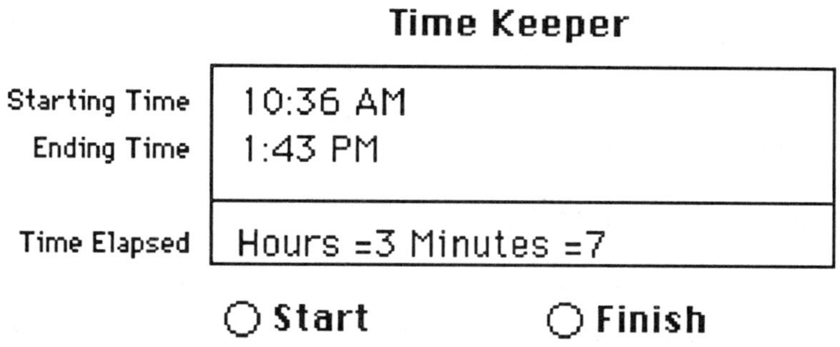

Time Keeper

| Starting Time | 10:36 AM |
| Ending Time | 1:43 PM |

| Time Elapsed | Hours =3 Minutes =7 |

○ **Start**   ○ **Finish**

Figure 6-8

Field: <u>Time Keeper</u>
Rectangle style
No lines showing
Graphic line across bottom third
no script

Button: <u>Start</u>
Radio button style
Button in background
script
```
on mouseUp
    global FirstTime
    get the time
    put it into FirstTime
    put it into line 1 of field "Time Keeper"
end mouseUp
```

Button: <u>Finish</u>
Radio button style
Button in background
script

```
on mouseUp
    global FirstTime
    get the time
    put it into SecondTime
    put it into line 2 of field "Time Keeper"
    - -Do the conversion
    convert FirstTime to seconds
    convert SecondTime to seconds
    - -Calculate Hours and Minutes
    put SecondTime - FirstTime into TimePassed
    put (TimePassed div 60) div 60 into Hours
    put (TimePassed div 60) mod 60 into Minutes
    put "Hours =" & Hours && "Minutes =" & Minutes¬
    into line 4 of field "Time Keeper"
end mouseUp
```

DateItems calculations. DateItems are used somewhat differently for calculations. Each of the items must be calculated separately since each represents a different category of time. Seconds are all lumped into one category, but dateItems are in seven categories that must be calculated separately. To see graphically how this works the card shown in Figure 6-9 presents the dateItems for the current date and a birthday entered by the user. The birthday data is entered in the *short date* format in the example, but any legitimate format for the date may be entered there using the Browse tool. The script is in the button, "Calculate Age." Using the first three dateItems, the script calculates the age of the person in years, months and days. The script is flawed, however, in that if the current date in months and days is less than the birthday month and days, the age is incorrect and the months and days are shown as negative values. In the next chapter we will see how, using conditional structures, this could be controlled.

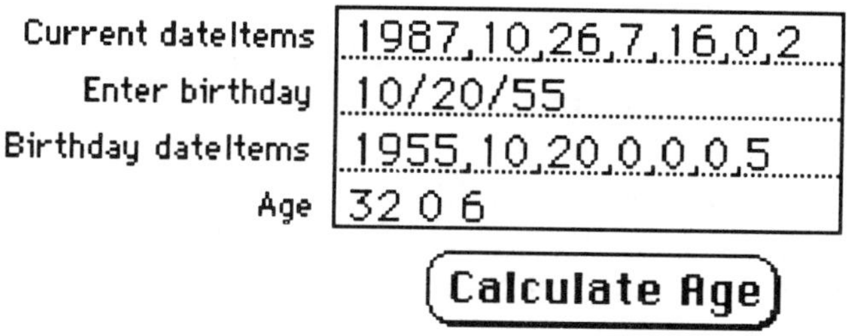

Current dateItems	1987,10,26,7,16,0,2
Enter birthday	10/20/55
Birthday dateItems	1955,10,20,0,0,0,5
Age	32 0 6

(Calculate Age)

Figure 6-9
Field: Field 1 (no name)
Rectangle style showing lines
Background field
no script

Button: Calculate Age
Oval button style
Show name
script

```
on mouseUp
    get the time
    put it into clock
    convert clock to dateItems
    put clock into line 1 of field 1
    get line 2 of field 1      - -Get birthday from field
    put it into birthday       - -Put in another container
    convert birthday to dateItems
    put birthday into line 3 of field 1
    - -Put current date into containers
    get item 1 of line 1 of field 1
    put it into year2
    get item 2 of line 1 of field 1
    put it into month2
    get item 3 of line 1 of field 1
    put it into day2
    - -Put birthday items into containers
    get item 1 of line 3 of field 1
    put it into year1
    get item 2 of line 3 of field 1
    put it into month1
    get item 3 of line 3 of field 1
    put it into day1
    - -Subtract
    put year2 - year1 into year
    put month2 - month1 into month
    put day2 - day1 into day
    - -Put it on the screen
    put year && month && day into line 4 of field 1
end mouseUp
```

Pay special attention to how line two in the field was used by the script to get the birthday and put it into another container. It would have been perfectly correct to have the line,

convert line 2 of field 1 to dateItems

used to do the conversion. However, had that been done, the date on the screen would have been changed from the short form to the dateItems form on line two. It would not have affected the calculations, but it was not what was desired in the format. Also, instead of getting the **time**, it would have been just as well to get the **date** in this particular instance.

The Number Function.

A function that returns a numeric value based on elements in a stack is the **number of...** function. It returns the number of chunks (characters, words, items, or lines) from a container or text string source; buttons or fields from current card or its associated background; and backgrounds or cards in a stack. Using the **number** function, it is possible to put something directly into a container or do calculation without first using **get**. For example,

put the number of buttons into msg

will put the numeric value of the current card's buttons into the message box. Try that line on the Home card to see how many buttons it has. The example in Figure 6-10 shows one application of using the number function.

With Version 1.2 the number function can tell you the number of cards in a given background.
Example:

get the number of cards of this background

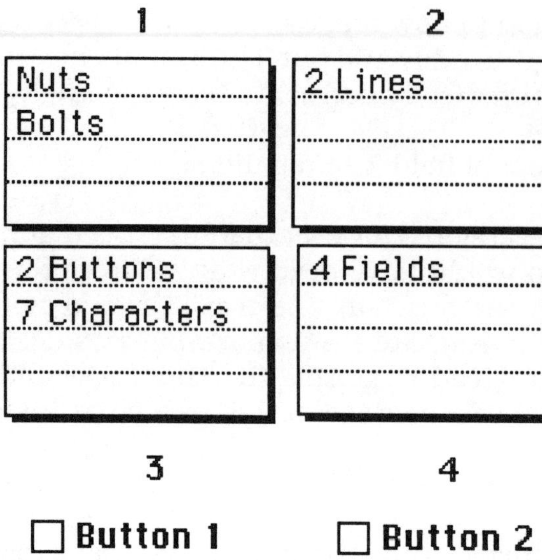

1   **2**

```
┌──────────────────┐   ┌──────────────────┐
│ Nuts             │   │ 2 Lines          │
│ Bolts            │   │                  │
│                  │   │                  │
│                  │   │                  │
└──────────────────┘   └──────────────────┘

┌──────────────────┐   ┌──────────────────┐
│ 2 Buttons        │   │ 4 Fields         │
│ 7 Characters     │   │                  │
│                  │   │                  │
│                  │   │                  │
└──────────────────┘   └──────────────────┘
```

3   **4**

☐ **Button 1**   ☐ **Button 2**

Figure 6-10

Fields: <u>1-4 (no names)</u>
Background fields
Show lines
Shadow style
no scripts

Button: <u>Button 1</u>
Check box style
Background button
script

```
on mouseUp
     put the number of lines in field 1 && "Lines" ¬
     into field 2
     put the number of fields && "Fields" into field 4
end mouseUp
```

Button: Button 2
Check box style
Background button
script

on mouseUp
    put the number of background buttons¬
        && "Buttons" into field 3
    put the number of chars of field 2¬
        && "Characters" into line 2 of field 3
end mouseUp

If you take all text out of Field 1, the value in Field 2 will be zero. That's because the number function only counts lines in a field if there is something there. Look at the scripts carefully and see if you can tell what each bit of information on the fields references.

Math Functions

There are 17 math functions in HyperTalk. Each will be presented with a brief example in the form of a script segment. At the end of this section some scripts will demonstrate possible applications of selected math functions.

abs   Returns absolute value of a number
Example: put abs (-18) into posWhole

annuity   Calculates present annuity by *rate* and
                periods.
Example: put monthPay * annuity (.011,12) into
                valueNow

atan   Returns arc tangent of number
Example: put atan (3.0) into bucket

average   Calculates mean of numbers.
Example: put average (2.5,3.3,3.7,3.2) into grade

compound   Calculates present or future value of
    compound interest by *rate* and *periods*.
Example: put valueNow * compound (.0875,12)
    into valueThen

cos   Returns cosine of angle in radians
Example: put cos(3.3) into pot

exp   Returns natural exponent
Example: put exp(4) into eVal

exp1   Returns natural exponent minus 1
Example: put exp1(4) into eValmin1

exp2   Returns power of 2
Example: put exp2(16) into sixteenBit

ln   Returns log to base e
Example: put ln(4) into logBase

ln1   Returns log of 1 plus value
Example: put ln1(2) into logJam

ln2   Returns log to base 2
Example: put ln2(2) into twoLog

max   Returns the maximum of number series
Example: put max(2,7,9,11,14) into most

min   Returns the minimum of number series
Example: put min(2,7,9,11,14) into least

sin   Returns sine of angle in radians
Example: put sin(8) into Apple

sqrt   Returns square root of number
Example: put sqrt(81) into niner

trunc   Removes fractions and turns number into integer
Example: put trunc(9.77) into wholeOne

Using a common statistic, the standard deviation, we will see how to use some of the math functions. Specifically, we will use **average** and **sqrt**, along with several mathematical operators. The script on this program will be fairly long due to the fact that we are still using the most simple script structure in HyperCard. Further on in the book we will see how to make a much simpler and more powerful version of the same thing.

To begin with, we will need the formula for standard deviation:

$$sd = \sqrt{\frac{\Sigma\,(x - \bar{x})^2}{n-1}}$$

Figure 6-11

sd	Standard deviation
Σ	sum
x	single item
$\bar{x}$	mean
n	number of items
$\sqrt{}$	square root

The standard deviation is a useful tool for determining the degree to which a set of numbers deviates from the average. A high standard deviation suggests a widely disparate set of numbers, while a low one suggests very little difference in values.

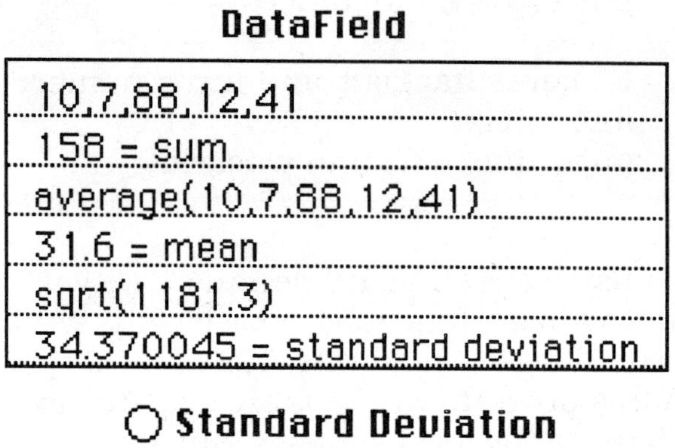

DataField

```
10,7,88,12,41
158 = sum
average(10,7,88,12,41)
31.6 = mean
sqrt(1181.3)
34.370045 = standard deviation
```

○ **Standard Deviation**

Figure 6-12

Field: <u>DataField</u>
Background field
Rectangle style
Lines showing
no script

Button: <u>Standard Deviation</u>
Radio style
name showing
script

on mouseUp
    - - First get the n and sum
    put number of items in line 1 of field 1 into n
    get item 1 of line 1 of field 1

```
put it into sum
get item 2 of line 1 of field 1
add it to sum
get item 3 of line 1 of field 1
add it to sum
get item 4 of line 1 of field 1
add it to sum
get item 5 of line 1 of field 1
add it to sum
put sum && "= sum" into line 2 of field 1

- - Second get the mean
put "average(" & line 1 of field 1 & ")" into¬
  line 3 of field 1
get value of line 3 of field 1
put it into mean
put mean && "= mean" into line 4 of field 1

- - Third get the sum of differences squared
get item 1 of line 1 of field 1
put ((mean - it) ^ 2) into sum2
get item 2 of line 1 of field 1
add ((mean - it) ^ 2) to sum2
get item 3 of line 1 of field 1
add ((mean - it) ^ 2) to sum2
get item 4 of line 1 of field 1
add ((mean - it) ^ 2) to sum2
get item 5 of line 1 of field 1
add ((mean - it) ^ 2) to sum2

- - Fourth divide sum of differences squared
- - by n - 1
put (sum2 /(n-1)) into hold

- - Fifth find the square root
put "sqrt("& hold & ")" into line 5 of field 1
```

```
          get value of line 5 of field 1
          put it && "= standard deviation" into¬
          line 6 of field 1
     end mouseUp
```

To use the standard deviation card, all you do is enter five numbers separated by commas into the first line of the field. Click the "Standard Deviation" button, and it calculates the values. It uses the values from the lines shown on the screen to compute values. Note in the script how it sets up the lines that it can use their values later for the calculations. Any container can be treated in the same way as lines in fields. By specifying the **value** of a line, HyperCard returns the *calculated results* of the line instead of the text in the line. For example, the following field and button use the local variable "calc" in the button script to get the results shown in Figure 6-13. The computed average of "6" is in line one, and the text string "average(5,6,7)" is in line two.

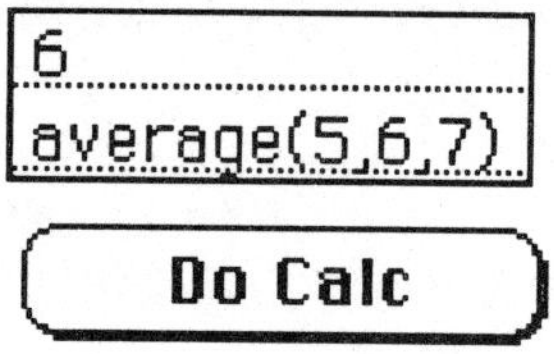

```
 6
 average(5,6,7)
```

```
 Do Calc
```

Figure 6-13

Button: Do Calc
Oval style
script

```
on mouseUp
     put "average(5,6,7)" into calc
     put value of calc into field 1
     put calc into line 2 of field 1
end mouseUp
```

Application: Foreign Money Exchanger

Money exchange rates change daily, and in order to keep up with what's worth what around the world, "HyperExchange" was developed. To use "HyperExchange," put the exchange rate in the "Exchange Rate" field. If the foreign currency unit is less than one dollar, just put the number of units in the first field. For example, if the dollar is worth 140 Japanese yen (¥), then type in 144 in the first field. If the currency unit is worth more than one dollar, put that amount in the last field labelled "Rates for currencies larger than dollar." That field will then calculate the exchange rate and put it into the "Exchange Rate" field for your. For example, if the $1.68 is worth one British pound (£), the exchange rate is .595238, as shown in Figure 6-14. Once the exchange rate is placed, put either a dollar amount in the "Number of Dollars" field or the foreign currency in the "Amount of Foreign Currency" field. Then either click "To Dollars" or "From Dollars." For example, if you wanted to find out how much 100 Dutch guilders was worth in dollars, you would put in the exchange rate and and 100 for "Amount in Foreign Currency" and then click the "To Dollars" button. Conversely, if you wanted to know how many Dutch guilders you could get for 100 dollars, you would put 100 in the "Number of Dollars" field and then click "From Dollars."

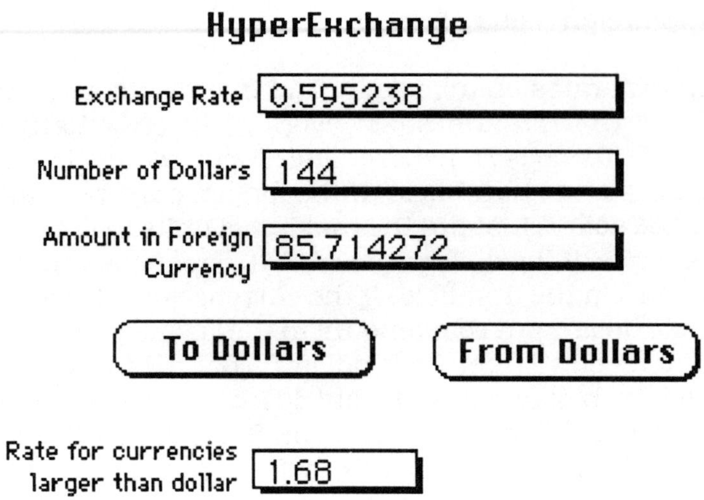

HyperExchange

Exchange Rate `0.595238`

Number of Dollars `144`

Amount in Foreign
Currency `85.714272`

(**To Dollars**)   (**From Dollars**)

Rate for currencies
larger than dollar `1.68`

Figure 6-14

Fields: <u>1 to 3 (no name)</u>
Shadow style
Background fields
no script

Field: <u>Great</u>
Shadow style
Background field
script

```
on closeField
    get field "Great"
    put (1 / it) into field 1
end closeField
```

Button: <u>To Dollars</u>
Button on card
Oval style name showing
script

```
on mouseUp
    get value of field 1
    put field 3 / it  into field 2
end mouseUp
```

Button: <u>To Dollars</u>
Button on card
Oval style name showing
script

```
on mouseUp
    get field 1
    put field 2 * it into field 3
end mouseUp
```

Summary

In the next two chapters, we will be examining new HyperCard structures, and this will extend your scripting power extensively. The scripts written in this chapter will be significantly reduced in size and there will be far more flexibility. However, the basic logic and mathematical computation ability learned in this chapter will be a crucial part of HyperCard scripting from now on. In using calculations and containers together, there is very little that you cannot accomplish with Hyper-Card. By breaking the problems down into discreet parts, it is much easier to deal with even the most complex mathematical problem. What is left is formatting the materials so that they can by seen by the user.

Decision Making, Interactions, and Screen Formats

7

Scripts for the User's Input

This chapter represents a turning point in the book since it introduces conditional structures. Up to this point, all of the scripts have been fairly sequential, even though the stacks themselves have not been. By its nature HyperCard is non-hierarchial and non-linear. However, up to this point the scripts themselves have not given the user a choice once a script has been launched. With conditional structures, all of that changes.

There are two basic conditional structures in HyperTalk; **if** and **repeat**. This chapter will deal with the **if** structure and show how to use it with other commands, functions and properties. We will pay special attention to using interactive commands that use data entered by the user to determine what to do next in the stack. In Chapter 8, we will examine how to use the **repeat** conditional.

In addition to examining conditional structures, we will examine screen formats as well. From within a script, it is possible to control certain aspects of what appears on the screen. Since these are often used in conjunction with conditional structures, they are introduced along with those structures.

If..then; If...then...else...end if

Conditionals are used with the operators we introduced in the last chapter in comparing one thing to one or more other things. Essentially, a conditional examines a set of statements as being true or false, and depending on the outcome, branches in one direction or another. It its simplest form, the "if...then" combination examines a single condition and does something if the condition if true. Make a button to use with the following script:

> **Button:** <u>Go Figure</u>
> Oval style

Card button
script

```
on mouseUp
    put 10 into pot
    if pot ≥ 7 then play boing
end mouseUp
```

In the second line, change "10 " to a value less than seven and execute the script a second time. If the value if less than seven, nothing will happen.

Instead of having a single action executed after a true condition, an "if...then" can cause several things to occur. However, this requires that the script have the various conditions on separate lines and the **end if** statement is placed at the end of the sequence of events. Change the "Go Figure" button's script to the following:

```
on mouseUp
    put 10 into pot
    if pot ≥ 7 then
        play boing                     - -#1
        put "It's true" into msg       - -#2
        wait 5 seconds                 - -#3
        go to Home                     - -#4
    end if
end mouseUp
```

When the conditional activity after an "if...then" is after a carriage return (the Return key has been pressed), you must end the single or multiple set of actions with **end if**.

When you want a branch to go in one direction or another, use the **else** statement. It can be used in a single line as the following script shows:

```
on mouseUp
    put 5 into pot
    if pot ≥ 7 then play boing else put ¬
    "it's not true" into msg
end mouseUp
```

On the other hand, like the multiple lines for multiple tasks, the "If.... then... else" sequence can be placed on several lines with more than a single task for each branch.

```
on mouseUp
    put 6 into pot
    if pot ≥ 7 then
        play boing           - -Branch #1
        go to first card
    else
        play harpsichord    - -Branch #2
        put "It still is not true" into msg
    end if
end mouseUp
```

To see a practical application of this structure, let's take a look at a stack that computes sales tax for a mail order business. If the customer is in the state, sales tax must be added to the bill, but if they are from out of state, no sales tax need be added. Make a field like that shown in Figure 7-1, and examine the script to see how it was able to know when and when not to add sales tax.

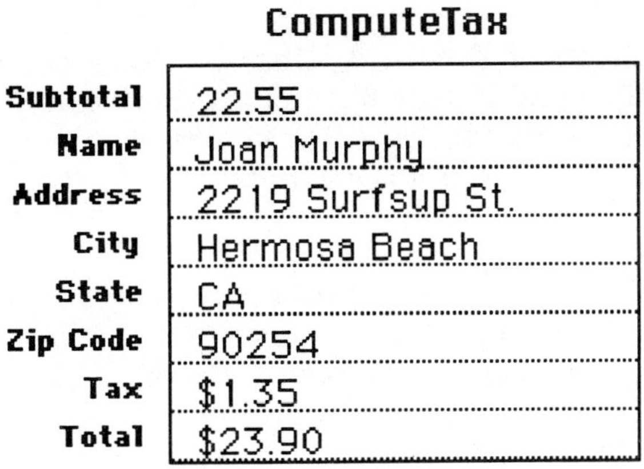

ComputeTax

Subtotal	22.55
Name	Joan Murphy
Address	2219 Surfsup St.
City	Hermosa Beach
State	CA
Zip Code	90254
Tax	$1.35
Total	$23.90

Figure 7-1

Field: ComputeTax
Background field
Rectangle style with lines showing
script

```
on closeField
    set numberFormat to "0.00"
    get line 1 of field "ComputeTax"
    put it into subTotal
    get line 5 of field "ComputeTax"
    if it is "CA" then
        put "$" & subTotal * .06 into line 7 of¬
        field "ComputeTax"
        put "$" & (subTotal * .06) + subTotal into¬
        line 8 of field "ComputeTax"
    else
        put "NA" into line 7 of field "ComputeTax"
        put "$" & subTotal into line 8 of¬
        field "ComputeTax"
    end if
end closeField
```

Instead of using a button, this script works as soon as the button is clicked outside of the field. Change the state to whatever state you want, and if the sales tax is other than 6%, change the line that computes it using .06 to whatever you need. Later we will use this routine in a larger, more complex stack.

Nested Conditionals. Before going on to interactional commands, there is one last class of conditionals to consider, "nested conditionals." These conditionals are multiple branches. Once a branch has been chosen, there are other branches within the chosen branch. For example, a situation of nested conditionals might include the following type of decision making:

Choose: England or France
    If England Choose: London or Cambridge
        If London Choose: North side or south side
        If Cambridge Choose: Darwin or Trinity
    If France Choose: Paris or Nice
        If Paris Choose: Left bank or Right bank
        If Nice Choose: Riviera or Beach
End

Within each set of choices, there are other choices that can only be taken if a certain branch was taken. If England is chosen instead of France, chosing between Paris and Nice is *not* a choice. To see an example of how nested loops work in Hyper-Card we will make a script that looks for two names in a stack. If one name is found, one set of actions will occur, while if the other name is found another set of actions will occur. Figure 7-2 shows a field and button that can contain information about one of two person's names being on the first line and their whereabouts on line two. Depending on (1) who's name is on line 1 and (2) their whereabouts, there will be a message either on the third line of the field or in the message box.

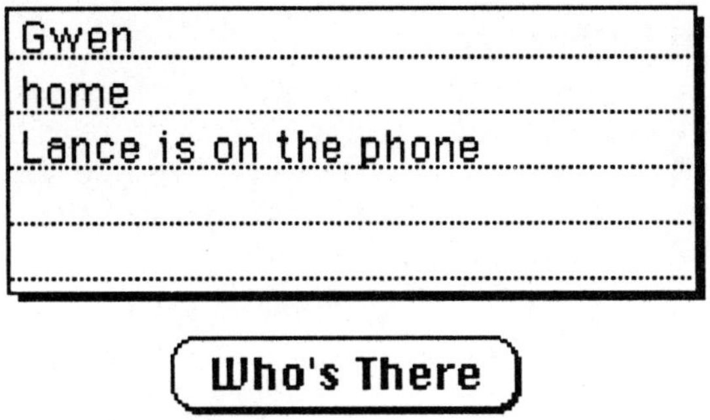

```
┌─────────────────────────────────┐
│ Gwen                            │
│ home                            │
│ Lance is on the phone           │
│                                 │
│                                 │
└─────────────────────────────────┘
```

    (**Who's There**)

Figure 7-2

Field: Field 1 (no name)
Background field
shadow style with lines showing
no script

Button: Who's There
Oval card button
script

```
on mouseUp
  If "Gwen" is in line 1 of field 1 then      - -If #1
    If "home" is in line 2 of field 1 then - -If #2
      put "Lance is on the phone" into line 3 of field 1
    else
      put "Lance called" into msg
    end if       - -End #2
  end if       - -End #1
  If "Lance" is in line 1 of field 1 then   - -If #3
    If "castle" is in line 2 of field 1 then - -If #4
      put "Gwen is at the drawbridge" into line 3 of field 1
    else
      put "Gwen dropped by" into msg
    end if       - -End #4
```

```
    end if      - -End #3
  end mouseUp
```

Change the names in lines one and two of the field and see the different messages. Also, note the two sets of nested conditionals, and how each "if.. then" is tied to an "end if."

Ask and Answer

The interactive mode in HyperCard scripts is the most dynamic since you can enter information while the script is being executed. The two main HyperTalk commands for prompting users for information are **ask** and **answer**. Both take information from the user and put it into a variable.

Ask. The **ask** command provides a dialog box with a line to write in any information you may want to use. Whatever is written is played in the "It" variable. For example, the following script asks what type of car a user wants and then stores that information in the first line of the field 1.

```
  on openField
      ask "What type of car would you like?"
      put it into line 1 of field 1
  end openField
```

As soon as the field is opened, the dialog box shown in Figure 7-3 appears.

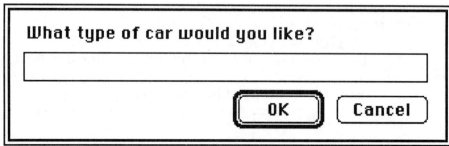

Figure 7-3

After entering the name of the car and either clicking the "OK" button or pressing the Return key, the script places the name in the first line of field 1 of the current card.

An option with **ask** is to enter a default name. For example, if a business had customers all over the world, but the great majority of them were in the United States, it would make sense to have "United States" as the default. Then it would not take as long to get to where you normally would want to go. The following button script asks a question and fills in the default answer.

```
on mouseUp
    ask "Which country?" with "United States"
    go to stack It
end mouseUp
```

Before the user writes anything in the dialog box, it appears with the default in the message area as shown in Figure 7-4.

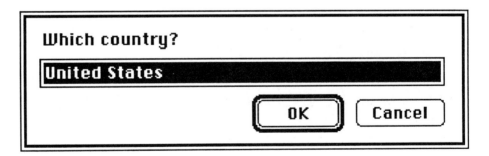

Figure 7-4

Either the word "United States" or the word that is entered by the user is placed in the "It" variable. Therefore, when told to proceed to "stack It," HyperCard sends the program to whatever name was entered in the dialog box or the default name. Clicking "OK" would result in HyperCard going to a stack named "United States."

You also can get the question and default answer from other sources. For example, it is possible to ask using a line from a field. For example, create two small background fields and a button as shown in Figure 7-5 and execute it. (The Message Box appears after the button is clicked and the dialog box completed.)

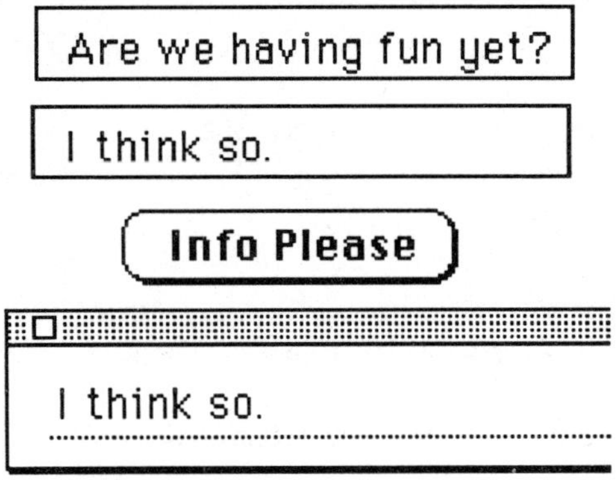

```
Are we having fun yet?
```

```
I think so.
```

```
( Info Please )
```

```
▫
I think so.
```

Figure 7-5

Fields: 1 and 2 (no names)
Background fields
Rectangle style, lines not showing
no script

Button: Info Please
Oval style card button
script

on mouseUp

```
        ask field 1 with field 2
          put It into msg
      end mouseUp
```

That little routine demonstrates how to get information from other places than the script to use it in a dialog box.

Ask Password. A final type of ask command is a special one for encrypting a password in a stack. Before we go into that, first let's take a look a password protection in general.

From the File Menu, the option of **Protect Stack...** delivers the dialog box shown in Figure 7-6. This allows the author to protect the stack in three ways:

1. Protect against deletion
2. Protect against unauthorized use
3. Limit user level.

```
┌─────────────────────────────────────────────────────┐
│ ┌───────────────────────────────────────────────┐   │
│ │                                                 │   │
│ │  Protect Stack:         Limit user level to:    │   │
│ │                            ○ Browsing           │   │
│ │                            ○ Typing             │   │
│ │  □ Can't delete stack      ● Painting           │   │
│ │                            ○ Authoring          │   │
│ │                            ○ Scripting          │   │
│ │  □ Private Access                               │   │
│ │  [ Set Password ]      [[ OK ]]   [ Cancel ]    │   │
│ │                                                 │   │
│ └───────────────────────────────────────────────┘   │
└─────────────────────────────────────────────────────┘
```

Figure 7-6

When the "Set Password" button is clicked, the dialog box shown in Figure 7-7 appears. Here the password is written twice, and "OK" selects that password until it is changed. Since you have to know the password to change it, either use a simple password to remember or write it down.

```
┌─────────────────────────────────────────┐
│                                           │
│   Enter new password here:                │
│   ┌─────────────────────────────────┐     │
│   │ Sherlock                        │     │
│   └─────────────────────────────────┘     │
│                                           │
│   Verify new password here:               │
│   ┌─────────────────────────────────┐     │
│   │ Sherlock                        │     │
│   └─────────────────────────────────┘     │
│                                           │
│  ( None )  (( OK ))  ( Cancel )           │
│                                           │
└─────────────────────────────────────────┘
```

Figure 7-7

The **password** parameter in **ask password** provides an additional level of stack security beyond the Protect Stack... level. When the user enters a password in the initial set up of the stack, that password is coded in a number placed in the It variable. This value can be placed somewhere out of sight in the stack such as a field where it can be saved. When the stack is used on subsequent occasions, it can then be referenced for comparison to the original one. To see how this works, create the card shown in Figure 7-8.

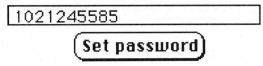

Figure 7-8

Field: Field 1 (no name)
Card field
rectangle style

Button: Set password
Oval style
Show name
script

```
on mouseUp
    ask password "Set password"
    put it into card field 1
end mouseUp
```

When you press the "Set password" button, type in the word "Hyper" in the dialog box. The number shown in the field in Figure 7-8 will appear. So even if someone finds the secret number, they still do not know what the password is.

To see how to set up a password, create a new stack with two cards. Put a card field on the **second** card. Go to the first card. From the Objects Menu choose "Card Info..." and *carefully* write the following script:

```
on openCard
    ask password "Enter Password"
    put it into card field 1 of card 2
    hide card field 1 of card 2
    doMenu Delete Card
end openCard
```

The above script got a little ahead by using the **doMenu** command, but for now it is enough to know that the fifth line deletes the card after it has been opened once. This sets up a one-card stack with the encrypted password hidden in a card field in the first card. Write the following script for the new first card.

```
on openCard
    ask password "Enter password"
    if It is card field 1 then
        beep
    else
        go home
    end if
end openCard
```

This now compares the password with the encrypted code in the hidden card field 1. Each time the stack is opened, the first card beeps its approval of the password or takes the user for a ride to the Home Stack.

Answer. The **answer** command is like **ask**, but instead of providing an area in which to write something, buttons are provided instead. It can have up to three buttons as choices, and while it is less flexible than ask, answer can provide a faster and cleaner interactive command. It takes the general form,

```
answer "question" with "replyA" or "replyB" or "replyC"
```

with the last two replies being optional, and quotation marks are required where indicated. For example,

```
answer "Which department?" with "Accounting"¬
    or "Budget" or "Dispersement"
```

uses all three replies and would appear as seen in Figure 7-9.

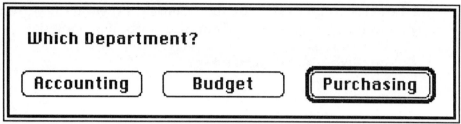

Figure 7-9

The actual text used in the replies goes into the "It" variable. If the "Budget" choice were clicked, then "It" would contain "Budget." The following script shows how this would be used with conditionals:

```
answer "Which department?" with "Accounting"¬
   or "Budget" or "Dispersement"
if It is "Accounting" then go to card "Accounting"
if It is "Budget" then go to card "Budget"
if It is "Purchasing" then go to card "Purchasing"
```

The answer command can be used for a reminder or any other kind of short message for someone. For example, the following card script is a little birthday reminder:

```
on openCard
  get the date
  if it is "11/2/89" then
    beep
    answer "Tomorrow is Mary's birthday!" with "OK"
  end if
end openCard
```

Similar reminders can be used for anything from over due bills to warnings about entering data. With only a single button, either clicking the "OK" or pressing the Return key will suffice to let the user carry on. Like ask, answer can get its text from any source that stores text. Thus, the script segment,

    put "What's up?" into query
    put "Stocks" into Juan
    put "Bonds" into too
    answer query with Juan or too

would put all of the information where required.

Building a "Do" Command

The **do** command is useful for developing scripts. The do command treats the contents of a source as a line of script. For example, if a line in a field contained,

    go to next card

in it, that line could be used as though it were script. The script line,

    do line 1 of field 1

would cause HyperCard to follow the command to "go the next card." When developing scripts, especially scripts that deal with screen formatting, if we can see the command line while developing a script, we can get a better idea of where everything goes. Once the script puts things exactly where you want them, the actual commands can be placed directly in the script.

Getting Around the Screen

Your Macintosh screen is a 512 by 342 matrix of dots called "pixels." Think of the screen as a giant checker board with 512 squares across and 342 squares down. HyperCard uses the this matrix to locate things on the screen in terms of X,Y (horizontal, vertical) coordinates. The upper left hand corner is position 0,0 and the lower right corner is 512, 342. Figure 7-10 shows all of the corner coordinates of the Macintosh screen.

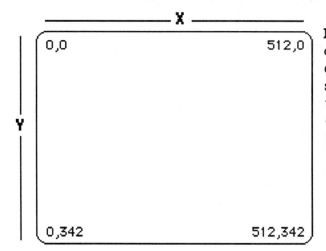

Note: The screens of Macintosh II computers and big screens that can be used with the standard Mac have different matrices. Use the new **screenRect** function to find the size of your screen on pages 250-251.

Figure 7-10

To get started, make a single background field and three buttons as shown in Figure 7-11. (The last two lines in the field are simply "fill" lines that provide something for HyperCard to "do" with the script in the Do Script button.)

Script Field

```
set the loc of tool window to 1,31
play silence
play silence
```

(**Show Tools**) (**HIde Tools**) (**Do Script**)

Figure 7-11

Field: Script Field
Background field
no script

Button: Show Tools
script

```
on mouseUp
    set the visible of tool window to true
end mouseUp
```

Button: Hide Tools
script

```
on mouseUp
    set the visible of tool window to false
end mouseUp
```

Button: Do Script
script

```
on mouseUp
    do line 1 of field 1
    do line 2 of field 1
    do line 3 of field 1
end mouseUp
```

In order to see and move things on the screen, it is necessary to set certain properties. We have discussed the **hide** and **show** commands, but we can also use **set the visible of** window property to true and false. For example, both the lines,

```
hide the tool window
set the visible of tool window to false
```

do the same thing. However, there are occasions when some logical outcome will determine whether or not you HyperCard to hide or show a property. For example, write the following script in the three lines of the field shown in Figure 7-11, and click Show Tools button and then the Do Script button.

```
put 5 into half
put (half = 10) into whole  - -False into whole
set the visible of tool window to whole - -whole=false
```

That will make the tool window disappear since the logic was determined to be "false" in line two. Since "false" was in the container named "whole," setting the truth value of visible to "whole" was the same as setting it to "false." With the "hide" and "show" commands, it would not be possible to use logical truth values that way.

To give you an idea of where things will end up with different values established with "set loc," use the card shown in Figure 7-11 with the following HyperTalk scripts, clicking Do Script to test each script:

```
set loc of tool window to (512/2), (342/2)
play silent
play silent

set loc of tool window to 1,31
play boing
play boing
```

Using different coordinates, see if you can place the tool window in all four corners of your screen and in the middle of the screen. If you can do that, you understand how to place objects correctly on the screen.

In addition to the **tool window** you can hide, show and move the **pattern window**, and **message box** (message window, message or msg). In addition to setting the window properties of loc and visible, it is possible to get the coordinates of windows, buttons and fields with **rect**(angle). The **rect** property returns the upper left and lower right coordinates of any window or field. Try the following scripts using the Script Field:

```
get the rect of tool window
put it into the msg
play silence
```

With the windows, it is possible to get the coordinates, but not to set them. However, with buttons and fields, it is possible to either get or set their size. Add a card field with a rectangle style to the card shown in Figure 7-11, and write the following script in the Script Field

```
set the rect of card field 1 to 20,20,100,100
set the loc of card field 1 to 50,50
hide menuBar
```

Not only did that script set the size and placement of the field, it also provided more work space on the screen by hiding the **menuBar**. Hiding and showing the **menuBar** allows more flexibility in screen formatting. However, it is important to remember to put the menuBar back on the screen when the stack is closed. (If you accidentally do that, just write in "show menuBar.)

* New For Version 1.2

More Rects

Version 1.2 has added several properties that can now be set on your screen. To begin with, the function **screenRect** returns the rectangle of the entire screen. In order to determine the rectangle size of your screen use the script in the message box shown in Figure 7-12.

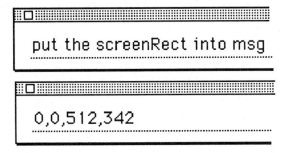

Figure 7-12

The values returned in the message box must be read in the following order:

1.	Left	0
2.	Top	0
3.	Right	512
5.	Bottom	342

All of the properties we will discuss in this section have the same Left, Top, Right, Bottom order. If you want to put something in the middle of the screen with a margin of 10 pixels around them the coordinates would be,

Left	(256-10)
Top	(171-10)
Right	(256+10)
Bottom	(171+10)

The new HyperCard 1.2 rectangle properties include:

the left of
the top of
the right of
the bottom of
the topLeft of
the bottomRight of (*or* botRight)
the width of
the height of

The targets can be buttons, fields or windows with all of the properties except width and height, which cannot be used with windows. The following samples show some uses.

set the left of card field 2 to 100
set the width of button 4 to 50
put the topLeft of field 3 into temp
set the bottom of tool window to 330

This next example, moves a button around the screen and changes its size using the various new properties. Note the use of abbreviations in the script.

400	Left
300	Top
200	Right
100	Bottom
200	Width
300	Height

Jump

Figure 7-13

Field: <u>R</u>
Card field
Shadow style with lines showing
AutoTab off
no script

Button: <u>Jump</u>
Rectangle card button with Icon#1019
script

```
on mouseUp
  — Set up
  — Note use of abbreviations for "card" and "field"
  put line 1 of cd fld "R" into Left
  put line 2 of cd fld "R" into Top
  put line 3 of cd fld "R" into Right
  put line 4 of cd fld "R" into Bottom
  put Left & "," & Top into TopLeft
  put Right & "," & Bottom into BottomRight
  put line 5 of cd fld "R" into Width
  put line 6 of cd fld "R" into Height
  put the width of button "Jump" into OW
  put the height of button "Jump" into OH

  — Move the button
  set the left of button "Jump" to Left
  wait 1 sec
  set the top of button "Jump" to Top
  wait 1 sec
  set the right of button "Jump" to Right
  wait 1 sec
  set the bottom of button "Jump" to Bottom
  wait 1 sec
```

```
        set the TopLeft of button "Jump" to TopLeft
        wait 1 sec
        set the BotRight of button "Jump" to BottomRight

        — Change the size of the button
        set the width of button "Jump" to Width
        wait 1 sec
        set the height of button "Jump" to Height
        wait 2 secs
        set the width of button "Jump" to OW
        set the height of button "Jump" to OH
    end mouseUp
```

Change the values in the field to get a clear idea of what can be done with the new rect properties. Re-write the script and substitute the field for the button and watch it jump around.

Another pair of new HyperCard 1.2 functions, **clickH** and **clickV**, give you the horizontal and vertical position of the cursor where the button was last clicked. If writing scripts with these two functions, it is important to refer to them as,

the ClickH
or
the ClickV

otherwise without the "the" they will not be recognized as functions.

To get a quick idea of what is happening, and to see how to have HyperCard do something while you have time to click the mouse, consider the following card script: (Remember to put a script in a card, choose **Card Info...** while holding down on the Shift key.)

```
on idle
  put the clickH && the clickV
end idle
```

Each time you click the mouse, there is a different pair of numbers in the message box. The script did not specify the message box as the container, but when no container is specified, the message box becomes the default container.

For a little fun with the new functions, create the button shown in Figure 7-14.

```
Dodge Button
```

Figure 7-14

Button: <u>Dodge Button</u>
Rectangle card button
script

```
on mouseWithin
  set the left of button 1 to the clickH
  set the bottom of button 1 to the clickV
end mouseWithin
```

Each time you click the mouse, and then put the mouse pointer in the area covered by the Dodge Button, the button will jump to the location that was last clicked. Go over the portion in Chapter 4 where mouseWithin was introduced if you have any trouble understanding what is happening with the script.

The Within Operator

✳ New For Version 1.2

A final HyperCard 1.2 word that can be used in locating positions on the screen is the **Within** operator. Basically, **Within** returns a TRUE or FALSE depending on whether a given point is *within* a given rectangle. The rectangle is specified in terms of four values designating the Left, Top, Bottom and Right side of the rectangle. For example, the lines

```
if the clickLoc is within "50,30,100,200" then beep
if the clickLoc is within field 2 then beep
if bottomRight of button 3 is within the rect of button ¬
4 then set the bottomRight of button 3 to "200,300"
```

are all perfectly correct ways of using the **Within** operator. The function **clickLoc** returns *both* the horizontal and vertical position of the last location clicked by the mouse. For a simple illustration of how a card can always locate the position of a click, use the following card script:

```
on idle
  if the clickLoc is within the screenRect ¬
  then put the clickH
end idle
```

Since the screenRect encompasses the entire screen, anywhere you click on the screen will be trapped and placed in the message box. This would be useful in a card where you want the user to click on the card in different positions.

Another new feature of HyperCard 1.2 is the use of the "me" variable as a container in fields. When an object refers to itself, it can use the "me" container. The field shown in Figure 7-15 contains a script that uses "me" with a field and the Within operator.

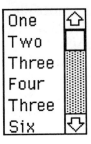

Figure 7-15

Field Within Me
Scrolling card field
script

on closeField
  if the clickLoc is not within the rect of me then¬
  select word 2 of card field 1
end closeField

Write anything in the field, and then click somewhere not on the field. The last action will cause the field to be closed. Since the script specifies that the clickLoc be somewhere outside the field ("not within me)", the action triggers the selection of the second word of the field. When discussing graphics, we will see how useful these functions, properties and operators are.

Cursor Formats

There are now eight cursors controlled by scripts; seven that are visible and one that is not. Figure 7-16 shows the original four and their associated numeric values, plus three new ones. Before Version 1.2, the cursor style was set with the associated numeric values. Now, with eight cursors, the original four can either be called up by name or number, and the new four by names only. From left to right the cursor names are:

1. iBeam
2. cross
3. plus
4. watch
5. busy
6. arrow
7. hand
8. none

Figure 7-16

Using the format,

    set cursor to <cursor name or 1-4>

you can change what is seen on the screen to let the user know what's going on. Using the button shown in Figure 7-17 put in the accompanying script and see how to set them up. We will also introduce another set of new 1.2 functions in the script. These functions work with "selected" materials.

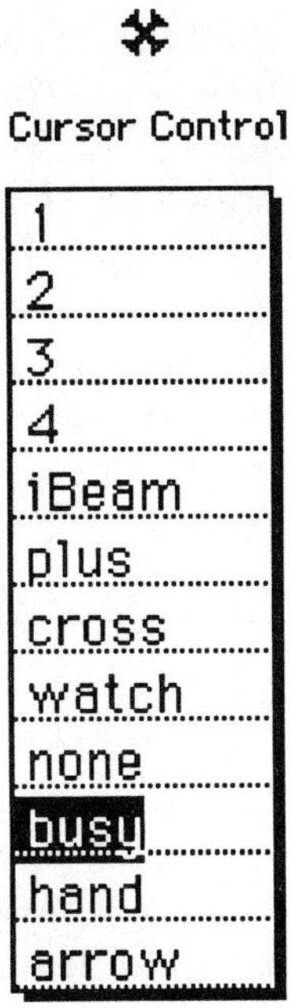

Cursor Control

| 1 |
| 2 |
| 3 |
| 4 |
| iBeam |
| plus |
| cross |
| watch |
| none |
| **busy** |
| hand |
| arrow |

Figure 7-17

Field: <u>No name</u>
Shadow style
Lines showing
No script

Button: <u>Cursor Control</u>
Iconstyle ID 1018
Auto hilite
script

on mouseUp
  set cursor to the selectedText
  wait 4 seconds
end mouseUp

Even though the script is short, it is very powerful. By selecting any of the numbers or cursor names in the fields, the cursor with the corresponding number or name will appear as soon as you click the button. In the following section we will see how to use other new 1.2 functions that handle selected text an numbers.

Special Note: You can design your own cursor style with the ResEdit resource editor. Using the technique described in Chapter 3 for making customized button icons, the CURS resource can be edited to a cursor of your choice.

The Selected Functions

In the previous example, we saw how **selectedText** functions to return the text material selected by dragging the mouse over it. The **selectedChunk** provides precise information about the characters chosen and the field in which they can be found. **SelectedField** returns the field with the selected materials, and **selectedLine** returns the line and field of the selected text.

These functions will prove very useful in developing stacks that require the user to select text from fields in making a choice. As we saw in the cursor example, all the user has to do to see the cursor of choice is to select one from the available list and click the button. Figure 7-18 shows a field before and after the select functions have been initiated. Note in the script how the selection has to be re-selected after each function has operated on the selected text. That is important to remember, for if your script requires more than a single access to selected text, it must be re-selected before the second "selected" function will operate.

Selector

Select me

Selector

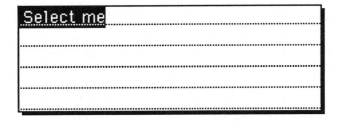

Select me	
char 1 to 9 of card field 3	selectedChunk
line 1 of card field 3	selectedLine
card field 3	selectedField
Select me	selectedText

Figure 7-18

Field: No name - card field 3
Shadow style
Lines showing
No script

Button: Selector
Icon ID# 8538
Auto hilite on
script

```
on mouseUp
  put the selectedChunk into line 2 of card field "Selected"
  select char 1 to 9 of card field "Selected"
  put the selectedLine into line 3 of card field "Selected"
  select char 1 to 9 of card field "Selected"
  put the selectedField into line 4 of card field "Selected"
  select char 1 to 9 of card field "Selected"
  put the selectedText into line 5 of card field "Selected"
end mouseUp
```

Experiment with different uses of the select functions. Like many of the various functions and commands in HyperCard, unless you experiment with them, you may neglect to employ them in stacks where they would be extremely useful.

Controlling What the User Sees

There will be occasions when your script will have to leave a stack, get some information and return to the stack from where it started. When this occurs, you may want to use the **lockScreen** option to prevent the user viewing the other screen and speed up the operation. To see how this works, make a new button and execute the following script.

```
on mouseUp
    set cursor to 4
    set lockScreen to true
    go to stack "Home"
    put the number of buttons into it
    go back
    put it into msg
end mouseUp
```

While the HyperTalk script goes to the Home Stack and gets the number of buttons, you see the "clock" cursor and the screen you started with. Change the third line in the script so that it reads,

>   set lockScreen to false

and try it again. It should have taken a little longer since it had to change screen images. If you had a script that went to several different stacks and cards, the lockScreen would save a more significant amount of time.

Special Visual Effects

The **visual effects** command adds a lot of style to your stacks. Visual effects are computerized "special effects." In applications where you want the user to pay attention, or just because it adds a little life to the stack, try out the various visual effects you can do. The following constitute the various effects:

barn door close	**barn door open**	**checkerboard**	**dissolve**
iris close	**iris open**	**plain**	**scroll down**
scroll left	**scroll right**	**scroll up**	**wipe up**
wipe down	**venetian blinds**	**zoom close**	**zoom in**
zoom open	**zoom out**		

These effects have one of four speeds:

>   **fast   slow[ly]   very slow[ly]   very fast**

Finally, the image can change to one of the following shades or the default "card shade":

>   **black card gray white**

The most effective use of the **visual** [effect] command is with the handler "on CloseCard." Several different effects can be done with a single handler, but if too many are included, they lose their effect. The following script shows how to use many effects together.

```
on closeCard
    visual scroll up slowly to gray
    visual scroll down to white
    visual wipe right to black
    visual wipe left to white
    visual barn door open to black
    visual barn door close to gray
end closeCard
```

Usually, only one or two will be used together. It can be very effective to use one "closing" effect followed by an "opening" effect. That makes it look like the last card closes while the next card opens. The following show some effective closings and openings.

```
on closeCard
    visual iris close to gray
    visual iris open to card
end closeCard
```

```
on closeCard
    visual checkerboard to black
    visual venetian blinds to white
end closeCard
```

```
on closeCard
    visual dissolve slowly to white
    visual zoom out slowly to card
end closeCard
```

Experiment with different effects to see what best works for communicating the "feel" you want the stack to have.

New Locks and Modify Control

There have been some upgrades in the "protection" script in HyperCard 1.2. In some situations, you will want to lock the screen while HyperCard goes to other cards and stacks, as was discussed elsewhere in this chapter. The new commands,

Lock Screen
Unlock Screen

have the same effect as "set lockScreen " to true or false. However, now the unlocking can be done with a visual effect. In the card shown in Figure 7-19, the field and button will be hidden from view after the button is pressed. Then the screen will be locked, and a message is written on the field. When the screen is unlocked, the images of the field and button slowly dissolve onto the screen. In addition, the button shows another way of controlling the speed on the spin of the "busy" (beach ball) cursor.

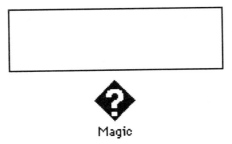

Magic

Figure 7-19

Field: <u>Card Field 1</u>
Rectangle style
Three lines not showing
No script

Button: <u>Magic</u>
Card button
Icon #3185 transparent
script

```
on mouseUp
  — Another "Beach ball" control
  repeat 15 times
    set cursor to busy
    repeat 20 times
    end repeat
  end repeat

  — Magic Show
  hide button "Magic"
  hide card field 1
  put "      Make a wish" into line 2 of card field 1
  lock screen
  wait 1 sec
  show card field 1
  show button "Magic"
  unlock screen with dissolve very slowly
end mouseUp
```

Note also that in using the visual effect script, there was no need to put in "visual" as we had done in prior examples. The line "with dissolve very slowly" did the trick.

There are going to be more and more occasions where you will want to write protect your creations. For example, suppose there is a set of data that has to circulate through a company. By write protecting the stack, it is possible to keep it from being changed permanently. With HyperCard 1.2 there are several options for protecting stacks.

To protect a stack, the standard way is to lock it from the Finder window. Select **Get Info...** from the **File** menu and click the "Locked" box as shown in Figure 7- 20 . This can also be done by opening the write protect window on a 3.5 inch diskette. Stacks on CD-ROMs and stacks on file servers with "read only" status also write protect the stacks.

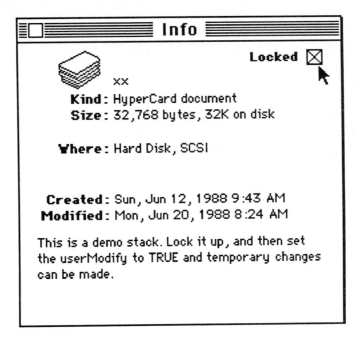

Figure 7-20

A new way to write protect a stack is with the **cantModify** property. This locks or unlocks a stack. The format is

> set the cantModify of <stack> to TRUE or FALSE

For example, to lock a current stack, the script,

> set the cantModify of this stack to true

would write protect that stack. A little lock symbol appears on the menu bar. Also, the new **cantDelete** property can be set from a script. Of course both delete and modify protection can still be obtained by using the **Protect Stack...** option from the **File** menu. These new properties allow it to be done more simply in a script.

The most important new 1.2 property is **userModify**. When userModify is set to TRUE, the user can write in locked stacks. However, as soon as a modified card is closed, all of the changes revert to the original. This can be a critical feature for CD-ROM and file server users, especially where several people must access the same stack simultaneously.

In developing educational stackware for CD-ROMs, or any other format that must be protected from permanent modification, the userModify property is especially important. For example, suppose a teacher wants to help students learn how to read by having them fill in blank spaces in a story. This requires that the child write in a field, but the text in the field must return to the original when the next student uses the stack. The button and fields in Figure 7- 21 shows how to employ userModify to have flexibility and protection at the same time.

 File   Edit   Go   Tools   Objects 🔒

Once upon a time there lived a child named ----------
who had a pet ----------, ---------- and (his/her)
-------- used to visit the ---------- located near
a big -------------. Whenever they visited the
----------, they would go see ------- who
lived in a cozy -----------.

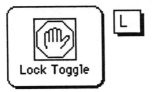

Lock Toggle

Figure 7-21

Field: <u>Story</u>
Rectangle style
Six lines showing
No script

Field: <u>Locker</u>
Shadow style
No script

Button: <u>Lock Toggle</u>
Icon# -15744
script

```
on mouseUp
  if char 1 of card field "Locker" = "L" then
    set the cantModify of this stack to FALSE
    put "U" into char 1 of card field "Locker"
  else
    set the cantModify of this stack to TRUE
    put "L" into char 1 of card field "Locker"
  end if
  set the userModify to TRUE
end mouseUp
```

Click the "Lock Toggle" button to get the letter "L" in the "Locker Field" and the lock symbol on the menu bar. Write something in the dashed spaces (− − − −). Now, go to another card or stack and then return. All of the changes you made are gone, and the text in the field appears as it does in figure 7-21.

Obviously, you would not want to have the write protection and then give the user something with which to toggle the lock on and off. Setting the userModify to TRUE or FALSE would be something most appropriately placed in a stack or card script.

Application: Mail Order Business

With the new commands, we are prepared to make a little more sophisticated application. One of the elements not discussed up to now is the matter of making a stack easy to use and flexible. The terms *user friendly* and *idiot proof* come to mind in discussing such human interfaces, but perhaps a better idea is to think of stack design in terms of *real world practical*. That is, when designing a stack, try to imagine the kinds of events that occur typically in the real world and make a stack that efficiently and effectively deals with those events.

Using a hypothetical company called "Doit Disks Co.", the application will be a mail order business stack for a company that sells different products pertaining to computer disks and drives. For the mail order business application, we will need a price list, containers for entering customer's names and addresses, quantity of different items ordered, an invoice number, the date, totals, shipping costs and tax. Also, we will need a script to total all of the orders, and we will include a warning in a dialog box if there are any problems with an order, such as damaged goods or bad checks.

Since prices in a business can change, we will use a separate card and background for the price list. The cards on the "invoice" will get their prices from the price list when they are created; so we will use the handler "on newCard" in a separate background. In that way, if the price list changes, the old prices will stay on the cards already created, but the new prices will be reflected on new cards. Figure 7-22 shows the first background. There is no script; just a single unnamed background field on a single card called "PriceList." Create it first.

Price List

Diskettes	12.99
Disk Drives	185.99
Hard Disks	599.22
Drive Cover	5.88
Disk Case	2.55
RAM Drive	16.55

Background #1
Figure 7-22

Card: PriceList
no script

Field: Field 1 (no name)
Background field

Rectangle with lines showing
no script

Next, make the second card on a new background, with the objects shown in Figure 7-23. Beneath the graphic disk (Doit Disk Co.) there is a transparent button, expanded to the size of the disk.

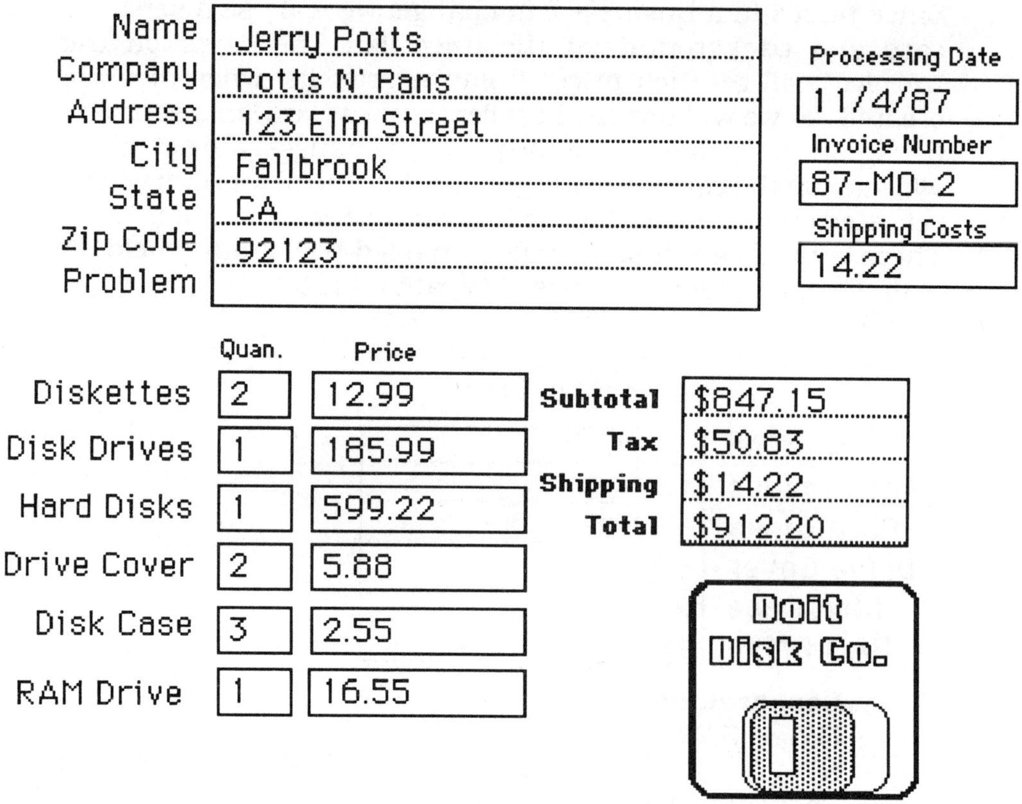

Name	Jerry Potts	
Company	Potts N' Pans	Processing Date
Address	123 Elm Street	11/4/87
City	Fallbrook	Invoice Number
State	CA	87-M0-2
Zip Code	92123	Shipping Costs
Problem		14.22

	Quan.	Price		
Diskettes	2	12.99	Subtotal	$847.15
Disk Drives	1	185.99	Tax	$50.83
Hard Disks	1	599.22	Shipping	$14.22
Drive Cover	2	5.88	Total	$912.20
Disk Case	3	2.55		
RAM Drive	1	16.55		

Doit
Disk Co.

Figure 7-23

272

Next, from the Objects Menu, choose "Bkgnd Info..." and put in the following script:

Background #2

```
on newCard
    put the date into field 2
    put the length of field 2 into temp
    put char (temp-1) to temp of field 2 into year
    put number of cards into num
    put year & "-MO-" & (num-1) into field "Invoice"
- -Get Current Prices
    get line 1 of field 1 of card "PriceList"
    put it into field "D1P"
    get line 2 of field 1 of card "PriceList"
    put it into field "D2P"
    get line 3 of field 1 of card "PriceList"
    put it into field "D3P"
    get line 4 of field 1 of card "PriceList"
    put it into field "D4P"
    get line 5 of field 1 of card "PriceList"
    put it into field "D5P"
    get line 6 of field 1 of card "PriceList"
    put it into field "D6P"
end newCard

on openCard
    if line 7 of field 1 <> empty then
        answer "Check problem on this one." with "OK"
    end if
end openCard

on closeCard
    visual iris close to gray
    visual iris open to card
end closeCard
```

Button: <u>Calculate</u>
Background button
Transparent (Beneath "Doit Disk Co." graphic.)
Name not showing
script

```
on mouseUp
  set numberFormat to "0.00"
put 0 into sum

 - -Quantities and Products
 if field "D1Q" <> empty then
   put field "D1Q" into sub1
    multiply sub1 by field "D1P"
    add sub1 to sum
  end if
  if field "D2Q" <> empty then
   put field "D2Q" into sub2
    multiply sub2 by field "D2P"
    add sub2 to sum
  end if
  if field "D3Q" <> empty then
   put field "D3Q" into sub3
   multiply sub3 by field "D3P"
   add sub3 to sum
  end if
 if field "D4Q" <> empty then
   put field "D4Q" into sub4
   multiply sub4 by field "D4P"
   add sub4 to sum
 end if
 if field "D5Q" <> empty then
```

```
    put field "D5Q" into sub5
    multiply sub5 by field "D5P"
    add sub5 to sum
   end if
   if field "D6Q" <> empty then
    put field "D6Q" into sub6
    multiply sub6 by field "D6P"
    add sub6 to sum
   end if

   - -Add them all up
   put "$" & sum into line 1 of field "Totals"
   put 0 into Tax
   if line 5 of field 1 is "CA" then    - -May change state
    put (sum * .06) into Tax          - -May change tax rate
    put "$" & Tax into line 2 of field "Totals"
   else
     put "$" & Tax into line 2 of field "Totals"
   end if
    put field "Shipping" into Ship
    put "$" & Ship into line 3 of field "Totals"
   put "$" & Sum + Tax + Ship into line 4 of field "Totals"
  end mouseUp
```

Background Fields- See Figure 7-20 pg. 267.

Field: Customer (#1)
Rectangle style
Seven lines showing
no script

Field: Date (#2)
Rectangle style
No lines showing
no script

Field: <u>Invoice (#3)</u>
Rectangle style
No lines showing
no script

Field: <u>Shipping (#4)</u>
Rectangle style
No lines showing
no script

Field: <u>D1Q - D6Q (#5-10)</u>
Fields for quantities
Rectangle style
No lines showing
Six fields titled D1Q through D6Q
no script

Field: <u>D1P - D6P (#11-16)</u>
Fields for prices
Rectangle style
No lines showing
Six fields titled D1P through D6P
no script

Field: <u>Totals   (#17)</u>
Field for totals
Rectangle style
Four lines showing
no script

If you put in something the "Problem" line of the customer field, a dialog box appears just to bring your attention to the problem. Once the problem is remedied, remove all text from that line and the dialog box will no longer appear each time you open that card. To print an "invoice," just select Print Card from the file menu. Use command-N to make a new card, but make sure you're at the *last* card when you do it. The all of the cards will be in chronological order. If they accidentally get out of order, use the **sort** command. From the Message Box, just type in,

sort by field "Invoice"

and everything will be in order again.

Summary

This chapter has provided a key structure for your arsenal of HyperTalk commands. The conditional structure allows decision making once information has been entered into the system or taken from another source from the system. Working in conjunction with the ask and answer commands, a script can pause to get information once a script has been launched. Since HyperCard is highly interactive to begin with, this feature, while still important, is not as dramatic as when it is combined with other programming environments.

Screen formatting from within a script is not required to the same degree as other computer languages since fields, buttons and graphics are placed into backgrounds and on cards using interactive tools. However, there will be a number of occasions where it will be important to do something from within a script that requires placing things on the screen. In the chapter on using graphic scripts, this will become more evident. In the meantime, the visual effect command and the effects you can create, add a lot to the way you can control a screen's image.

Recurrent Procedures and Script Menu Control

8

The Computer as a Simple but Fast Thinker

Behind all of the "smartness" of computers is a simple basic structure that evaluates whether a line is "on" or "off" that is translated into ones and zeros. The ones and zeros, binary numbers, are translated at high speeds into other things that eventually result in what we see on the screen. In looking at the **repeat** command, we can see how to deal with problems the same way. Break a problem down into simple parts and do each little part very fast so the computer looks "smart."

Forms of Repeat

There are many different types of parameters to use with repeat. We will look at each one and suggest how it might be used in an application. Make a card with a test button and a couple of background fields like the one in Figure 8-1 to launch the different scripts we will examine in this section. Once out of the background, write the indicated text in Field 1.

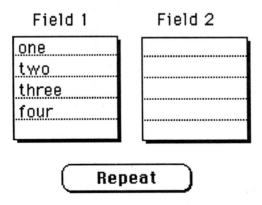

Figure 8-1

Repeat *number*. The first form of repeat is,

```
repeat N times
end repeat
```

This form is similar to a FOR....NEXT loop in BASIC. For example, the following script takes the information in the first field and copies it into the second field.

```
on mouseUp
 put 1 into lineGet
  repeat 5 times
    put line lineGet of field 1¬
    into line lineGet of field 2
    add 1 to lineGet
  end repeat
end mouseUp
```

Had we used this repeat structure in the "Mail Order" application in the last chapter, the script for transferring the data from the "PriceList" field to the "Customer" card would have been much shorter.

Repeat until. The second repeat structure waits until it encounters a certain condition to stop repeating. This is useful for scripts that search for certain occurrences either in existing sources or ones entered by the user. Using our test card in Figure 8-1, write the following button script:

```
on mouseUp
  put empty into It
  put 1 into lineGet
  repeat until It is "Three"
    get line lineGet of field 1
    add 1 to lineGet
```

```
    end repeat
    put it into line 1 of field 2
  end mouseUp
```

In an interactive role, repeat can be used with answer or ask to stop when a certain condition has been met. For example, in searching through a stack for a card, the following button script will search a stack until the desired card has been located.

Button: <u>Go Find</u>
Card button
Oval shape with name showing
script

```
on mouseUp
  put empty into It
  repeat until It is "Yes"
    answer "Is this the card?" with "Yes" or "No"
  go next card
  end repeat
end mouseUp
```

Put that button on the "Address" stack and flip through the cards until you find what you want.

Repeat while. This is the opposite of repeat until. As long as a condition is true, the the loop repeats itself. Using the test card shown in Figure 8-1, this next script shows another way to move everything from one field to the next.

```
on mouseUp
  put 1 into It          — Initialize container
  put 1 into lineGet
  repeat while It <> empty   — While it's not empty
    get line lineGet of field 1
    put it into line lineGet of field 2
```

```
      add 1 to lineGet
    end repeat
  end mouseUp
```

The script could have been written using "until" the It container was equal to "empty" just as well. "While" and "until" are two sides to the same coin, but in some situations it may be necessary to use one or the other. This is especially important if using nested loops or both "while" and "until" repeats in the same handler. Also notice that we did *not* use the line,

```
    put line lineGet of field 1 into line lineGet of field 2
```

because had we done so, the "It" container would never have been used in the script. The result would have been an endless loop.

Repeat forever ... exit repeat. This structure is used with an If...then statement. The **repeat forever** command keeps repeating until it encounters **exit repeat**. This format is useful for embedding in nested loops and multiple conditions. Using the test card shown in Figure 8-1, the following script uses the repeat forever to move things from one field to the other.

```
  on mouseUp
    put 1 into lineGet
    repeat forever
     put line lineGet of field 1¬
      into line lineGet of field 2
      if lineGet = 4 then exit repeat — The way out
      add 1 to lineGet
    end repeat
  end mouseUp
```

Repeat with var = start to finish. This form of repeat is similar to a FOR ... NEXT structure in BASIC. With the sample button and fields, it turns out to be the most economical to write in terms of script. In the following script, the variable "x" was used. (For programmers familiar with BASIC, this would have been equivalent to FOR X = 1 TO 4.)

```
on mouseUp
  repeat with x = 1 to 4      — x = local variable
    put line x of field 1 into line x of field 2
  end repeat
end mouseUp
```

The important aspect of this arrangement is that the repeat loop generates values for the variable, and it is not necessary to have a separate line increment the variable's value.

Repeat with var = start down to finish. To count backwards, there's a "down to" parameter. This decrements the value of the variable each time it is repeated.

```
on mouseUp
  repeat with x = 4 down to 1
    put line x of field 1 into line x of field 2
  end repeat
end mouseUp
```

It's virtually the same as using repeat with *to* except that the count is downwards instead of upwards.

Using Repeat Structures: A Sort Example

Those familiar with programming are well aware of what can be done with loop and repeat structures. For those new to programming, some practical examples may help. In the last chapter, we briefly introduced the sort command in HyperCard. There also are occasions when you will need to sort something other than cards. For example, instead of having a list of names with telephone numbers on separate cards, you decide to put them on a single card in a scrolling files. After adding names for a while, you decide you would like them in alphabetical order. Since the sort command only works with sorting cards and not lines in a field, you decide you need a sort routine that puts all of the names in alphabetical order. Assuming the last names are first, shown in Figure 8-2, by writing a script using repeat statements, we will see how to get everything sorted out.

The most basic sort algorithm is called a "Bubble Sort." It is called that since it "bubbles up" elements in a list from the bottom. Using "nested loops" of repeat statements, we will do this in a script. Two words are compared, and if the first is "greater than" the second, the two words are swapped. If not, then the script gets the next pair of words and does the same thing all over again. This process would require a very long script without a repeat statement; however, with repeat, it is fairly short. You can use any names and phone numbers you want, but for practice try the perfectly backward list supplied in the example field.

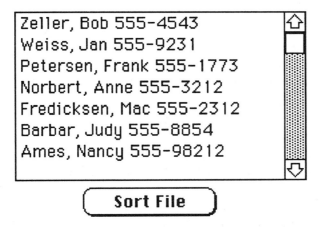

Zeller, Bob 555-4543
Weiss, Jan 555-9231
Petersen, Frank 555-1773
Norbert, Anne 555-3212
Fredicksen, Mac 555-2312
Barbar, Judy 555-8854
Ames, Nancy 555-98212

Sort File

Figure 8-2

Field: <u>Field 1 (no name)</u>
Background field
Scroll style with no lines showing
no script

Button: <u>Sort File</u>
Oval style
Card button
script


```
on mouseUp
  get the number of lines in field 1
  put (it-1) into N
  put 2 into flag2                      — Set flag2
  repeat while flag2=2                   — O u t s i d e
"loop"
    put 0 into flag                      — reset flag
    repeat with x= 1 to N                — Inside "loop"
      put line x of field 1 into alpha — First word.
      put line (x+1) of field 1 into beta    — S e c o n d
word.
      if alpha <= beta then next repeat      — C o m p a r e
them.
      put beta into temp                 — Swap
      put alpha into beta                — Reverse the
      put temp into alpha                — lines.
      put alpha into line x of field 1 — Put them back
      put beta into line (x+1) of field 1       — sorted.
      put 1 into flag
      put x into N
    end repeat                           — Inside "end"
    if flag <>1 then put 0 into flag2
  end repeat                             — O u t s i d e
"end"
end mouseUp
```

That script was fairly complicated for a beginner, but it shows how important the repeat structure can be for a script. Go over the script and see if you can follow all of its decision making and repeat loops. The bubble sort is fairly slow, but for a partially sorted list it is very efficient. When you're ready to see the list sorted, click the "Sort File" button.

＊ New For Version 1.2

Another new set of functions concern identifying the what the **find** command has located. These functions let the user write scripts for the "found material." There are four new **find functions:**

1. foundChunk
2. foundField
3. foundLine
4. foundText

These functions all follow the issue of a find command. Without selected materials, they return nothing. The format for each is,

the foundFunction

For example, the script segment

find whole "Joe"
put the foundText into line 1 of field 3

first issues a find command and then, using the foundText function, moves the word to a specified line and field. A more likely place to employ the found functions is where the information to be found is unknown until the user enters it. For example, the card shown in Figure 8-3 illustrates this feature.

FindStuff

Figure 8-3

Field: <u>No Name</u>
Shadow style
lines showing
No script

Button: <u>FindStuff</u>
Icon # 31685
Card button
script

```
on mouseUp
  hide msg
  ask "Find what? "
  find it
  select the foundChunk
  put the foundText
end mouseUp
```

The line,

select the foundChunk

darkens the entire word found. With foundText, you cannot use it with select. (Substitute foundText for foundChunk an try it.) Using the found functions, you can have the find commands locate a whole string with a partial string search (e.g. using "Eli" to find "Elizabeth"), and then use the functions to operate with the found string.

FoundField and foundLine return information in a different form. The foundLine function is very useful for picking up more than just the found word. It picks up the entire line. For example, lets use the field from the sort example. You have a list of names and telephone numbers. As the list gets longer, you want something to quickly jump to the name and number and highlight it for you. The next sample card shown in Figure 8-4 does that for you, and it lets you know in which field the name was found. (The last operation is simply for illustration of what happens when using the foundField function.)

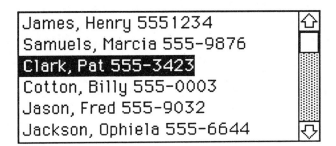

Find Phone Friends

Figure 8-4

Field: <u>Card Field 1</u>
Scroll format
No script

Button: <u>Find Phone Friends</u>
Icon# 10610
script

```
on mouseUp
  hide msg
  ask "Name segment"
  find it
  select the foundLine
  put the foundField
end mouseUp
```

Experiment with this little card. Add names beyond the bottom of the visible portion of the field. HyperCard will find and highlight the name or name segment you seek. (You could just put the button on the card with your sorted phone list.)

Arrays

Non-programmers may never have head of arrays as they are typically used in programming, but the concept is a very useful one, and one that relates to repeat structures. Basically, arrays are simply orderly sets of variables. It usually helps to think of arrays in terms of rows and columns:

	Columns				
	<u>1</u>	<u>2</u>	<u>3</u>	<u>4</u>	<u>5</u>
1	A	B	C	D	E
2	F	G	H	I	J
Rows 3	K	L	M	N	O
4	P	Q	R	S	T
5	U	V	W	X	Y

Table 8-1

Examining the characters in Table 8-1, we can describe each letter in terms of Row/Column. For example, the letter "H" can be described as, 2/3 since it is in Row 2, Column 3. The table is a "Two Dimension" array. The two dimensions are the "rows" and "columns."

Translating Table 8-1 into HyperCard is simple. Each column can be a word or item, and each row a line in a field or other variable. Figure 8-5 shows how Table 8-1 would look in a field with separate items.

```
A,B,C,D,E
F,G,H,I,J
K,L,M,N,O
P,Q,R,S,T
U,V,W,X,Y
```

Figure 8-5

Now the letter "H" is "line 2/item 3."

There are many uses for arrays. For example, a researcher may want to analyze data collected with cross tabulation. A simple survey may want to determine if there were any differences between boys and girls in their reaction to a movie. This would give us two dimensions; 1) gender and 2) attitude toward movie. From this, it would be possible to derive the matrix shown in Figure 8-6

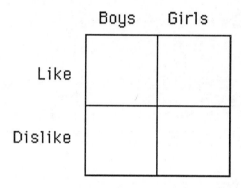

Figure 8-6

To re-create that matrix with HyperCard, we could use four fields. The data could be placed in a separate data field in an array format. Each line represents a different respondent, and the two numbers represent gender and whether or not they liked the film. The coding would be simple:

Gender   1=boy 2=girl
Like   1=yes 2=no

By placing the data in a scrolling data field, we can enter as many cases as we want. The data are entered as two numbers separated by a comma. Since all data are stored as text, we could have used "b" for boy and "g" for girl or any other code we wanted. However, using "1" and "2" we can better illustrate the array matrix concept. Figure 8-7 shows the five fields and one button for the matrix.

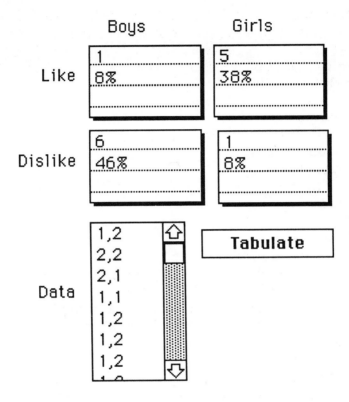

Figure 8-7

By writing a script that tabulates the data, we can see if there is any apparent relationship between gender and whether or not a certain film was liked. The sample data indicates girls generally liked the film and boys did not. Both the numbers and percentages are shown in the fields, the latter helping to establish a trend in situations where there are a very large number of cases to tabulate.

Fields: <u>C11,C12,C21,C22</u>
Background fields

Shadow style
no scripts

Field: <u>Data</u>
Background field
Scroll style
no script

Button: <u>Tabulate</u>
Rectangle shape
Card button
script

```
on mouseUp
  set numberFormat to "##"
  put the number of lines in field "Data" into N
  repeat with x=1 to N
    put item 1 of line x of field "Data" into alpha
    put item 2 of line x of field "Data" into beta
    if alpha=1 and beta = 1 then add 1 to field "c11"
    if alpha=1 and beta = 2 then add 1 to field "c12"
    if alpha=2 and beta = 1 then add 1 to field "c21"
    if alpha=2 and beta = 2 then add 1 to field "c22"
  end repeat
  repeat with x=1 to 4
    get value of field x
    put (it/N) *100 & "%" into line 2 of field x
  end repeat
end mouseUp
```

To get data from a table where the data are arranged in terms of items and lines, one repeat structure can loop through the lines and the other through the items. For example, Figure 8-8 shows a central field where the lines are treated as rows and the separate items as columns. Using a nested repeat loop, it is a simple matter to total the rows and columns. To make the totals stand out, we will set their fonts to bold underline.

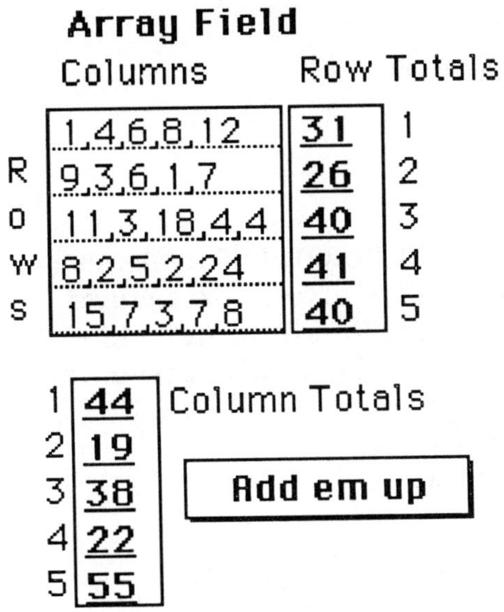

Array Field

Columns   Row Totals

R
o
w
s

1,4,6,8,12	**31**	1
9,3,6,1,7	**26**	2
11,3,18,4,4	**40**	3
8,2,5,2,24	**41**	4
15,7,3,7,8	**40**	5

1	**44**
2	**19**
3	**38**
4	**22**
5	**55**

Column Totals

Add em up

Figure 8-8

Field: <u>Array</u>
Background field
Rectangle with five lines showing
No script

Field: <u>ColTotal</u>
Card Field
Rectangle with no lines showing
No Script

Field: <u>RowTotal</u>
Card Field
Rectangle with no lines showing

No Script

Button: <u>Add em up</u>
Card button
Rectangle with name showing
script

```
on mouseUp
 — Set the font and style
   set textFont of card field "RowTotal" to Geneva
   set textFont of card field "ColTotal" to Geneva
   set textStyle of card field "RowTotal" to bold,underline
   set textStyle of card field "ColTotal" to bold,underline

 — Run through the array
   repeat with row=1 to 5
     repeat with col=1 to 5
       get item col of line row of field "Array"
       add  it to line row of card field "RowTotal"
       add it to line col of card field "ColTotal"
     end repeat
   end repeat
end mouseUp
```

By adding more fields, cards and stacks it is possible to increase the dimensions of the arrays. Nested loops are the means to store and retrieve arrays, and the various sources are the locations to place them.

Creating Your Own Commands and Functions

In specific applications, or just in general, you may find yourself writing the same line over and over again. For example, a common line in any stack may be,

get the number of lines of field 1

or some similar line. To see how this works, write the following script in a stack background:

```
on getLines
        get the number of lines in field 1
        put it into msg
end getLines
```

Now, whenever the command "getLines" is used in that stack, the number of lines in Background Field 1 will appear in the Message Box. To test it, choose Stack Info... from the Objects Menu and click the "Script" button in the dialog box. Write the above script in the editor, and then create a background field, if one does not exist, and write the following script in a button:

```
on mouseUp
   getLines
end mouseUp
```

When you click the button, the number of lines in Field 1 will appear in the message box. Once you have created a new command, that new command can be further used to create more commands. To see how this works, go back to the stack script and change it so that it will be as the following:

```
on getLines
   get the number of lines in field 1
   put it into msg
end getLines

on lnBeep
   getLines
   beep
end lnBeep
```

Change the button script to,

```
on mouseUp
  lnBeep
end mouseUp
```

When the button is clicked this time, not only does it get the number of lines and put them into the Message Box, it "beeps" as well. As you become more and more familiar with the kinds of words you will need all the time, you can begin placing them in the background of the Home Stack. Then all of the stacks you have with that Home Stack can use the commands you created there. The ability to define commands is a very powerful extender of HyperTalk, and you should experiment with it to maximize your work with HyperTalk.

Besides commands, you can define functions as well. Defining a function is very much like defining a command. It goes inside a handler beginning with **function** instead of **on**. Furthermore, the **return** statement is required to set up the expression used for the function. The following format is used:

```
function test [parameters]
    return something
end test
```

A simple useful function would be one for finding the amount an item would cost is a tax were added to it. We will name the function "wTax" to indicate that is what the item would cost "with tax." This assumes a 6% sales tax, but you can make the tax rate anything you want.

```
function wTax Cost
  return Cost + (Cost * .06)
end wTax
```

To use the function, put it into a container. From the Message Box, try writing,

> put wTax(17) into msg

and the total 18.02 will appear as soon as you press Return.

It is possible to write functions that include commands and multiple parameters. For example, let's take a look at creating a function to find someone's year of birth if they provided their age and the month of birth. It involves getting the date, converting it and using conditional structures.

```
function birthYr age,month
  get the date
  convert it to dateItems
  if item 2 of it > month then
    return item 1 of it - age
  else
    return item 1 of it - (age+1)
  end if
end birthYr
```

That's a fairly complex function, but if you have an application where it is required to use such a function, it is simpler to do it once, and then just write the function that re-do the whole thing every time you need it. Create the following button script on a card with a background field with at least two lines:

```
on mouseUp
  put line 1 of field 1 into age
  put line 2 of field 1 into month
  put birthYr(age,month) into msg
end mouseUp
```

Using DoMenu and Choose

The **doMenu** and **choose** commands are like robotic arms in a script. They work on menu items just as through you had used the mouse to grab them. The format does not require you specify which menu is chosen; only the menu command or tool. To use doMenu, the format

        doMenu menuCommand

selects what you want. For example,

        doMenu "New Card"

creates a next card. This would be very useful if you wanted to create several cards all at once. The script,

        repeat with x = 1 to 10
            doMenu "New Card"
        end repeat

would rapidly create 10 new cards. Likewise, using a script, not only can you quickly create new objects, you can place and name them as well. For example, suppose a social scientist or market researcher needed a data entry card requiring a given number of buttons for different responses from a questionnaire. The following button script would not only generate the needed number of buttons, it would proportionately space them and name them sequentially. (See Figure 8-9.) When it is finished it goes to the script editor of the first button. The **edit script** command is used to go to the button from a script.

        on mouseUp
          doMenu New Card
          put the number of this card into cardNo
          set the name of card cardNo to "Test"

```
repeat with x=1 to 6
  doMenu New Button
  set loc of button x to (x+200),(x*30+20)
  set name of button x to ("Response #" & x)
end repeat
Edit script of button 1
end mouseUp
```

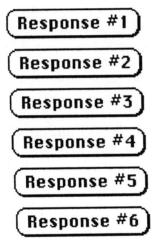

Figure 8-9

Now that the buttons are generated, you're all set the write the scripts. Once the scripts have been written in the button in the first card, the New Card command can duplicate the card.

When writing scripts for non-programmers, you will not want to end up with the user in the script editor. To automatically write scripts, depending on what the user needs, use the **set** command. Using the format,

> set the script of [object] to [script]

the named object will be given the script specified. The problem is putting in the necessary carriage returns. For example, if you write the script,

> set the script of Button 1 to "on mouseUp beep end mouseUp"

the script will generate an error message. That's because the whole thing is in a single line. One way to get around this is to have the script placed in a field and transfer the field contents to the script. Create the card field and button shown in Figure 8-10, and put it in the same stack as the button that created the buttons shown in Figure 8-9. We will now write a button script that will generate scripts for all six of the buttons in Figure 8-9 What's more, the script-generating script will put a different value into all of the different buttons.

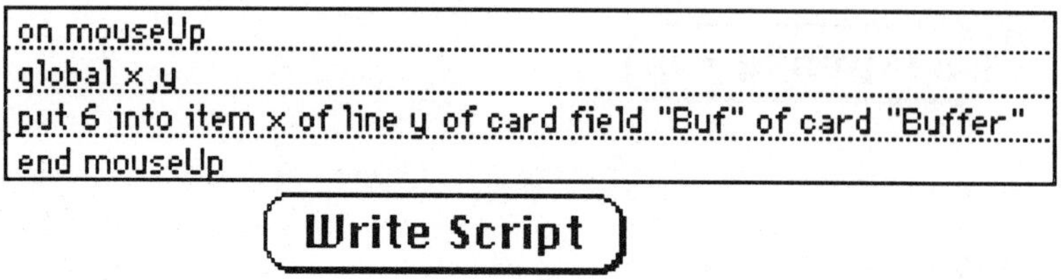

```
on mouseUp
global x,y
put 6 into item x of line y of card field "Buf" of card "Buffer"
end mouseUp
```

(**Write Script**)

Figure 8-10

> **Field**: Scripter
> Card field
> Rectangle style with four lines showing
> *no script*

Button: <u>Write Script</u>
Oval card button
script

```
on mouseUp
  repeat with x=1 to 6
    add 1 to word 2 of line 3 of card field "Scripter"
    set the script of button x of card Test¬
    to card field "Scripter"
  end repeat
end mouseUp
```

Since the x variable in the script changes the contents of the "Scripter" field, each time the script goes through the loop, the value of the second word is incremented. Thus, for example, the third button script would read,

```
on mouseUp
  global x,y
  put 3 into item x of line y of card field¬
  "Buf" of card "Buffer"
end mouseUp
```

providing it with an appropriate value in the second word of the third line. The "item x" and "line y" reflect possible global variables that could be used in another script to organize the data generated by clicking the response buttons into a card field called "Buf" in a card named "Buffer."

Choose

The **choose** command will be used a lot when we start dealing with the paint properties, but it is a good one to learn now so that we can see how to use the rest of the menu elements. Basically, the **choose** command makes the chosen tool box tool current. For example, choose button tool

makes the button tool the current one. It would be useful while developing a script to have the emerging script end with "choose button tool" so that you could go right back to editing. Once the script was perfected, it would end with "choose browse tool" or some other tool choice. The following tools are available:

browse	button	field	select
lasso	pencil brush		eraser
line	spray	rectangle	round rect
bucket	oval	curve	text
regular polygon			

In later chapters we will more fully use choose with other commands.

Application: Data Entry Utility

The application for this chapter will build on what was begun with the examples shown in Figures 8-9 and 8-10. What we want is a stack that will be easy for the end user to operate from the "Paint Level" of HyperCard with no programming abilities required. The plan is to develop a program that requires the user to do a minimum amount of work to create a stack of that can be used as a general data entry utility. All of the data will be stored in a "field array" for later analysis. The user must supply the following:

    1. The maximum number of responses in any question.
    2. The number of questions.
    3. The size of the sample.

From this, the initial card will generate the correct number of response buttons and question cards and know when to exit the cycle through the questions. The get started, it is necessary to create two cards, one called "Start" and the other called "Buffer." Figure 8-11 shows the Start card.

Create Stack

Data Entry

Scripter Field

```
on mouseUp
global x,y,z
put 0 into item x of line y of card field "Buf" of card "Buffer"
put 1 into z
end mouseUp
```

Info Field

Max responses	4
Number of Questions	3
Size of Sample	3

Figure 8-11

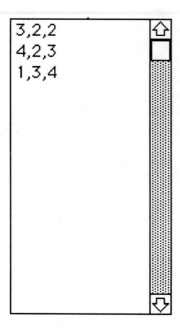

Figure 8-12 (After data entry. It is blank at the outset.)

Card: Start

Button: Create Stack
Transparent button with icon #27056
card button
script

```
on mouseUp
  global x,y,z
  put 1 into z
  put 0 into x
  put 0 into y
  put line 1 of card field "Info" into Responses
```

```
put line 2 of card field "Info" into Questions
put line 3 of card field "Info" into N

— Make the Response Card Script
doMenu New Card
put "on closeCard" into line 1 of CdScript
        put "global x,y,z" into line 2 of CdScript
        put "if z=0 then play boing" into line 3 of CdScript
        put "add 1 to x" into line 4 of CdScript
        put "put 0 into z" into line 5 of CdScript
        put "end closeCard" into line 6 of CdScript
        put "on enterKey" into line 7 of CdScript
        put "go to next card" into line 8 of CdScript
        put "end enterKey" into line 9 of CdScript
        set script of card 2 to CdScript

        — Make the buttons
        repeat with x=1 to Responses
          doMenu New Button
          set autoHilite of button "New Button" to true
          set loc of button x to (x+400),(x*30+20)
          set name of button x to ("Response #" & x)
          add 1 to word 2 of line 3 of card field "Scripter" of card
"Start"
          set the script of button x of card 2¬
          to card field "Scripter" of card "Start"
        end repeat

        — Make enough response cards for questions
        repeat with x=1 to (Questions-1)
          doMenu Copy Card
          doMenu Paste Card
        end repeat

        — End of Form Button
        doMenu New Button
```

set icon of button "New Button" to 14953
set showName of button "New Button" to false
set style of button "New Button" to transparent
    set rectangle of button "New Button" to
300,300,350,350
set name of button "New Button" to "NextData"
put "on mouseUp" into line 1 of StartOver
put "global x,y" into line 2 of StartOver
put "if y=" & N && "then go to last card" into line 3 of
StartOver
put "else" into line 4 of StartOver
put "put 0 into x" into line 5 of StartOver
put "add 1 to y" into line 6 of StartOver
put "go to card 2" into line 7 of StartOver
put "end if" into line 8 of StartOver
put "end mouseUp" into line 9 of StartOver
set the script of button "NextData" to StartOver

— Back to the start
go to card 1
put 0 into word 2 of line 3 of card field "Scripter"
choose browse tool
end mouseUp

Button: Data Entry
Transparent button with icon #20186
card button
script

on mouseUp
  global x,y,Q
  put 1 into y
  put 1 into x
  put line 2 of card field "Info" into Q
  go next card
end mouseUp

Field: <u>Scripter</u>
card field
lock text
rectangle style with four lines showing
no script

Special Note: There is text in the Scripter field that is used as script in the buttons generated by the "Create Stack" button, but the field itself has no script.

Field: <u>Info</u>
card field
rectangle style with three lines showing
no script

Card: <u>Buffer</u>

Field: <u>Buf</u>
Scroll style
card field
no script

When the "Create Stack" button is clicked, the script generates a set of cards between the "Start" and "Buffer" cards. Depending on the information the user supplies in the Info box, there will be greater or fewer response buttons and cards generated. On the last card a special button is placed so the user can go back to the first question. When the sample is exhausted, it automatically goes to the last card where all of the data is waiting on the "Buf" field.

The response buttons are placed on the right hand side of the cards generated. This allows the user to place his/her question to the left of the buttons. Figure 8-13 shows a sample card representing the last card generated. The "Return Arrow" button on the bottom has been moved to place it better in relation to the response buttons as shown in Figure 8-13.

3. Do you think that by reducing taxes the government can stimulate the economy and reduce the deficit?

(Response #1)

(Response #2)

(Response #3)

(Response #4)

Figure 8-13

The Enter Key (not the Return Key) is used to move to the next card. This was chosen instead of a button so the user could click with one hand on the mouse and press a key with the other hand. If the user forgets to click a response button, a "Boing" reminds him/her the question is without a response. This can be later remedied by inserting the correct response code in the "Buf" field on the "Buffer" card. Figure 8-12 shows what the data looks like after a sample of three persons with three questions has been completed.

Special Note: The data generated can be put into a file, but at this stage we have not yet seen how to do that with HyperCard. By copying the data and then pasting it into a word processor file and saving it as text, it can be put in a text file.

Summary

The repeat structures shown in this chapter add a lot to your scripting power and should be used to cut down on the amount of typing required for a script. Not only will less script take less time, it will make for faster execution of the program. It's a lot easier to have your computer repeat a procedure than to do it yourself by writing more script.

Like the Alamo, "Remember the Array!." Think of an array as something that will help organize containers. Using the repeat structures, it is possible to access containers in an array style. With the HyperCard items, lines, fields, cards, words and backgrounds, it is possible, and relatively simple, to arrange containers into multi-dimensional arrays.

With the script control of menu items, not only can you do less script authoring yourself, you can actually make the computer write the script for you. As we saw in the example of the data entry stack, each card and button had scripts written by the master script. As we will see further in the chapter on graphics, script menu control lets you write your own "artistic" script with the computer doing all of the work for you.

Files and Printing With HyperCard

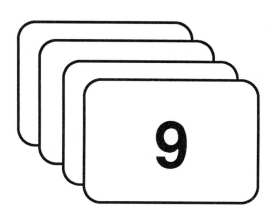

9

Files and HyperCard

At first glance, files with HyperCard may appear to be redundant. The fields and cards within HyperCard make up a very powerful database environment themselves, and adding more file handling capabilities might seem to be using an older, less efficient method for dealing with files. To a large extent that is true, and when using files with HyperCard, it should not be in the traditional mind set, but rather for very specific purposes.

For those new to programming, the files being discussed are ASCII or text files that are stored on disk. The files contain information in ASCII format, but the data themselves are not formatted into buttons, fields or anything else. In HyperCard, we have been storing information in fields in a format we can see, and with which we can easily modify, add and delete information. So who needs files?

There are two reasons for HyperCard file handling capabilities: 1) conserving disk space and 2) importing and exporting information between HyperCard and different applications. Files store information in a far more compact fashion than do HyperCard files. This is a minor reason, but one that may become important if you have either very big files or very limited disk storage space. More importantly, we will see how to import and export files between HyperCard and other applications with the file commands. This means you can use information generated with another program and transfer it to HyperCard or vice versa.

Creating Files

To create a file, use the **open file** command. It has the format,

    open file "NameOfFile"

with the name of the file in quotation marks. A container name can be used instead, and typically is when using the **ask** command in conjunction with **open**. The command prepares the file for reading or writing.

To put data into a file, use the **write** command. *Before* you can write to a file, it must first be *opened*. **Write** has the format,

> write "something" to file "NameOfFile"

where "something" can be text in quotation marks or a container. For example,

> write field 1 to file "Test"

would take the entire contents of background field 1 and put them into the file named "Test."

To examine the contents of a file, HyperCard employs the **read** command. As with the write command, it is necessary that the file be opened first. Either the format,

> read from file "NameOfFile" until "character"

or

> read from file "NameOfFile" for [integer value]

will take the contents of the file and place them into the "It" container. From that point, the contents can be placed anywhere that any other thing in a container could be stored. For example, the script segment,

> read from file "Friends" until tab
> put it into Folks

takes the contents of the file called "Friends" and puts it into the HyperCard container called "Folks."

Finally, once everything in a file has been written to or read from, it must be closed. The **close** command does this. The format is simply,

> close "NameOfFile"

and it serves to satisfy disk requirements that an open file be closed.

To get an idea of some uses of files, make a single background field and two card buttons as shown in Figure 9-1.

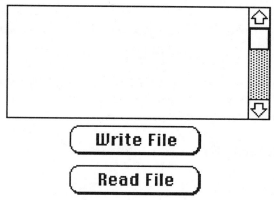

Figure 9-1

The goal is to write a script that will take the information out of a HyperCard stack and place it all into a single container. We will use a scrolling field container so we will be able to see everything. The card will take all of the data out of the sample stack called "Address" and put the data into a file with a name of your choosing. Then, the "Read File" button's script will put all of the data in the file into the background field.

Field: <u>Field 1 (no name)</u>
Background scrolling field
no script

Button: <u>Write File</u>
Oval card button
script

```
on mouseUp
  set lockScreen to true
  push card
  ask "Name of file to create"
  put it into NameOfFile
  open file NameOfFile
  go to stack "Address"
  put number of cards into CardNum
  repeat with x=2 to (CardNum)
    go to card x
    write field 1 to file NameOfFile
    write field 2 to file NameOfFile
    write field 3 to file NameOfFile
  end repeat
  close file NameOfFile
  pop card
  hide message box
  set lockScreen to false
end mouseUp
```

Button: <u>Read File</u>
Oval card button
script

```
on mouseUp
  ask "Name of file to open"
  put it into NameOfFile
```

```
   open file NameOfFile
   read from file NameOfFile until tab
   put it into field 1
   if it is empty then close file NameOfFile
end mouseUp
```

Scroll through the field window and see how the data were stored. Notice there are no carriage returns between fields. The name and address field runs right into the phone field, and the phone field runs into the date field. By placing the **return** constant between fields, you can keep them separate. For example, the lines from the "Write File" button script could be changed to read,

```
   write field 1 to file NameOfFile
   write return to file NameOfFile    - -Insert a return
   write field 2 to file NameOfFile
```

and insure there was a return after each file segment.

After you have finished writing the file to disk, compare the difference in size of the stack named "Address" and the file make up of the data from the stack. With the stack tested, we found the following:

Address stack	25,143 bytes	27.5K on disk
Address file	2,896 bytes	5K on disk

That's a big savings in disk space, but unless you're really strapped for space, do not waste your time converting Hyper-Card information to ASCII files for space alone.

To get a better idea of how data can be stored and retrieved between applications and HyperCard, we will create a Hyper-Card file with one format and then retrieve the information in a different format. Create one button and five background fields as shown in Figure 9-2. Only write text in Field 1. When you press the "compass" button, the button script will put Field 1 into a file and then break up the file and put it separately into Fields 2-5.

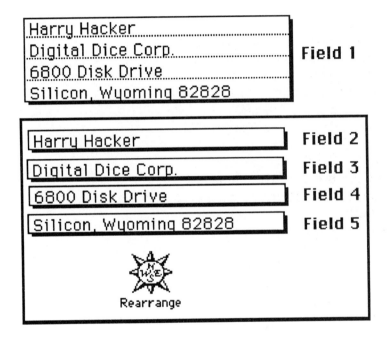

Figure 9-2

Field: Field 1 (no name)
Background field
Shadow style with four lines showing
no script

Fields: Fields 2-5 (no names)
Background fields
Shadow style with no lines showing

no scripts

Button: <u>Rearrange</u>
Card button
Icon style 9761
script

```
on mouseUp
  - -Put Field 1 into a file
  ask "File name please."
  put it into NameOfFile
  open file NameOfFile
  write field 1 to file NameOfFile
  close file NameOfFile

  - -Take it out of the file and
  - -put it into four separate
  - -fields
  open file NameOfFile
  repeat with x = 2 to 5
    read from file NameOfFile until return
    put it into field x
  end repeat
end mouseUp
```

When you get data from another application's file, or even another HyperCard file, the arrangement of that data may not be what you need. The above routine can be used to rearrange it in manner useful to you. However, if there are not carriage returns at the end of lines, it may be necessary to insert them as discussed previously in this chapter.

Using ASCII Characters

Text or ASCII characters have been mentioned throughout the book, but they really have not been discussed in much detail.

For those familiar with computers and programming, ASCII characters are nothing new, but for programming novices, there are a few things to learn. Basically, ASCII, which stands for American Standard Code for Information Interchanges, is a set of numbers that stand for certain characters. The "return" character, for example, is ASCII number 13. Since you cannot see a character for a return, computer languages have either developed special words, such as **return** in HyperCard, or they use the ASCII value. To use ASCII values directly in HyperCard there are two HyperCard functions available;

CharToNum
NumToChar

CharToNum changes a character into an ASCII number, and **NumToChar** changes an ASCII value into a character. To get familiar with ASCII functions, create the card shown in Figure 9-3. It will translate to and from ASCII code for you and make an ASCII chart. When you click the button "ASCII Chart," all of the different characters and their decimal ASCII values will appear in the field. (**Note:** There is only one real button in Figure 9-3. The one labelled "Phony Button" is not a button at all but a graphic. The "ASCII Chart" button is a real button.)

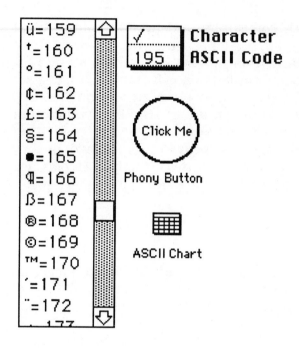

Figure 9-3

Field: <u>Field 1 (no name)</u>
Background field
Scroll style field
no script

Field: <u>Field 2 (no name)</u>
Background field
Shadow style with two lines showing
script

```
on closeField
   if line 1 of field 2 is not empty then
      put line 1 of field 2 into Alpha
```

```
      put CharToNum of Alpha into line 2 of field 2
   else
     if line 2 of field 2 <> empty then
       put line 2 of field 2 into ASCII
       put NumToChar of ASCII into line 1 of field 2
     else
       exit closeField
     end if
   end if
end closeField
```

Button: <u>ASCII Chart</u>
Card button
Icon number 15972
script

```
on mouseUp
  repeat with ASCII = 0 to 255
    put the NumToChar of ASCII & "=" & ASCII into¬
    line (ASCII + 1) of field 1
  end repeat
  play boing
end mouseUp
```

By scrolling through Field 1, you can see all of the different ASCII codes used in your Macintosh. The "play boing" line near the end of the button script was to let you know when the script had finished getting everything in order. (It takes a long time.) The "phony button" is a place on the card to click once an ASCII character or number has been placed in Field 2. Since the script is a field script, the program has to know there is a "closeField" condition to execute.

It is necessary to erase any of the old characters to convert from an ASCII value to a screen character since the script first looks to see if there is an alphanumeric character in the first line of

Field 2. If there is, it ignores the part of the script with instructions for converting from ASCII to characters.

The value of knowing ASCII lies in cleaning up other files you may get for HyperCard. Often "junk" in the form of control characters may invisibly mess up a file, and you may not know what it is. Those little squares (,) that show up in some files constitute some type of control character that can be removed only by selecting and deleting by hand. By converting the information to ASCII code, you can identify and remedy the problem with a program.

This next card will show how to go through a file and get rid of unwanted control ASCII characters. For purposes of illustration, we will use two fields. The first field will have a control character in it, and the button script will take out the control character and put the fixed text in the second field. The "washing machine" button in Figure 9-4 is a graphic on top of a transparent button. The button "cleans" out the control characters.

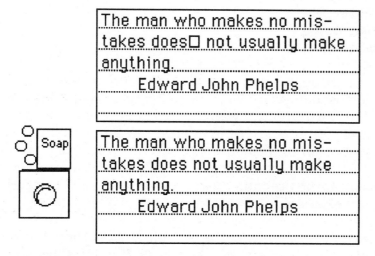

Figure 9-4

Fields: <u>Field 1 and 2 (no names)</u>
Background fields
Rectangle style; lines showing
no scripts

Button: <u>Cleaner</u>
Transparent style (over graphic)
Name hidden
Card button
script

```
on mouseUp
  put 1 into lineCount
  repeat with x=1 to number of chars in field 1
    get char x of field 1
    if CharToNum of it is 13 then add 1 to lineCount
    if CharToNum of it > 31 and CharToNum of it < 218¬
        or  CharToNum of it is 13 then
      put it into char x of line lineCount of field 2
    end if
  end repeat
end mouseUp
```

To put a control character in the first field (the top one in Figure 9-4) use the shift-option-1 key combination. To use the card with files, put the exported file into field 1, and put field 2 into a file.

Printing With HyperCard

Most of the printing work can be handled efficiently and effectively using the HyperCard menus. Printing cards and stacks simply involves choosing the format for printing from the menus and clicking the choices you want. However, there are some occasions where you will want to use a printing command in your script. For example, if there are different stacks and/or cards that you want printed, it may be easier to have a script go find and print everything while you work on something else. Likewise, there are print commands that allow you to print non-HyperCard materials with non-HyperCard applications and then return to HyperCard when the job is finished.

The first set of commands are used to print HyperCard cards and stacks. The following sequence is used:

Open printing [with dialog]
Print card
Close printing

Between the **open printing** and **close printing** commands, any or all cards in a stack can be printed with the **print card** command. With **print card**, the number of cards, including *all*, may be specified or a card descriptor can be used. For example, the following script segment shows a typical use of printing commands using multiple stacks:

opening printing
go to stack "News"
print 5 cards
go to stack "Business"
print card "FirstQuarter"
go to stack "Customers"
print all cards
close printing

When a number of cards is specified, the first card up to the number of cards is specified. Thus, the line,

print 5 cards

prints the first five cards. On the other hand, if you wanted to print the last five cards or some other combination of cards not in the first set of a stack, it would be necessary to use a different structure. For example, the following script segment would print the fourth through seventh cards:

```
open printing
repeat with x= 4 to 7
print card x
end repeat
close printing
```

Thus, even though the print commands are somewhat limited, using other HyperCard structures, there's not much you cannot print.

Printing With Dialog. Using the option to have the dialog box appear gives the same options for printing out cards as discussed in Chapter 2. When the script is executed instead of using the default parameters of full size printing of cards with two cards to a page, the entire range of options appears. The following button script   shows the option of printing the "Help" stack using the dialog box:

```
on mouseUp
        go to "Help" stack
        open printing with dialog
        print all cards
        close printing
end mouseUp
```

By choosing the option to print with the dialog box, the user could take a big stack like the Help one and print the cards at half size, getting eight on a page instead of only two.

Printing with Invisible Fields. Up to this point, mostly we have employed fields with visible lines and styles. However, with printing, it is important to begin thinking about how text and graphics are going to look when they are printed on paper instead of just what they look like on the screen. For example, Figure 9-5 shows how two fields are used to make a letterhead. The top portion of the figure shows the surrounding fields of the letterhead, while the bottom portion shows how it looks when it is printed out.

Amalgamated Ink, Co.
12345 Wells Street
Spotts, New Jersey 12345

Amalgamated Ink, Co.
 12345 Wells Street
Spotts, New Jersey 12345

Figure 9-5

It is important to remember that formatting for the screen is not the same as formatting for the printed page. What looks good on your Macintosh screen does not necessarily look good on paper and vice versa.

Printing With Other Resources. When you want something printed with another application program, such as MacWrite, Excel or any other program that does printing, *do not use* the **open printing - print card - close printing** sequence. Instead, the HyperCard command format,

> print "document" with "application"

will take any printable document and print it using the specified application. For example, the line,

>   print "Letter 1" with "Word"

would print the document called "Letter 1" using the word processor program "Word." Both the document and application may require a pathname sequence to automatically locate each. For example,

>   print "hd: letters: Letter 1" with "Word 4.0: Word"

would find Letter 1 on the hard disk in a folder called "letters," and the application program Word, would be found on a disk called "Word 4.0." Once everything has been printed, control returns to HyperCard. Containers may hold the name of either or both the document or application. Thus, the line,

>   print noteZ with field 1

assumes that the local variable "noteZ" contains the name of the document and field 1 has the name of the application.

Other Controlling Commands

Besides controlling the printer and files, HyperCard has a number of commands to control other devices and HyperCard activities. This section will discuss using various such commands.

Dial. The dial command has two different basic configurations. First, the command followed by a telephone number in quotes will simulate the sound of a touch tone dial. For example,

>   dial "1-619-555-1721"

would "dial" the 11 digit long distance number. With a special box attached to the serial port, you can actually dial numbers with this command. If you have a modem, you also can dial through it using the parameter "with modem" after the number dialed. For example,

> dial "555-4321" with modem

would dial the number through your modem. That uses the default modem setting "ATS0=0DT." With Apple modems and Hayes compatible modems, the settings are listed in modem manuals. With partially Hayes compatible modems, the code "ATDT" (dial touch tone) worked well. For a simple modem dialer, the field and button in Figure 9-6 illustrates how to use the selection container in a script with the **dial** command.

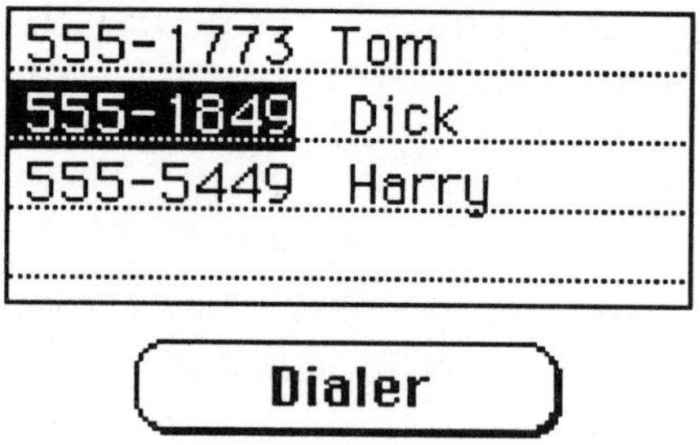

```
555-1773 Tom
555-1849 Dick
555-5449 Harry

```

```
(  Dialer  )
```

Figure 9-6

Button: <u>Dialer</u>
Card button
Oval style with name showing
script

```
on mouseUp
  dial selection with modem "ATDT"
end mouseUp
```

If your modem is connected to your telephone, you can set up an automatic phone dialer with a name and address stack.

Send

The **send** command can be a little tricky, but it makes it possible to control various actions from a HyperCard script that usually take a mouse action or typing to complete. The **send** command has the following form:

> send "message" to "object"

The message can be a system message or a command.

There are two different types of practical actions you can take with the **send** command. First, it is possible to initiate actions on other cards through a script. For example, suppose a button on a certain card needed to be "clicked" to initiate a "mouseUp" condition. The script segment,

> go to card x
> send "mouseUp" to button "beep"

would go to the indicated card and click the button called "beep." This type of script would be useful in a situation where a certain set of steps would lead to the user pushing the button anyway. At the same time, pushing the button would be optional if another set of steps were used in a stack.

A second general use for the **send** command is in situations where a script in one object needs to be used elsewhere. For example, if a card script were written on one particular card, and you wanted to use that same script on another card, it would be possible to use **send** to get the script command and use it on a different card. Figure 9-7 shows a card that can be added to a stack for purposes of illustration. Put it in the last card position or create a new stack, and add a card.

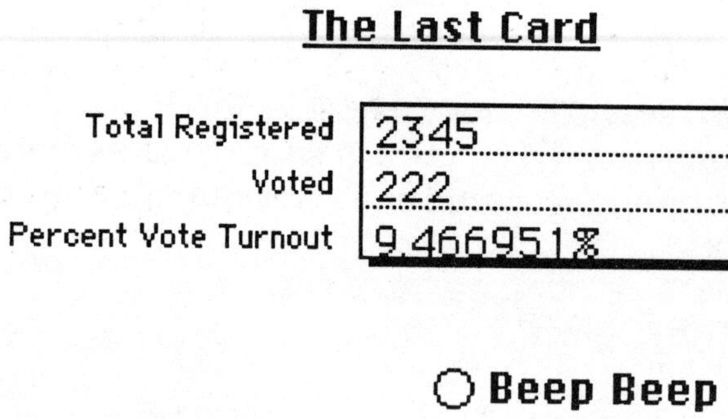

The Last Card

Total Registered	2345
Voted	222
Percent Vote Turnout	9.4669951%

○ **Beep Beep**

Figure 9-7

Field: <u>Field 1 (no name)</u>
Background field
Shadow style with three lines showing
no script

Card: <u>Percenter (last card in stack)</u>
script

```
on percent
  put (line 2 of field 1) / (line 1 of field 1) into pot
  multiply pot by 100
  put pot  & "%" into line 3 of field 1
end percent
```

Button: <u>Beep Beep</u>
Radio style button
script

```
on mouseUp
  beep
  beep
end mouseUp
```

Type in two numbers in the field on the last card. Test it by writing in the word "percent" in the message box and pressing the Return key to make sure it works properly.

On any other card, create the field and button shown in Figure 9-8.

☐ **Sender**

Figure 9-8

Field : <u>Field 1 (no name)</u>
Background field
Shadow style with three lines showing
no script

Button: <u>Sender</u>
Card button
Check box style
script

```
on mouseUp
  push card
  send "percent" to last card
  set lockScreen to true
  go to last card
  send "mouseUp" to button "Beep Beep"
  pop card
  set lockScreen to false
end mouseUp
```

As you can see when the "Sender" button is clicked, the command "percent" created by the card script on the last card is used on the current card's field. That is because both used background field 1. Had the command "percent" been used on the current card without the send command getting it from the last card, it would not have worked. To get the button to "beep" on the last card, it was necessary for the script to go first to the last card and click the button there. Had the line, send "mouseUp" to button "Beep Beep" been issued without first going to the last card, it would not have worked.

Application: HyperCard Mailing List Converter

A number of mailing list companies sell mailing lists on disks in ASCII format. These lists are full of codes that can be used for selecting different customer features. Transferring these to HyperCard make it possible to use the information in a very powerful and flexible environment. The application shown in Figure 9-9 can be used to transfer these files into HyperCard. The particular mailing list used to develop the program had each record separated by a return. That made it easy to develop a card that would generate a stack that would place each customer on a separate card. Also included are find, two printing and stack clearing buttons. The print routine prints out two customer information pieces per page, but it would probably only be used for single labels. For multiple labels, you would be better off using the "Print Report" button. The find button asks for a string to find, and the "Clear Stack" button deletes all of the stack except the first card.

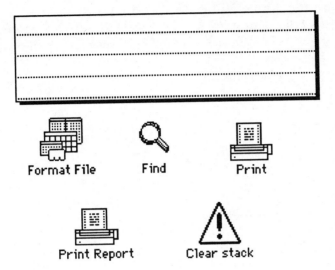

Format File   Find   Print

Print Report   Clear stack

Figure 9-9

Field: <u>Field 1 (no name)</u>
Background field
Shadow style with lines showing
(Adjust   the number of lines showing)
no script

Button: <u>Format File</u>
Card button
Transparent style
Icon number 18814
script

```
on mouseUp
   ask "File name please."
   put it into NameOfFile
   open file NameOfFile
   put 2 into x
   repeat while it <> "|"
      doMenu "New Card"
```

```
      read from file NameOfFile until return
      put it into field 1 of card x
      add 1 to x
      if it is empty then
        close file NameOfFile
        exit repeat
      end if
    end repeat
  end mouseUp
```

Button: <u>Find</u>
Card button
Transparent style
Icon number 8538
script

```
on mouseUp
  ask "Find what?"
  find it
end mouseUp
```

Button: <u>Print</u>
Card button
Transparent style
Icon number 1007 (1008 for laser)
script

```
on mouseUp
  ask "Begin printing with which card?"
  put it into alpha
  ask "End printing with which card?"
  put it into omega
  set style of field 1 to transparent
  set showLines of field 1 to false
  open printing
  repeat with x=alpha to omega
```

```
        print card x
       end repeat
       close printing
       set style of field 1 to shadow
       set showLines of field 1 to true
      end mouseUp
```

Button: <u>Print Report</u>
Card button
Transparent style
Icon number 1007 (1008 for laser)
script

```
on mouseUp
  doMenu Print Report...
end mouseUp
```

Button: <u>Clear Stack</u>
Card button
Transparent style
Icon number 2
script

```
on mouseUp
  go to card 2
   repeat with x=2 to (number of cards)
     doMenu "Delete Card"
   end repeat
end mouseUp
```

Try different scripts with different types of mailing lists. Once you get your mailing list established, it might be a good idea to delete the Clear Stack button, just to be on the safe side.

Graphics
and
Sound

10

Script Driven Graphics and Making Music

In this chapter, we look at graphics and sound. We have discussed graphics in terms of the tools available, while leaving the use of these tools to the user's artistic ability and stack requirements. Various examples have used simple sound techniques. This chapter deals with how to access and use graphics and sound from a script. The examples provide some practical applications of graphics and sound.

When to Script Graphics

Using the mouse and keyboard for creating graphics will get most of the graphic work done in HyperCard. However, there are certain situations where it will be useful to write a script that will do something with graphics. For example, if you want a graphic view of data, a script that automatically sets up a proportional chart is more precise and simpler than one you have to draw and estimate the length of graph lines to represent different values.

Graphic Properties

There are fourteen graphic properties that can be set.

brush	**centered**	**filled**	**grid**	**lineSize**
multiple	**multiSpace**	**pattern**	**polySides**	**textAlign**
textFont	**textHeight**	**textSize**	**textStyle**	

Using the **choose** command, first select a tool, and then these properties are established using the **set** command. Depending on the property, there will be different parameters.

The **brush** tool can be set to one of 32 brush styles. Using the format, set brush to [1-32]

establishes the brush stroke characteristics. Figure 10-1 shows the different strokes with the accompanying values to the left of the stroke.

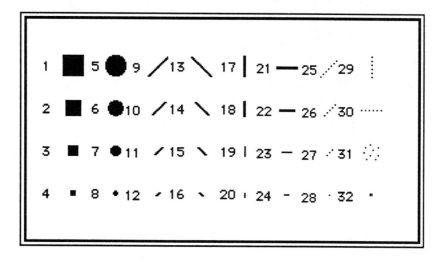

Figure 10-1

The **pattern** is set in a similar way as is brush. Each pattern is represented by one of 40 values as seen in Figure 10-2.

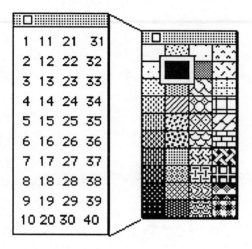

Figure 10-2

To set the **pattern** for the basket-weave display, the line

    set pattern to 37

would be used.

The **lineSize** property establishes the size of lines, including the lines that make up polygons and curved figures. Figure 10-3 shows the values to be set for the different line widths. Note that the values are in increments of two after four.

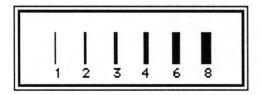

Figure 10-3

The script segment,

> set lineSize to 4

is an example of setting a line width property.

The four other paint properties that use integer values to establish a property characteristic include,

> **multiSpace**   **polySides**   **textSize**   **textHeight**

MultiSpace establishes the space between multiple images with values from 1 to 9, and **polySides** can be set from 3 to 50 to establish the number of sides a polygon will have. Using the *paint* text tool, **textSize** and **textHeight** determine the size of the text and the vertical space between letters to any integer value.

The remaining paint text tool properties are set to specific descriptive properties. The **textAlign** property can be set to *left*, *right* or *center*. The **textFont** property can set the font to any available font in your system. For example,

> choose text tool
> set the textFont to Chicago

would use the Chicago face font with the paint text tool. This should not be confused with **textStyle** which establishes the type style of a type face. For example, with the Chicago type face, you can have bold, plain, italic or some other style or combination of styles with that single face. The script segment,

> set textStyle to bold, underline

would set the type face to a combined bold and underline style. Four paint properties are turned on or off with the setting of **true** or **false**. They include the following:

grid   filled   centered   multiple

For example,

set multiple to true

would initiate the multiple drawing feature of HyperCard. Setting the property to **false** turns it off.

Using the Graphic Tools in Scripts

The two commands used most in graphic scripts are **click** and **drag**. The **click** command has the same effect as pointing to a spot on the screen and clicking the mouse. Similarly, **drag** has the same effect as holding down the mouse button and moving the mouse. The position for clicking and dragging are in terms of the 512 by 342 matrix that makes up the screen positions discussed in Chapter 7.

To get an idea of what you can do with the various tools and properties, make a button with the following script:

Button: <u>Paint It</u>
Oval button
script

on mouseUp

  - -Paint an X
  set pattern to 12   - -solid black
  choose brush tool
  set brush to 30
  drag from 10,10 to 300,300
  set brush to 22

```
        drag from 10,300 to 300,10

        - -Make a rectangle and fill it
        choose rectangle tool
        set lineSize to 6
        drag from 100,100 to 200,200
        choose bucket tool
        set pattern to 15
        click at 150,110

        - -Click and Type
        choose text tool
        click at 150,250
        set textAlign to center
        set textFont to Chicago
        type "Right here"
        choose browse tool

    end mouseUp
```

Experiment with the paint tools and properties to see if you can get them all working in expected ways.

The real use of scripted graphics lies in their ability to calculate positions and do a better job than you could by hand. To give an idea of what can be done by the computer, we will use the **random** function to generate "abstract" art. Random has the format,

```
        random (source)
```

where source is an integer number. The integer establishes the maximum random number that can be generated. Closely examine the following button script to see how it generates random patterns and lines.

Abstract Artist

Button: <u>Abstract Artist</u>
Card button
Icon # 26884
Transparent style
script

```
on mouseUp
  choose brush tool
  repeat 30
    set brush to random(32)
    set pattern to random(40)
    drag from random(512),random(342)¬
      to random(512),random(342)
  end repeat
  choose browse tool
end mouseUp
```

Each time you click the button, you get a different "painting." Be careful, though, because this can take up a lot of memory and may lead to a system crash if you click the button too many times before erasing the old painted patterns.

Graphics to Get Attention

A moving object will catch the eye better than a static one. In order to get the user's attention, animated graphics can be a big help, and besides, they're fun. To animate a painted object, you first create it either by hand or from a script, then you select it with the **lasso** tool, and finally you drag it across the screen with the **drag** command. By using the **click** command with the

commandKey in combination with the **lasso** tool selected, it is possible to select the unified paint object with a single line of script. The speed of the movement can be controlled by the **dragSpeed** property. For example, the following button script shows how to use several different paint tools together to create an eye-catching "Welcome" card.

```
on mouseUp
  choose text tool
  click at 250,170
  set textSize to 50
  set textFont to Geneva
  type "HI"
  choose brush tool
  set brush to 6
  click at 500,330
  choose lasso tool
  click at 500,330 with commandKey
  set dragSpeed to 300
  drag from 500,330 to 50,50
  play boing
  drag from 50,50 to 10,250
  play boing
  drag from 10,250 to 300,300
  play boing
  drag from 300,300 to 292,125
  play boing
  choose line tool
  set lineSize to 6
  drag from 250, 175 to 295,175
  choose browse tool
end mouseUp
```

After you have executed the script, you can see how the card is more likely to get someone's attention than a static display of the same salutation.

Likewise, for presentations, animated graphics are good atten-
tion-getters. For example, in a presentation of current and
projected sales, the card shown in Figure 10-4 gives life to the
stacked graph. Clicking the button both shows and animates
the bars.

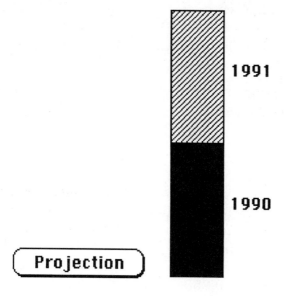

Figure 10-4

       Button: <u>Projection</u>
       Card button
       Oval style
       script

```
on mouseUp
  choose rectangle tool
  set filled to true
  set pattern to 12
  set dragSpeed to 100
```

```
        drag from 200,300 to 240,200
        set pattern to 14
        drag from 200,200 to 240,100
        choose text tool
        set textFont to Chicago
        set textSize to 12
        click at 245, 250
        type "1990"
        click at 245,150
        type "1991"
    end mouseUp
```

Hiding and Showing Pictures

The addition of **Hide Picture** and **Show Picture** helps the HyperCard programmer use graphics more effectively. Any graphics on a card can be hidden with the Hide Picture command and be brought back to the screen with Show Picture. The following are the basic formats:

    show/hide picture of <card/background>
    show/hide <card/background> picture

A new property, **showPict**, performs similar fuctions with the format,

    set showPict of <card/bkgnd> to <TRUE/FALSE>

With either the command or property, it is possible to combine screen locking and visual effects with hiding and showing pictures. Figure 10-5 shows the components of a card and background graphics with a button script illustrating how to use special visual effects with graphics.

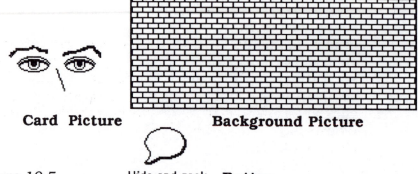

Card Picture   **Background Picture**

Figure 10-5   Hide and seek   **Button**

First draw the background picture, and then the card or
foreground picture in the same screen area as the brick wall.

> **Button**: <u>Hide and seek</u>
> Icon ID# 14767
> *script*
>
> on mouseUp
>   hide background picture
>   hide card picture
>   lock screen
>   show card picture
>   unlock screen with iris open very slowly
>   lock screen
>   show background picture
>   show card picture
>   unlock screen with checkerboard slowly
>   lock screen
>   hide card picture
>   unlock screen with dissolve very slowly
>   wait 2 sec
>   set the showPict of this background to false
>   set the showPict of this card to true
> end mouseUp

Calculated Graphics: Making Graphs

From the above discussion, it should be clear we can write scripts to make charts. We will start with simple bar graphs, and then gradually work up to more sophisticated charts and graphs. The first task will be to determine how to convert any set of values into values that can be translated into plotted points on the screen.

Bar Graphs

To make a proportional bar graph, it is necessary to establish a ratio of vertical points on the screen to plotted values. Of the 342 vertical points, only 340 will be used. That will provide a little room at the bottom the screen. If the maximum value to be plotted is less than 340; then the ratio will increase the number of vertical plot points. While if it is more than 340, the number will be proportionately decreased. To determine the maximum value of a set of numbers, the script will use the **max** function. Then, 340 will be divided by the maximum value to get a ratio. Each value will be multiplied by the ratio. For example, suppose the maximum value of a set of numbers to be plotted was 1200. The ratio to be established would be,

$$340 \div 1200 = .283$$

which would be used to multiply any value. All other values would be proportional to the maximum value.

$$1200 \text{ X } .283 = 340$$
$$800 \text{ X } .283 = 226.67$$
$$50 \text{ X } .283 = 14.15$$

Since we cannot plot a fraction, we will have to use the **round** function to round off any fractions. The rest of the script will deal with drawing a rectangle from the bottom of the screen to 340

minus the rounded proportional plot point. We must subtract
the value from 340 since the higher the position on the screen,
the lower the value. Figure 10-6 shows what a typical graph
would look like with the data placed in a scrolling field.

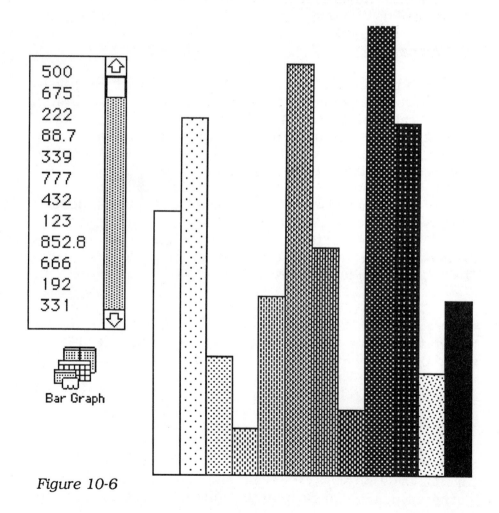

Figure 10-6

Card: <u>Graph</u>
script

```
on closeCard
  show menuBar
end closeCard
```
Field: <u>Field 1 (no name)</u>
Background field
Scroll style
no script

Button: <u>Bar Graph</u>
Card button
Icon number 18814
script

```
on mouseUp
  hide menuBar
  hide tool window
  get the number of lines in field 1
  put it into Plots
  repeat with x=1 to plots
    put line x of field 1 into item x of line 1 of temp
  end repeat
  put max(temp) into maxVal
  put (340/maxVal) into ratio
  choose rectangle tool
  doMenu "Select All"
  doMenu "Clear Picture"
  set filled to true
  set lineSize to 1

- -Draw the bars
  repeat with x=1 to plots
    set pattern to x
```

```
    put ((line x of field 1) * ratio) into yAx
    drag from (20*x + 80),340 to ¬
        (20*x + 100),(round(340-yAx))
  end repeat
end mouseUp
```

To provide more room for labels, move the bottom portion up and the top portion down. For fatter bars increase the multiple on the third from the last script line and decrease it for thinner bars. There will be an error message if the number of values exceeds the horizontal parameters of the screen. Thinner bars will allow a larger set of values to be entered.

Line Graphs

If you understand how to make bar graphs, line graphs will be very simple. The only major difference is in the appearance of the graph; not the logic of the script. Figure 10-7 shows a line graph with a script very similar to the bar graph shown in Figure 10-6.

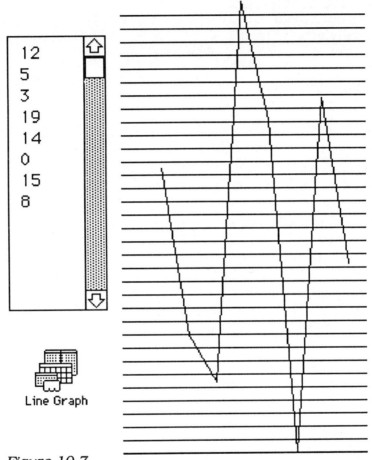

Figure 10-7

Card: <u>Graph2</u>
script

```
on closeCard
  show menuBar
end closeCard
```

Field: <u>Field 1 (no name)</u>
Background field
Scroll style
no script

Button: <u>Line Graph</u>
Card button
Icon number 18814
script

```
on mouseUp
  hide menuBar
  hide tool window
  get the number of lines in field 1
  put it into Plots
  repeat with x=1 to plots
     put line x of field 1 into item x of line 1 of temp
  end repeat
  put max(temp) into maxVal
  put (340/maxVal) into ratio
  choose line tool
  doMenu "Select All"
  doMenu "Clear Picture"
  set lineSize to 1

  - -Draw horizontal lines
  repeat with x=1 to 34
    drag from 90,x*10 to 500,x*10
  end repeat

- -Draw line graph
 repeat with x=2 to plots
   put ((line x-1 of field 1) * ratio) into yAx1
   put ((line x of field 1) * ratio) into yAx2
        put  round(340-yAx1)into alpha
        put round(340-yAx2)into beta
```

```
        drag from (20*x+80),alpha to (20*x+100),beta
    end repeat
    choose browse tool
end mouseUp
```

Graphic Graph

The final graph we will examine before learning to how to play music is one type of pictorial bar graph. Instead of using the vertical axis, this one will use the horizontal axis. Figure 10-8 shows a partial picture of a "Rabbit Graph" using what appears to be a drawn graphic. In fact, it is a character in the Geneva font character set. The rabbit character is created using shift-option-~ keys. Since only twelve 24-point rabbits would fit on the horizontal screen, it was necessary to base the ratio on 12 instead of 340 as we did with the other graphs. Other fonts that can be installed in the Macintosh, such as "Cairo" and "Zapf Dingbats," have several graphic characters that can be substituted for the rabbit font. (**Note**: When you type the rabbit font in the script editor, it will not look like a rabbit since all script is typed in the Monaco font. There will be three stacked lines instead.)

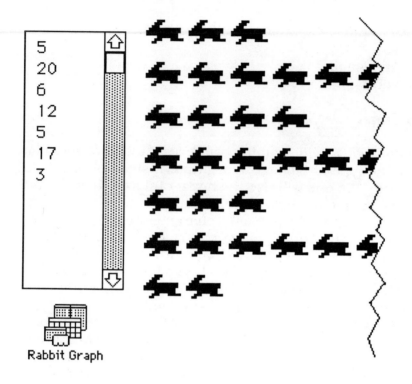

Rabbit Graph

Figure 10-8

Card: <u>Graph3</u>
script

on closeCard
  show menuBar
end closeCard

Field: <u>Field 1 (no name)</u>
Background field
Scroll style
no script

Button: <u>Rabbit Graph</u>
Card button
Icon number 18814
script

```
on mouseUp
  hide menuBar
  hide tool window
  get the number of lines in field 1
  put it into Plots
  repeat with x=1 to plots
    put line x of field 1 into item x of line 1 of temp
  end repeat
  put max(temp) into maxVal
  put (12/maxVal) into ratio
  choose text tool
  doMenu "Select All"
  doMenu "Clear Picture"
  repeat with x=1 to plots
    put line x of field 1 into item x of line 1 of temp
  end repeat

  set textFont to Geneva
  set textSize to 24
  doMenu "Select All"
  doMenu "Clear Picture"
- -Plot those rabbits
  repeat with x=1 to plots
    put ((line x of field 1) * ratio) into yAx
put round(yAx) into rabbit
click at 100,x*32
repeat with y=1 to rabbit
  type "Ÿ"         - -Shift-option-~
end repeat
end repeat
end repeat
```

```
        choose browse tool
      end mouseUp
```

Making Music

Up to this point, there have been scripts with some "boings" and harpsichord sounds. In this section, we will examine the full power of HyperCard to make music. The general format for music is the following:

play "instrument" [tempo] ["notes"]

The instrument or voice is the type of sound the play command generates. Only "boing" and the harpsichord voices come with HyperCard, but other instruments or voices, such as the saxophone, flute and human voice, are available as external commands from other sources. They can be installed using the ResEdit resource editor. The tempo controls the speed at which the notes are played with 100 being a medium speed. Higher tempo speeds are faster.

The notes parameter is broken into four parts,

noteName accidental octave duration

with each note separated by a space. The note's name is taken from actual musical notes, **a** through **g**. Following the note may be a sharp or flat represented by the pound sign, **#** and lowercase **b**, respectively. (A b-flat would be "bb.") Third, the octave's middle 'C' is 4, with higher and lower octaves represented by higher or lower values. Finally, the note's duration is tied to note names.

w=whole note	h=half note
q=quarter note	e=eight note
s=16th note	t=32nd note
x=64th note	

For a dotted or triplet note use "." or "3" after the note. A dotted half note of F sharp in octave five would look like the following:

f#5h.

The octave and the duration of a note is passed on to the next note if no new ones are specified. To experiment with music, make a card like that shown in Figure 10-9. First make the "Make Scale" button and click it with the browse tool to draw the bars. The individual notes are graphics on top of transparent buttons.

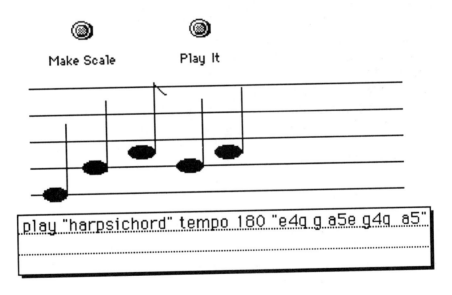

Figure 10-9

Button: <u>Make Scale</u>
Background button
Icon #1015
script

```
on mouseUp
  - -Make Scale
  choose line tool
  repeat with x=1 to 5
    drag from 20,x*20+70 to 300,x*20+70
  end repeat
end mouseUp
```

Button: Play It
Background button
Icon #1015
script

```
on mouseUp
  do field 1
end mouseUp
```

Buttons: Musical Notes
Each note is a graphic overlay on a
transparent button
scripts-(**Note:** Each script begins with 'on mouseUp' and
ends with 'end mouseUp'. The single line for each note
between these handlers is shown below. Each note is a
single button.)

```
on mouseUp
    play "harpsichord" tempo 180 "e4q"    - -note 1
    play "harpsichord" "g"                - -note 2
    play "harpsichord" "a5e"              - -note 3
    play "harpsichord" "g4q"              - -note 4
    play "harpsichord" "a5"               - -note 5
on mouseUp
```

Change the text in the field to try out different combinations of
sound. Start by changing the harpsichord voice to the "boing"
one.

Application: Graphing Your Stocks

One way to attempt to predict how stocks will perform on the stock market is to find another stock or other indicator that goes up or down before another stock. For example, if oil stocks go down, that may be followed by an increase in the value of certain stocks that rely on people travelling by automobile for vacations. Other times, a decline or rise in what appears to be a wholly unrelated stock or indicator will affect certain stocks. By having a graph program that sets two or more charting lines on the same graph, it is easier to see what occurs. This application will do that for you.

To generate a better screen appearance, button and fields are hidden until they are used. In Figure 10-10, the "Print Graph" button is visible, but after the first time the "Reset" button is used, it only appears when the graph is on the card. The two fields and the "Stock Comparison" button disappear when the graph is plotted as well. Figure 10-11 shows how the screen looks when the graph is on the screen.

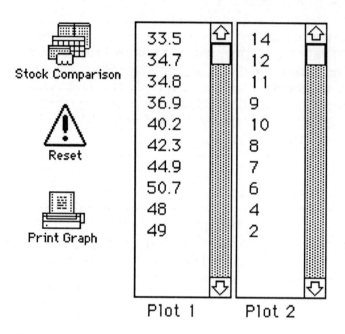

Figure 10-10

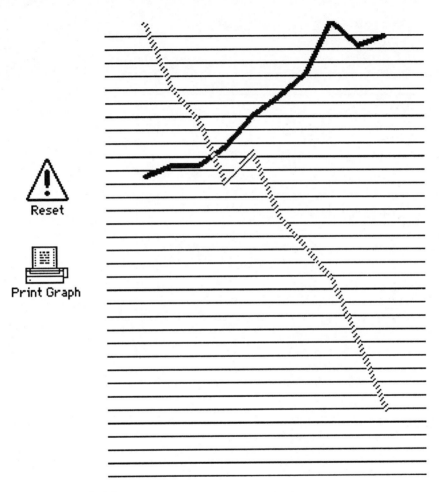

Figure 10-11

Fields: <u>Fields 1 & 2 (no names)</u>
Background fields
Scroll styles
no scripts

Button: <u>Stock Comparison</u>
Transparent style
Icon #18814
script

```
on mouseUp
  hide field 1
  hide field 2
  hide card button 1
  hide menuBar
  hide tool window
  hide pattern window
  choose line tool
  doMenu "Select All"
  doMenu "Clear Picture"

  - -Find Maximum Values
  get the number of lines in field 1
  put it into Plots
  repeat with x=1 to plots
    put line x of field 1 into item x of line 1 of temp
  end repeat
  put max(temp) into maxVal
  put (340/maxVal) into ratio
  put it into Plots2
  repeat with x=1 to plots2
    put line x of field 2 into item x of line 1 of temp
  end repeat
  put max(temp) into maxVal
  put (340/maxVal) into ratio2

- -Draw horizontal lines
set lineSize to 1
repeat with x=1 to 34
  drag from 90,x*10 to 500,x*10
end repeat
```

```
choose brush tool
set brush to 8
      set filled to true
      set pattern to 12

      - -Draw the Two Plots
      repeat with x=2 to plots
        put ((line x-1 of field 1) * ratio) into yAx1
        put ((line x of field 1) * ratio) into yAx2
        put  round(340-yAx1)into alpha
        put round(340-yAx2)into beta
        drag from (20*x+80),alpha to (20*x+100),beta
      end repeat

      set pattern to 14
      repeat with x=2 to plots2
        put ((line x-1 of field 2) * ratio2) into yAx1
        put ((line x of field 2) * ratio2) into yAx2
        put  round(340-yAx1)into alpha
        put round(340-yAx2)into beta
        drag from (20*x+80),alpha to (20*x+100),beta
      end repeat

      choose browse tool
      show button "Print Graph"
end mouseUp
```

Button: <u>Reset</u>
Transparent style
Icon #2
script

```
on mouseUp
  choose select tool
  doMenu Select All
  doMenu clear picture
```

```
        show field 1
        show field 2
        show button 1
        choose browse tool
        show MenuBar
        hide button "Print Graph"
  end mouseUp
```

Button: <u>Print Graph</u>
Transparent style
Icon #1007
script

```
on mouseUp
  hide button "Print Graph"
  hide button "Reset"
  doMenu "Print Card"
  show button "Print Graph"
  show button "Reset"
end mouseUp
```

By adding another field and adding further scripts to the "Stock Comparison" button, it is possible to have more than two different plots charted. Also, depending on the figures being compared, you might want to use a single ratio instead of two separate ones as was done in this sample. If the number range between the sample figures is relatively close; then it would not hurt to have a single ratio to give a more accurate view of exactly how two sets of values differ. However, by using a single ratio, it is almost impossible to determine patterned changed when the ranges of two sets of data are very different. The lower set tends to be "flattened" out on the chart.

Using
MultiFinder

What Is MultiFinder?

MultiFinder is a control system that allows more than a single application to be in memory at once. This means that you can have several programs working in conjunction with one another. For instance, if you are using HyperCard and need to use a word processor or a graphics program momentarily, it is possible to have the other program "in the background" waiting to be used. A click of the MultiFinder icon quickly transfers control to the other application. Then, after using the other application, another click of the icon returns you to HyperCard. This saves a lot of time compared with first quitting one program, and then starting up another, and then going through the whole thing again to get back to the first program.

Special Note: Using HyperCard with MultiFinder can really speed things up for you if you have it and Finder working together under Multifinder. Normally, it is necessary to shut down HyperCard and your Mac in order to return to the desktop. However, with HyperCard operating under MultiFinder, all you need to do is to click the icon in the upper-right corner of the screen to switch to Finder and the desktop without shutting down HyperCard and possibly your Mac.

The term "multitasking" is applied to MultiFinder. This means several tasks can be carried out simultaneously. For example, while your printer is printing out a file, you could be working on a new HyperTalk script. The computer handles more than one task at a time. However, since most applications require the user's attention and input, only a few actual multitasking operations would be practical. Rather, it is better to think of MultiFinder as a rapid applications switching device with some multitasking functions.

Installing MultiFinder

To install MultiFinder, open the **Installer** application on your System Disk and choose your computer type from the dialog window. If your system is an older one that has been updated with additional memory and a double-sided internal drive along with the newer ROMs that come with the double-sided internal drive, choose the Macintosh Plus configuration. Figure 11-1 shows the screen that appears when the Installer application is run. After selecting your system, click "Install." Your system then will be installed along with Multifinder.

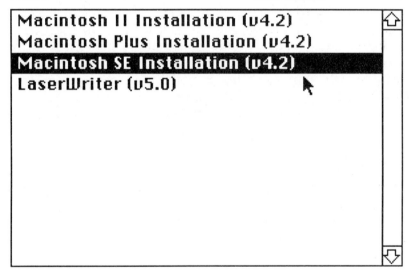

Figure 11-1

Using the System Tools Disk 2, another Installer application will install the correct printer. Launch the second Installer program in the same way you did the first. It will be on a different System Tools disk with printer tools. If you have a LaserWriter, then you have the option of installing either **LaserWriter** or **Background LaserWriter**. Apple Computer, Inc. does not recommend installing the Background LaserWriter unless you have a hard disk. This is because the system uses a "spooled files" system that is written to your startup disk during printing. This is done with the **PrintMonitor** that is installed when the Background LaserWriter option is taken. Usually there will not be enough room for everything else on the system disk and the spooled files. However, if you minimize your System by removing little-used fonts, especially font sizes that you do not use and other non-essential documents from the startup disk, you can use the Background LaserWriter on a non-hard disk system. The printed documents will have to be short, however, and have a minimum of graphics. For certain types of business letters, especially where multiple copies are required, this may be a good way to use the multitasking function of MultiFinder without a hard disk drive. While multiple copies of the letter are being printed, you can work on something else on your Mac. This saves a lot of time when you have more than a single job to complete on your Mac at once.

Likewise, the non-hard disk configuration works well for printing single HyperCard cards, even ones with a lot of graphics to be printed. When using the **PrintMonitor** (background printing which allows you to work on another project while your Mac prints something to a LaserWriter) with HyperCard, though, it is necessary to have at least two megabytes of memory. Also, when the PrintMonitor is at work, some of the other activities may be slowed or even garbled a little as your Mac does two things at once. On minimal systems, such as a Mac Plus or SE with two megabytes of memory and no hard disk, this is more noticeable. On Mac II systems with five megabytes of memory and a 40 megabyte hard disk, the background printing may go wholly unnoticed.

Finally, certain applications do not work with the PrintMonitor (background printing). These are programs that come with their own printing resource, such as Adobe's *Illustrator* and versions of *PageMaker* before version 2.0. In these cases, the background printing must be turned off prior to attempting to print a file. (Newer versions of all software for the Macintosh family of computer, including *Illustrator*, are expected to be compatible with background printing.) Figure 11-2 shows the screen during printer installation.

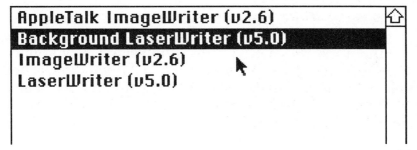

Figure 11-2

Setting the MultiFinder Startup

Once the printer and system are installed, it is necessary to set the Startup from the Special menu to actually use MultiFinder. After starting up your Mac with the disk with the installed system and printer, first choose the applications you wish to be launched when you turn on your computer. Select the items you want in the startup by darkening them as shown in Figure 11-3. This is done by clicking each with the Shift key held down or by dragging the arrow key around the desired files.

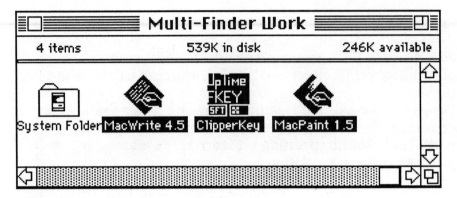

Figure 11-3

Next, choose "Startup" from the Special Menu. Figure 11-4 shows the dialog box that appears. Click the MultiFinder option, and then the "OK" button. Your disk now will be configured to start up with MultiFinder and launch the selected items. You will notice when the configured MultiFinder disk is used as the startup disk all of the applications chosen take time to be activated. The last to be activated will be in the foreground and the others in the background.

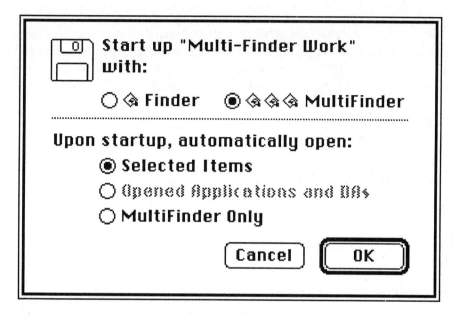

Figure 11-4

From this point on, when you start up your Mac with the MultiFinder configured hard disk or a 3 1/2 inch disk, MultiFinder will be operating. You can tell by the small icon in the upper right hand corner of your screen what application is running and that it is indeed under MultiFinder. Figure 11-5 shows what Microsoft's word processor program, *Word*, looks like when it is being used.

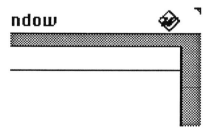

Figure 11-5

It can be difficult to tell which icon is being used due to their small size. However, just remember they are simply miniature. For example, Figure 11-6 shows the relative size difference between a full-sized HyperCard icon and the little ones used with MultiFinder.

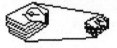

Figure 11-6

Working in the MultiFinder Environment

When under MultiFinder control, there are a number of things that can be done differently than when using the standard Finder. Applications are either in the "foreground" or "background." A *single* foreground application is *interactive* at any one time, while several applications may be open in the background. However, other applications may be *working* in the background, such as PrintMonitor printing pages to a Laser-Writer. Figure 11-7 shows a screen showing three different applications open at once. The active application is the Microsoft *Word* document. The menu bar belongs to the *Word* application, but Finder and *MacPaint* are also open in the background.

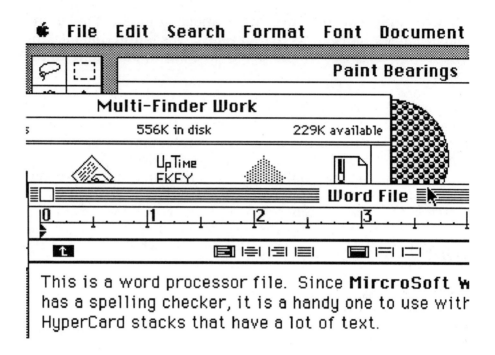

Figure 11-7

To change the foreground application, do one of three things:

1. Click the icon in the upper right hand corner.
2. Click the application.
3. Pull down the Apple Menu from the menu bar and select the application.

Unless there are numerous applications, the third method was found to be the least efficient. With six or seven applications open at the same time on a system with a monster amount of RAM memory, selecting the exact application desired may prove to be the fastest way to activate a specific program. Normally, though, only two or three applications and the Finder are opened at the same time. In that case it was found that clicking the icon is simplest way to bring different applications to the foreground.

Under MultiFinder, it is possible to move the screen placement of a foreground application. By dragging the application by the bar across the top of the window, it can be moved. You will be able to see behind the application to the desktop and other opened applications. Some applications, such as earlier versions of MacPaint, cannot be moved but take up the whole screen. However, they do move to the background when another application is brought to the foreground. Figure 11-7, above, shows a MacPaint document taking up the whole screen in the background so that the desktop is not visible.

Memory and MultiFinder

As handy as MultiFinder may be, it does take up a lot of memory. To find how much memory is used with a given set of opened applications choose "About the Finder" from the Apple Menu. Figure 11-8 shows what you will see. The bar graphs show how much memory is allocated to each application and how much it has used. Both the *HyperCard* and *Word* applications have used up about half of their allocated memory.

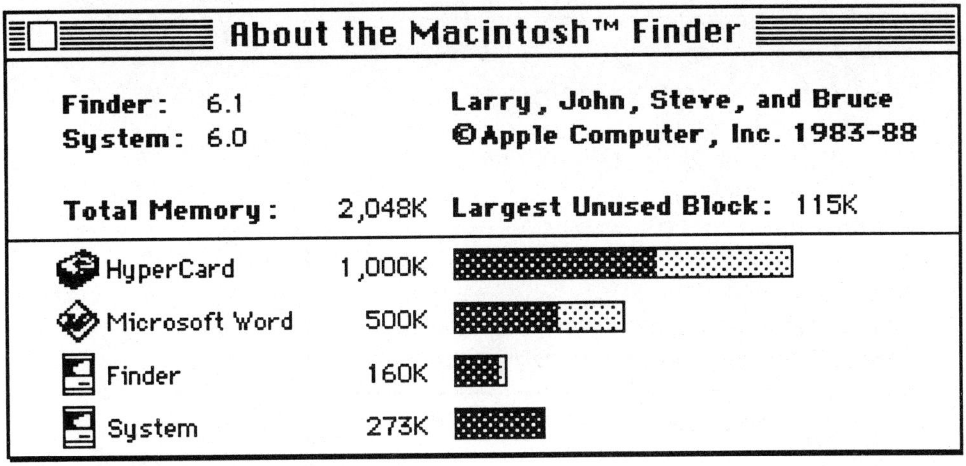

```
▤□▥▥▥▥▥ About the Macintosh™ Finder ▥▥▥▥▥

  Finder:  6.1          Larry, John, Steve, and Bruce
  System:  6.0          ©Apple Computer, Inc. 1983-88

  Total Memory:   2,048K  Largest Unused Block:  115K

  ▦ HyperCard       1,000K  ███████████▒▒▒▒▒
  ◈ Microsoft Word    500K  ██████▒▒
  ▣ Finder            160K  ▓▓
  ▣ System            273K  ██████
```

Figure 11-8

To change the amount of memory for a given application, *first* quit the application. Then, from the Finder, select the application and choose "Get Info" from the File menu. From the Info window, you can change the amount of memory allocated for the application. The box in the lower right hand corner is used for changing the amount of memory. Figure 11-9 shows an Info window for Microsoft *Word* where the amount of memory was changed from 384K to 450K.

```
╔══════════════════ Info ══════════════════╗
║  ▣                                        ║
║   ◈W◈                          Locked ☐   ║
║         Microsoft Word                    ║
║   Kind: application                       ║
║   Size: 357,260 bytes, 349.5K on disk     ║
║                                           ║
║  Where: Word 3.01, external drive         ║
║                                           ║
║                                           ║
║  Created: Wed, Jul 15, 1987 1:25 PM       ║
║  Modified: Tue, Aug 11, 1987 9:28 AM      ║
║  ┌─────────────────────────────────────┐ ║
║  │ Microsoft Word for the Macintosh Version 3.01 │
║  │                                       │ ║
║  │                                       │ ║
║  │                                       │ ║
║  └─────────────────────────────────────┘ ║
║      Suggested Memory Size (K):  384      ║
║      Application Memory Size (K): ┌─────┐ ║
║                                   │ 450 │ ║
║                                   └─────┘ ║
╚═══════════════════════════════════════════╝
```

Figure 11-9

If you find that MultiFinder eats up too much RAM with certain
applications or slows things down, you can turn on your
Macintosh so that MultiFinder is not launched. Use the Multi-
Finder startup disk and turn on your Mac. As soon as "Welcome
to Macintosh" appears on the screen, hold down the command
key, and MultiFinder will not be launched. Instead the Finder
will take control and not use the memory that MultiFinder does.
Of course, when this is done, none of the MultiFinder advan-
tages can be used even though the startup disk has MultiFinder
on it.

If lack of memory is becoming a problem, your Mac will let you know in a number of ways. This will be especially evident when background printing is taking place and there are several opened applications. Some evidences of crowded memory include:

1. Missing text from a foreground document. The text in a word processing program will look like someone carved a chunk out of it. Usually this problem disappears after the printing is completed or some background applications are closed.

2. You type something and there is a delay between the time you type it and when it appears on the screen.

3. One of the applications unexpectedly shuts down. The system does not crash (be thankful for that), but an application just stops all by itself and the helpful message, "Your application has unexpectedly quit" lets you know what happened.

4. Desk accessories have distorted characters.

If you get a message that a specific application does not have sufficient memory, increase the memory as described above and illustrated in Figure 11-9. After changing memory allocation to an application, it is necessary to restart your Mac.

Summary

This short chapter has introduced MultiFinder. One important thing to get out of this chapter is that you really should upgrade your RAM to at least two megabytes. It doesn't matter whether you have a Mac Plus, an SE or a Mac II, MultiFinder takes up a lot of memory, and unless you increase the amount of memory, you will not be able to take full advantage of it. This is doubly true for HyperCard. In the scripting mode, HyperCard 1.2 requires 700K of RAM. That only leaves 324K for everything else if you only have one megabyte of RAM. Apple Computer, Inc., as well as several third party developers, have RAM memory upgrades. Along with upgrading RAM, get a hard disk drive. That will go a long way toward getting the most out of your system. This is vitally important with regard to using the PrintMonitor and background printing.

Once there's sufficient memory on your Mac, use MultiFinder to get the most out of its capabilities. As more and more applications are written with MultiFinder in mind, the more important it is to be familiar with it. Companies that develop software for the Macintosh will begin using the background processing capabilities available under MultiFinder. In the same way that printing can tie up the Mac, so too can transferring data over a modem, making large speardsheet calculations and scanner processing. With new software that will allow such programs to be processed in the background, it is a good idea to be familiar with MultiFinder on your particular system. In the meantime, the ability to quickly go from one application to another, and to transfer text, data and graphics, makes MultiFinder worth the time spent mastering it.

Using
XCMD's

What are XCMD's and XFCN's?

The extra commands and functions (XCMD's and XFCN's) are simply commands and functions you add to your HyperCard application or stacks. In the same way that HyperCard Version 1.2 has new commands and functions not found in earlier versions of HyperCard, XCMD's and XFCN's allow you to add commands and functions to existing or new versions of Hyper-Card. So, let's see how to get XCMD's and XFCN's into your stacks.

Where to Get XCMD's and XFCN's

There are basically two places to find XCMD's and XFCN's: 1) learn assembly language, Pascal or 'C' programming languages and write them yourself; or 2) get them through public domain or commercial sources.

If you plan to write XCMD's and XFCN's yourself, take a look at *XCMD's For HyperCard* by Gary Bond. Also, get Volumes One through Five of *Inside Macintosh*, and become familiar with how the Macintosh operating system works. It is far beyond the scope of this book to explain how to write XCMD's, but if you do choose that route, you will find it very rewarding.

To use the growing library of XCMD's, you will need to use the most recent version of a public domain program called *ResEdit*(Resource Editor). This powerful little program was introduced in Chapter 3 when we discussed making your own icons. The best place to get ResEdit is from your local Macintosh club.

At the same time you are getting your hands on ResEdit, look at the public domain XCMD's that are available from your local Macintosh club. Apple Computer, Inc. and Macintosh clubs have worked to get the ball rolling on distributing various public domain XCMD's. Likewise, check your local computer or software store. A number of commercial XCMD's are also becoming available for enhancing HyperCard.

Installing XCMD's

To install XCMD's with ResEdit, we will use an example of an XCMD stack called **sendSerial**. This new command will allow you to write stacks to send data out your modem port to a device connected to that port.

Special Note: Since you have to be careful using ResEdit, install XCMD's on a copy of the HyperCard application on a separate disk. Also, you will find that older versions of ResEdit will not work when MultiFinder is installed. Just use Finder during installation. Once the XCMD's are installed, though, they work fine with MultiFinder.

Use the following steps to install sendSerial into a copy of HyperCard:

1. After opening ResEdit, your screen will display several windows. Choose the window with SendSerial and select it by clicking it as shown in Figure 12-1

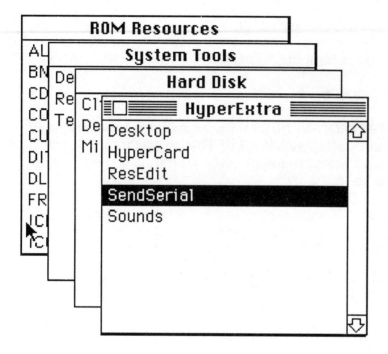

Figure 12-1

2. After opening the SendSerial stack, you will see a window with "XCMD." Open the XCMD resource.

3. Next, select the "XCMD "SendSerial" ID=222" line and choose **Copy** from the **Edit** menu.

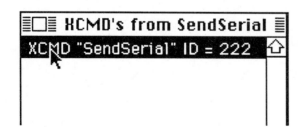

Figure 12-2

4. Close the SendSerial windows and open the stack or application into which you want to install the SendSerial XCMD . In this example, we will install it directly into to HyperCard application. Begin by opening the XCMD resource in HyperCard as shown in Figure 12-3.

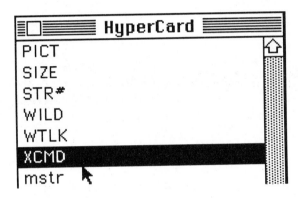

Figure 12-3

5. When the XCMD resource window is open, you may see more or different XCMD's depending on what XCMD's have been installed in your HyperCard application. However, once you have opened this window; simply, choose **Paste** from the **Edit** menu.

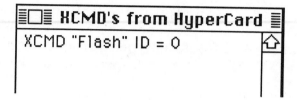

Figure 12-4

Once you paste in the XCMD, close all of the windows and save the changes in HyperCard when asked to do so. From now on, when you run the HyperCard with the XCMD installed, you can use the command just as any other command.

Using XCMD's

Once you have your XCMD installed, the next step will be to use it. Usually, XCMD's have sufficient documentation in the stacks in which they are installed; so it is no problem learning the how to use the commands. Many of the XCMD's stacks are "share ware," in which case there is a small donation requested by the XCMD author, and since the authors go through the trouble of providing not only the XCMD's but also the documentation, it is a small price to pay for the added HyperCard power.

The sendSerial command has two parameters in the format,

    sendSerial "string", baud rate

Besides placing straight text in the string parameter, you may also place hexadecimal numbers. Hexadecimal numbers are base-16 numbers the computer uses in various functions, especially with printers. To distinguish hexadecimal numbers from regular string values, a carat sign (^) is placed before the hexadecimal number. Once sendSerial sees the carat, it expects a two digit value from "$00" to "$FF." (Dollar signs are used to designate hexadecimal values.) For example, decimal value "13" (carriage return on most printers) is "D" in hexadecimal. Since a two digit number is expected, it is necessary to put in "0D" instead of just "D." So the script,

sendSerial "^OD Print This ^OA", 9600

would send hexadecimal value $0D, the string "Print This" and the hexadecimal value $0A out the serial port at 9600 baud. (9600 is the default value also; so the 9600 is actually unnecessary. If you were sending something through a 1200 baud modem, the baud value would be necessary.)

Finally, as with other text strings, it is perfectly correct to put the text into a container and have the object of the command be the container without using the quote marks. For example, the lines

put "Send me!" into capsule
sendSerial capsule, 2400

would send the message "Send me!" out the modem port at 2400 baud.

To illustrate using sendSerial, the "memo word processor" shown in Figure 12-5 will print the contents of a field to a printer hooked up to the modem port. An ImageWriter printer was used for the example; so if you have a different type of printer, you might want to check your user's manual for the hexadecimal values for a line feed ($0A) and carriage return ($0D) in the button script. Most dot matrix and daisy wheel type printers will use those parameter values; so it should not be a problem. Remember to connect your printer to the modem port. The port has a little phone next to it.

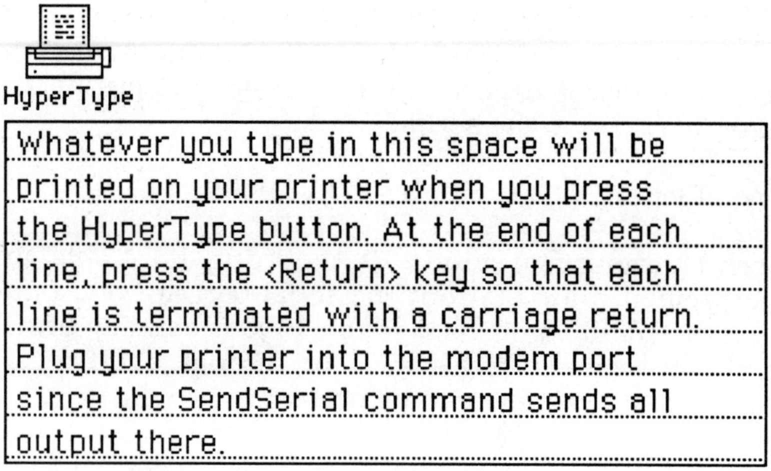

HyperType

Whatever you type in this space will be printed on your printer when you press the HyperType button. At the end of each line, press the <Return> key so that each line is terminated with a carriage return. Plug your printer into the modem port since the SendSerial command sends all output there.

Figure 12-5

Field: *No Name*
Card field
Rectangle style
No script

Button: *HyperType*
Card button
Icon ID #1017
script

```
on mouseUp
 repeat with x=1 to number of lines in card field 1
  put line x of card field 1 into typeMe
  sendSerial "^0D" & typeMe & "^0A",9600
 end repeat
end mouseUp
```

That should provide a quick introduction to using XCMD's. Try some of the other ones available through your Macintosh club and software store.

Quick Look Up and Example Glossary

This glossary is for a quick reference to the commands, functions, constants and properties used in HyperCard. More detailed explanations and examples are found in the body of the text, and they should be referenced through the Table of Contents or Index. Each command, function and constant have short descriptions and an example. The properties are listed with relevant objects. At the end of the Glossary is a list of abbreviations legal to use in HyperCard.

Commands

add

Adds value to container.
Example: add 3 to total

answer

Sets up user input for one of three fixed choice replies.
Example: answer "Finished" with "Yes" or "No"

ask

Sets up user input for open ended reply.
Example: ask "Name of file?"

beep

Emits a beep sound.
Example: beep

choose

Selects a tool from tool palette.
Example: choose eraser tool

click

Same as clicking the mouse at screen location with or without key.
Example: click at loc 100,150 with ShiftKey

close	Closes open file. **Example:** close file "StockData"
convert	Date and time container conversion. **Example:** convert dateTime to dateItems
delete	Removes specified data from container. **Example:** delete line 2 of field 3
dial	Dials phone through special interface or modem. **Example:** dial "555-4321" with modem
divide	Divides value of container by another value. **Example:** divide Share by 3
do	Executes command from container. **Example:** do line 2 of field 1
doMenu	Selects from menu bar with script. **Example:** doMenu "New Card"
drag	Works to drag mouse from script. **Example:** drag from 20,20 to 150,200
edit script	Goes to script editor from script. **Example:** edit script of card button 2
find	Locates string in current stack and/or field. **Examples:** find "technology" in field 2 find whole "Charles Darwin" find string "me"

get	Extracts contents/value of expression and puts into It variable. **Example:** get number of lines in field 1
global	Declares a variable to be global. **Example:** global total, taxPer
go	Transfers to specified card or stack. **Example:** go card 15
hide	Removes image from screen. **Example:** hide "tool window"
hide picture	Removes card or background graphic from screen **Example:** hide card picture
multiply	Multiplies value of container by another value. **Example:** multiply Total by 10
open	Executes document with applications. **Example:** open "memos" with "Word"
open file	Opens channel between HyperCard and disk file. **Example:** open file "names"
open printing	Prepares for printing with our without dialog box. **Example:** open printing with dialog
play	Executes sound of instrument. **Example:** play "harpsichord"
pop	Goes to last card "pushed". **Example:** pop card

print	Prints specified card(s). **Example:** print 7 cards
push	Establishes specified card as next to be "popped". **Example:** push this card
put	Places string or value into container. **Example:** put 15 into Total
read	Reads contents of open file to specified point. **Example:** read from file "News" until "\"
reset Paint	Replaces all paint options to default. **Example:** reset Paint
select	Selects specified text segment in field. **Example:** select foundChunk
set	Establishes configuration of properties. **Example:** set filled to true
show	Places hidden images on screen. **Example:** show field 3
show picture	Displays card or background graphic on screen **Example:** show background 2 picture
sort	Places cards in stack in specified order. **Example:** sort by first word of second field
subtract	Subtracts value from container. **Example:** subtract 10 from subTotal

type	Writes text into field or background from script. **Example:** type "This is all."
visual effect	Initiates effects when changing cards. **Example:** visual effect iris open slowly
wait	Stops script for specified time in ticks/seconds. **Example:** wait 2 seconds
write	Writes contents of something to an open file. **Example:** write field 1 to file "nameData"

Functions

charToNum	Returns ASCII values of character. **Example:** get charToNum "v"
clickH	Returns horizontal position where last mouse click occurred. **Example:** put the ClickH into Lateral
clickLoc	Returns the location where last mouse click occurred. **Example:** get the clickLoc
clickV	Returns vertical position where last mouse click occurred. **Example:** put the ClickV into Vertical
commandKey	Reads commands key's position. **Example:** wait until the commandKey is down

date	Returns the date. **Example:** put the date into msg
foundChunk	Returns the characters and field of text located with the find command. **Example:** put the foundChunk into SegX
foundField	Returns the field number of text located with the find command. **Example:** put the foundField into AreaG
foundLine	Returns the line number and field of text last located with the find command. **Example:** put the foundChunk into WhatLine
foundText	Returns the text last located with the find command. **Example:** put the foundText
length temp	Returns number of text characters in container. **Example:** put the length of field 1 into
math functions	*See pages 221 -223.*
mouse	Returns constant *up* or *down* depending on whether or not the button is pressed. **Example:** if mouse is down then go next card
mouseClick	Returns true or false if mouse is clicked in handler. **Example:** if mouseClick then show field 1

mouseH	Returns number of horizontal pixels mouse is from left side of screen. **Example:** if mouseH < 20 then beep
mouseLoc	Returns X and Y of mouse location. **Example:** type "Here" at mouseLoc
mouseV	Returns number of vertical pixels mouse is from top of card window. **Example:** put mouseV into field 1
number of	Returns number of buttons, fields, back grounds, cards or chunk items in speci fied source. including backgrounds. **Example:** get the number of cards in this stack
numToChar	Returns character of ASCII number. **Example:** if numToChar of temp < 65 then beep
offset the beginning of string.	Returns the number of characters from source string to beginning of specified **Example:** get offset ("Smith", field 3)
optionKey	Returns constant *up* or *down* depending on whether or not option key is pressed. **Example:** if optionKey is down then go next card
param	Returns parameter value of specified parameter in list. **Example:** put param of 2 into sourceParam

paramCount	Returns number of parameters passed. **Example:** if there paramCount is > 1 then edit script
params	Returns entire parameter list and mes sage name. **Example:** if params = "closeCard" then
beep	
random	Generates a random integer between one and specified value. **Example:** put random (256) into msg
result	Returns explanation of error if any. **Example:** put result into field 2
round	Returns number rounded off to nearest whole. **Example:** put round (total) into field 4
seconds	Returns number of seconds from Janu- ary 1, 1904 to current time set in Macintosh. **Example:** put (the seconds - timeThen) into howLong (*Note*: Seconds used with the **wait** command count actual seconds and are not the same as the seconds function.)
shiftKey	Returns constant up or down depending on whether or not shift key is pressed. **Example:** if shiftKey is up then add 32 to char x

sound	Returns name of current sound being played or string "done" if no sound is being played. **Example:** if sound = "done" then play secondChorus
target	Returns string with original recipient of message. **Example:** put id of the target into field 3
ticks	Returns the number of 1/60th of a second since Macintosh was restarted. **Example:** put the ticks into timeStart
time	Returns text string with time in default short form with option of "the long time." **Example:** put time into msg
tool	Returns name of current tool. **Example:** put the tool into msg
trunc	Truncates all fractions from number. **Example:** put trunc (total) into whole
value	Treats string in a source as an expression. **Example:** if the value of field 1 is > 55 then beep

Constants

down	State when key or mouse button is pressed down. **Example:** if mouse is down then beep

empty	Null state equivalent to " ". **Example:** if field 1 is empty then show field 2
false	Result of negative logical expression or state of condition. **Example A:** if it is false then beep **Example B:** set the visible of msg to false
formFeed	ASCII value 12. **Example:** if it is formFeed then close file "Zed"
lineFeed repeat	ASCII value 10. **Example:** if it is lineFeed then next
pi	Generates value 3.14159265358979323846. **Example:** put pi * radius ^ 2 into field 2
quote	Puts quotation marks around text. **Example:** put quote & "Heck" & quote into msg
return	ASCII value 13. **Example:** put return after last word of field 1
space	ASCII value 32. **Example:** put space in item 3 of line 1 of field 6
tab	ASCII value 9. **Example:** it is tab then close file "Test"

true	Result of positive logical expression or state of condition. **Example A:** if it is true then beep **Example B:** set the visible of msg to true
up charVal	State of key or mouse button when not pressed. **Example:** if shiftKey is up then add 32 to
zero — ten	Functions same as 1 through 10. **Example:** add five to field two

Properties

Global

blindTyping	true/false
cantDelete	true/false
cantModify	true/false
cursor	1-4, iBeam,plus, cross, watch, none,busy, arrow, hand
dragSpeed	pixels per second
editBkgnd	true/false
language	depends on translator resource
lockMessages	true/false
lockRecent	true/false
lockScreen	true/false
numberFormat	set with # or 0
powerKeys	true/false
showPict	true/false
userLevel	1-5
userModify	true/false

Window

loc(ation)	h,v (horizontal,vertical)
rec(angle)	h,v,h,v
visible	true/false

Painting

brush	1-32
centered	true/false
filled	true/false
grid	true/false
lineSize	1-4,6,8
multiple	true/false
multiSpace	1-9
pattern	1-40
polySides	3-50
textAlign	left, right, centered
textFont	font name
textHeight	number
textSize	number
textStyle	style name

Stack

freeSize	value
name	any string
script	any stack script
size	in bytes

Background and Card

id	number
name	any string
number	number in stack
script	any background or card script

Field

autoTab	true/false
id	number
loc(ation)	number, number
lockText	true/false
name	any name
number	number
rect(angle)	h,v,h,v
script	any field script
scroll	number
showLines	true/false
style	transparent, opaque, rectangle, shadow or scrolling
textAlign	left, right, centered
textFont	font name
textHeight	number
textSize	number
textStyle	style name
visible	true/false
wideMargins	true/false

Button

autoHilite	true/false
hilite	true/false
icon	number
id	number
loc(ation)	number, number
name	any name
number	number
rect(angle)	h,v,h,v
script	any button script
scroll	number
showName	true/false

style	transparent, opaque, rectangle, round rect, check box or radio button
textAlign	left, right, centered
textFont	font name
textHeight	number
textSize	number
textStyle	style name
visible	true/false

Abbreviations

Abbreviations followed by (1.2) indicate that the abbreviation was introduced in HyperCard Version 1.2

abbreviated	abbr, abbrev
background	bg (1.2), bkgnd
backgrounds	bgs (1.2), bkgnds,
button	btn
buttons	btns (1.2)
card	cd (1.2)
cards	cds (1.2)
character	char
field	fld (1.2)
fields	flds (1.2)
gray	grey (1.2)
location	loc
middle	mid
message	msg
picture	pict (1.2)
polygon	poly
previous	prev
rectangle	rect
regular	reg
second	sec (1.2) {Time sec only.)
seconds	secs (1.2)
ticks	tick (1.2)

Index

Here's how to receive your free catalog and save money on your next book order from Scott, Foresman and Company

Simply mail in the response card below to receive you free copy of our latest catalog featuring computer and business books. After you've looked through the catalog and you're ready to place your order, attach the coupon below to receive $1.00 off the catalog price on your next order of Scott, Foresman and Company Professional Books Group business or computer books.

— —

❑ YES, please send me my free catalog of your latest computer and business books! I am especially interested in

❑ IBM   ❑ Programming
❑ MACINTOSH   ❑ Business Applications
❑ AMIGA   ❑ Networking/Telecommunications
❑ APPLE IIc, IIe, IIɢs   ❑ Other_____

Mail response card to: Scott, Foresman and Company
                           Professional Books Group
                           1900 East Lake Avenue
                           Glenview, IL 60025

— —

Publisher's Coupon
No Expiration Date

SAVE $1.00

Limit one per order. Good only on Scott, Foresman and Company Professional Books Group publications. Consumer pays any sales tax. Coupon may not be assigned, transferred, or reproduced. Coupon will be redeemed by Scott, Foresman and Company, Professional Books Group, 1900 E. Lake Ave., Glenview, IL 60025.

Customer's Signature_____

— —